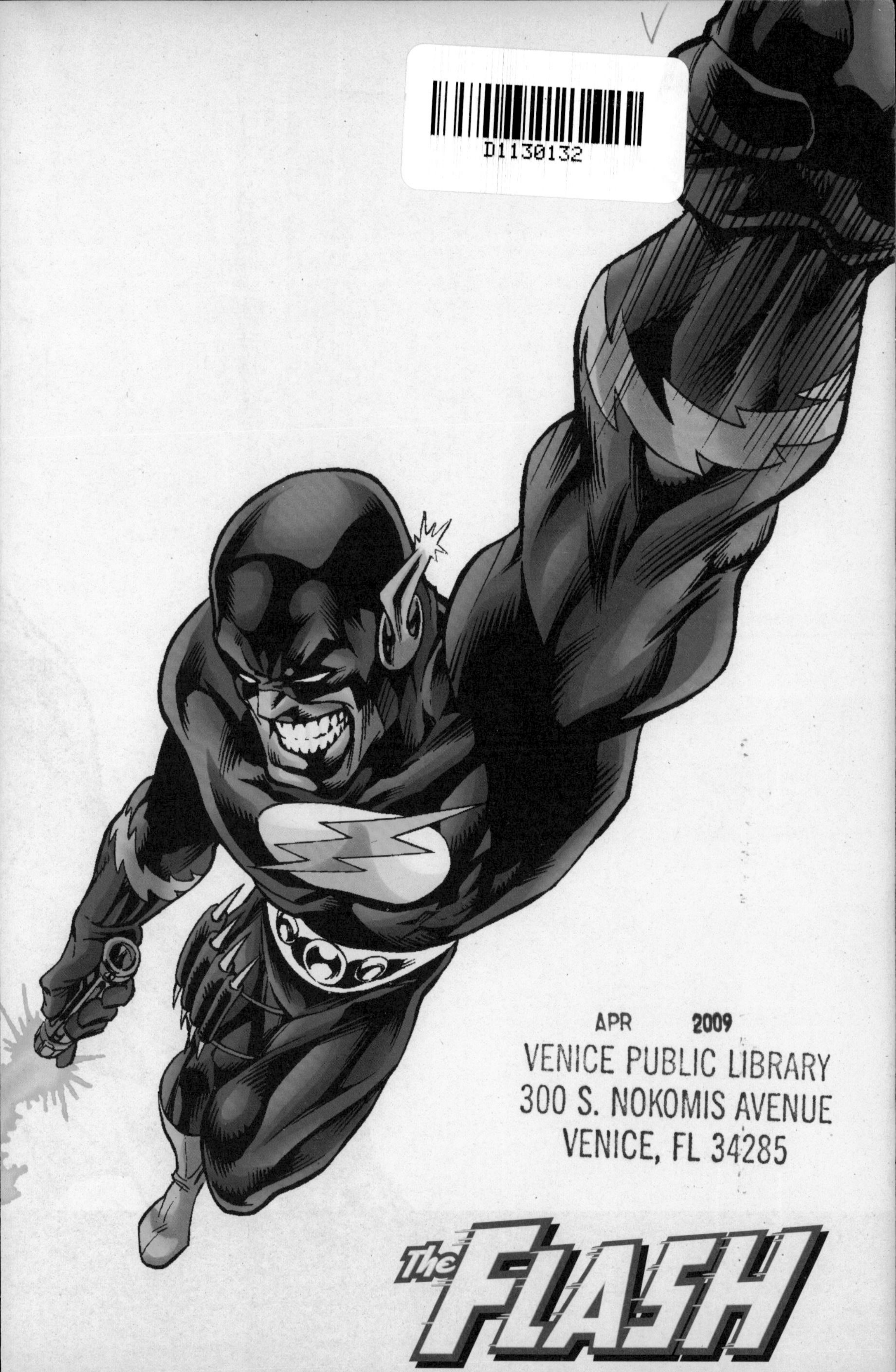

The FLASH
WONDERLAND

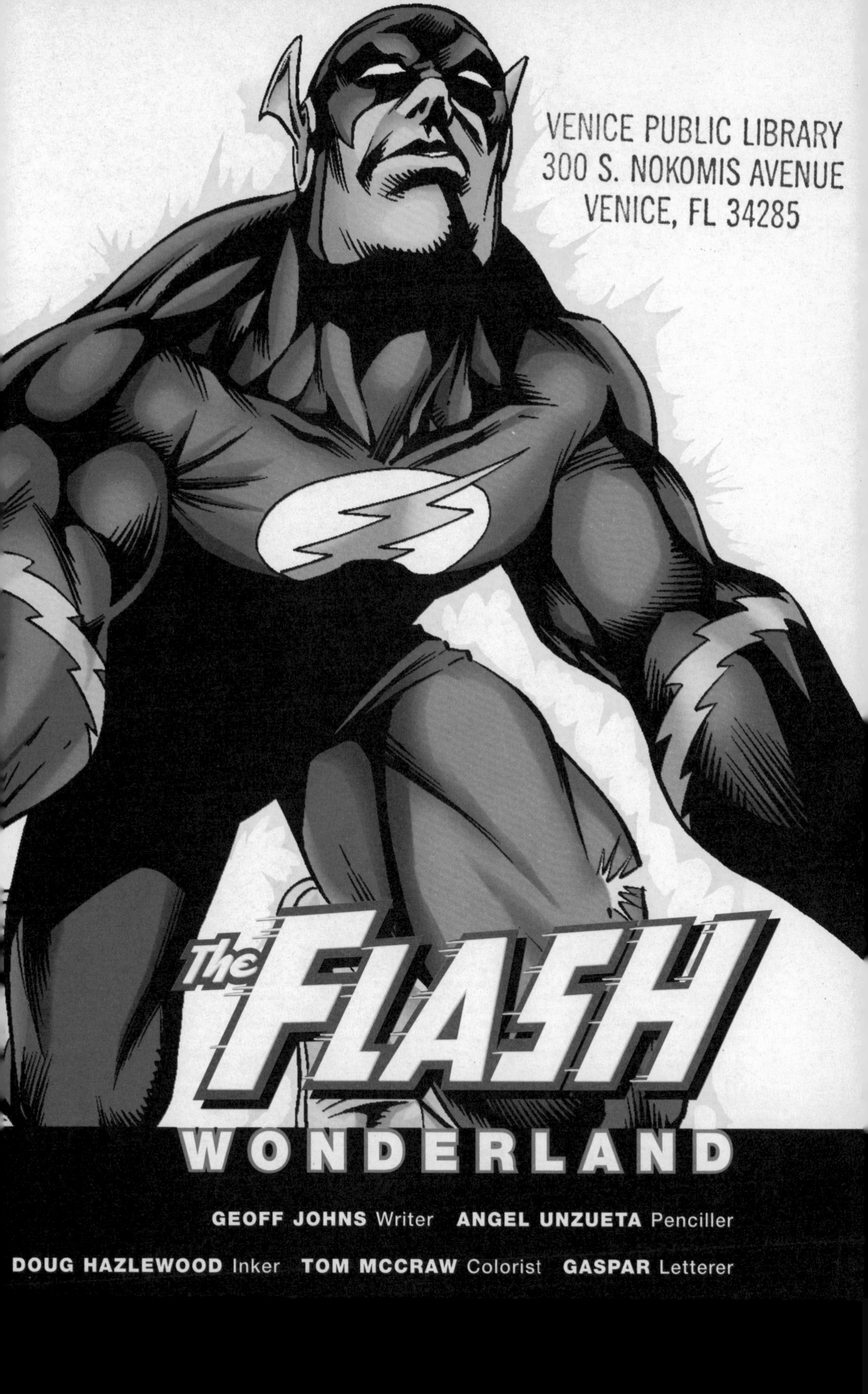

The FLASH
WONDERLAND

GEOFF JOHNS Writer **ANGEL UNZUETA** Penciller

DOUG HAZLEWOOD Inker **TOM MCCRAW** Colorist **GASPAR** Letterer

3 1969 01935 4785

Dan DiDio Senior VP-Executive Editor   Joey Cavalieri Editor-original series   Bob Joy Editor-collected edition   Robbin Brosterman Senior Art Director   Paul Levitz President & Publisher   Georg Brewer VP-Design & DC Direct Creative   Richard Bruning Senior VP-Creative Director Patrick Caldon Executive VP-Finance & Operations Chris Caramalis VP-Finance John Cunningham VP-Marketing Terri Cunningham VP-Managing Editor   Alison Gill VP-Manufacturing   Hank Kanalz VP-General Manager, WildStorm   Jim Lee Editorial Director-WildStorm Paula Lowitt Senior VP-Business & Legal Affairs   MaryEllen McLaughlin VP-Advertising & Custom Publishing   John Nee VP-Business Development   Gregory Noveck Senior VP-Creative Affairs   Sue Pohja VP-Book Trade Sales   Cheryl Rubin Senior VP-Brand Management Jeff Trojan VP-Business Development, DC Direct Bob Wayne VP-Sales

Cover art by Brian Bolland

FLASH: WONDERLAND

DC Comics, 1700 Broadway, New York, NY 10019
A Warner Bros. Entertainment Company
Printed in Canada. First Printing.
ISBN: 1-4012-1489-4
ISBN: 978-1-4012-1489-0

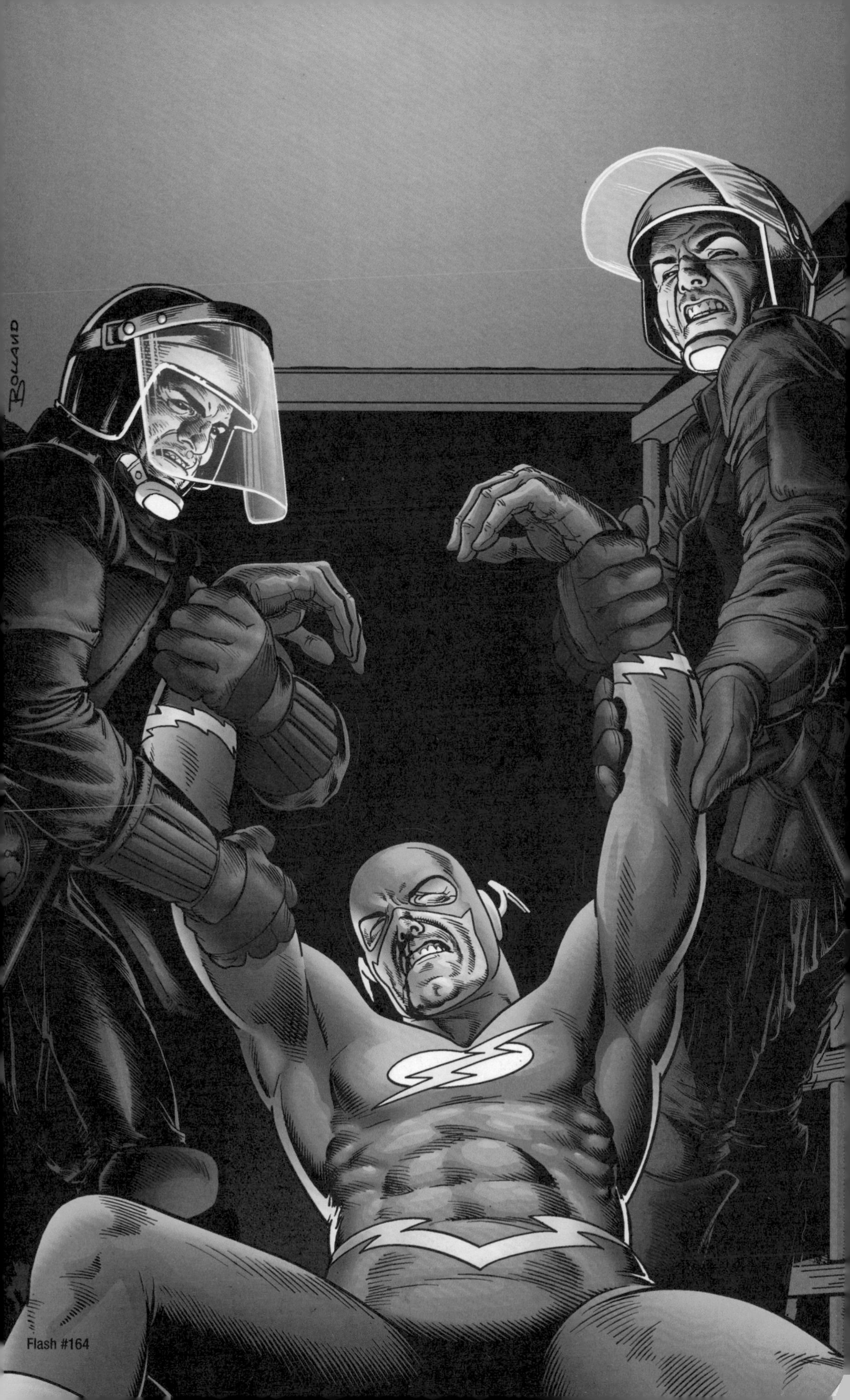
BOLLAND
Flash #164

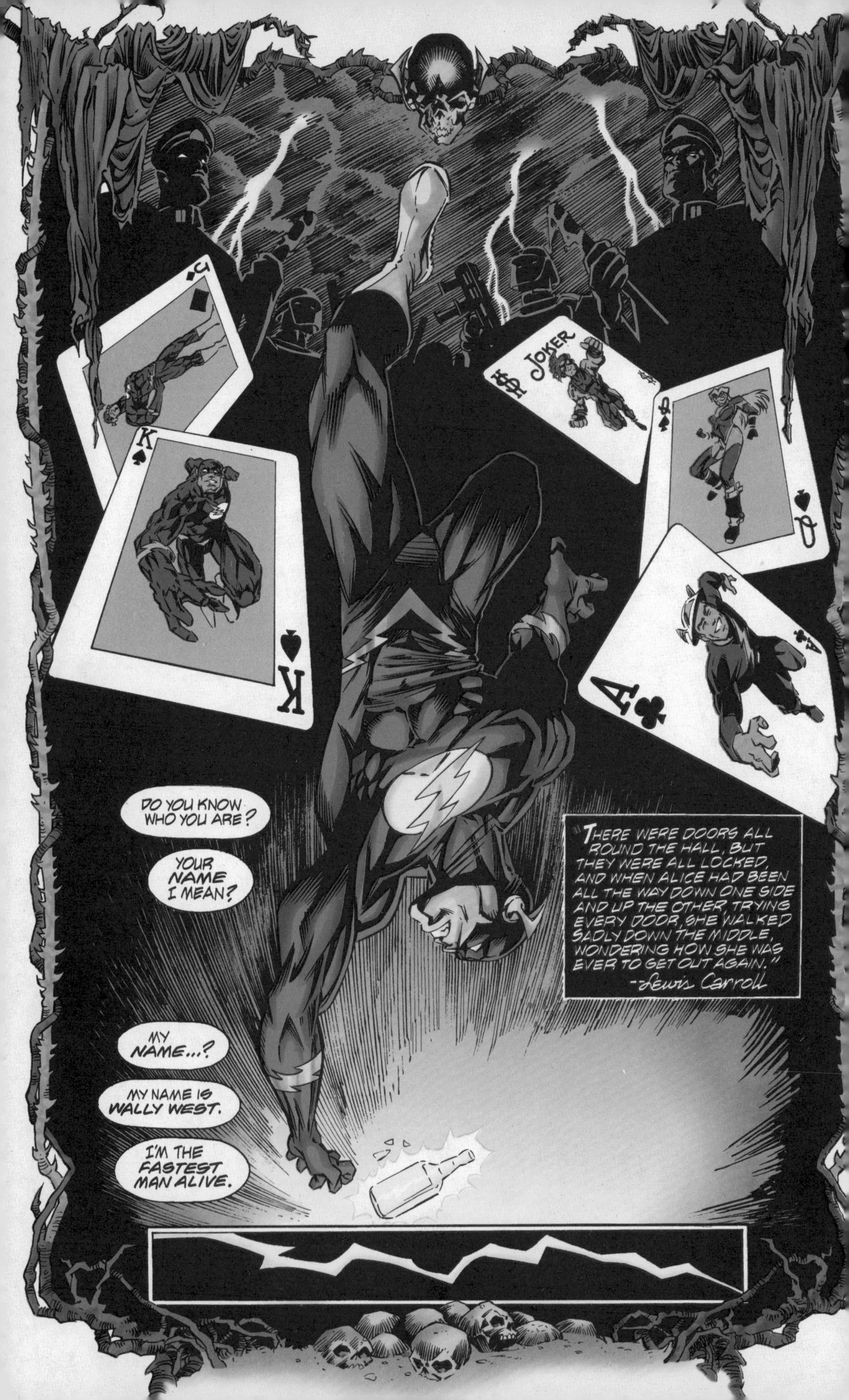

JOKER
DO YOU KNOW WHO YOU ARE?
YOUR NAME I MEAN?
"THERE WERE DOORS ALL ROUND THE HALL, BUT THEY WERE ALL LOCKED, AND WHEN ALICE HAD BEEN ALL THE WAY DOWN ONE SIDE AND UP THE OTHER, TRYING EVERY DOOR, SHE WALKED SADLY DOWN THE MIDDLE, WONDERING HOW SHE WAS EVER TO GET OUT AGAIN."
-Lewis Carroll
MY NAME...?
MY NAME IS WALLY WEST.
I'M THE FASTEST MAN ALIVE.

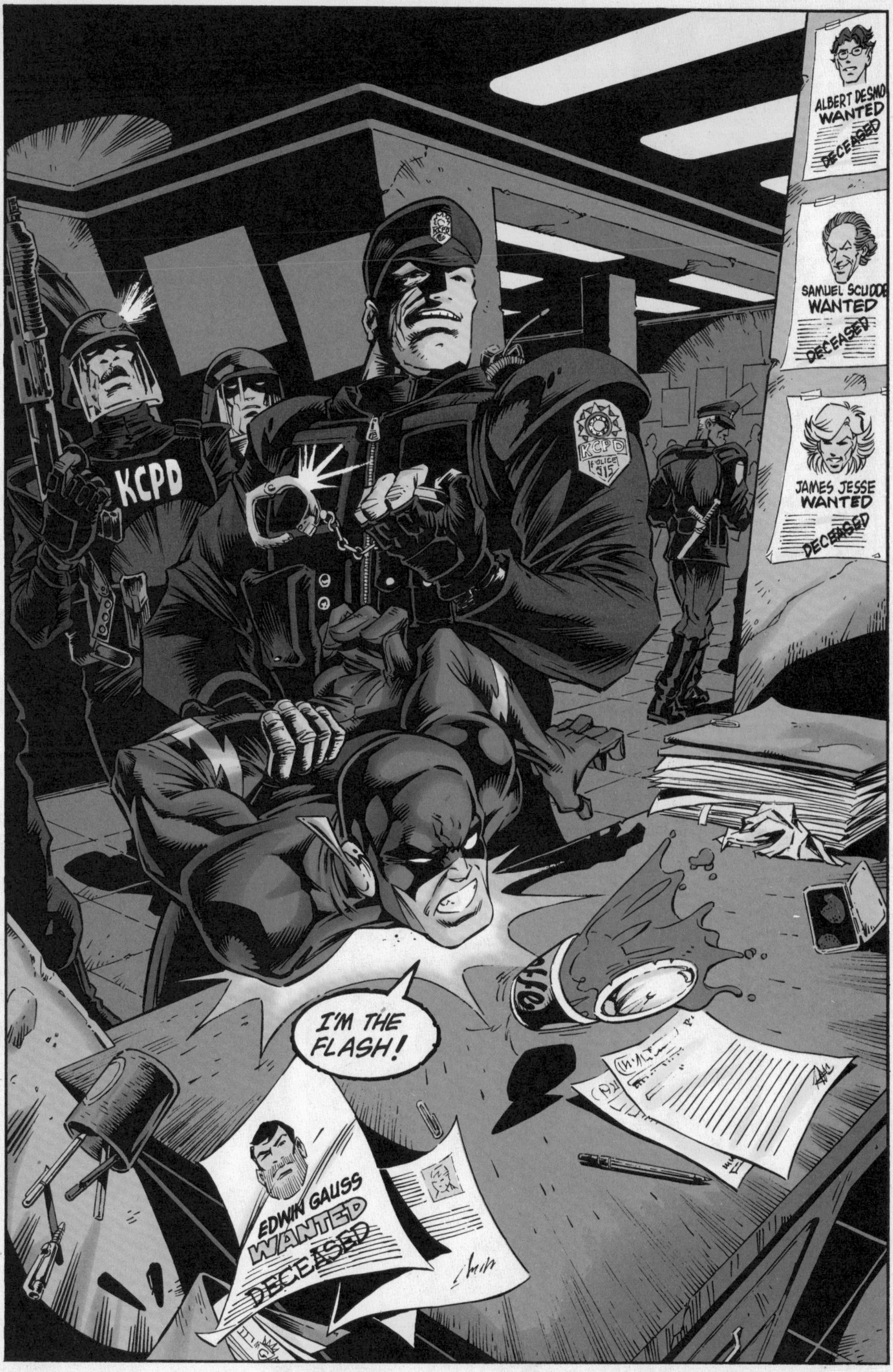
ALBERT DESMO
WANTED
DECEASED
SAMUEL SCUDDE
WANTED
DECEASED
JAMES JESSE
WANTED
DECEASED
KCPD
KCPD
POLICE
515
I'M THE FLASH!
EDWIN GAUSS
WANTED
DECEASED

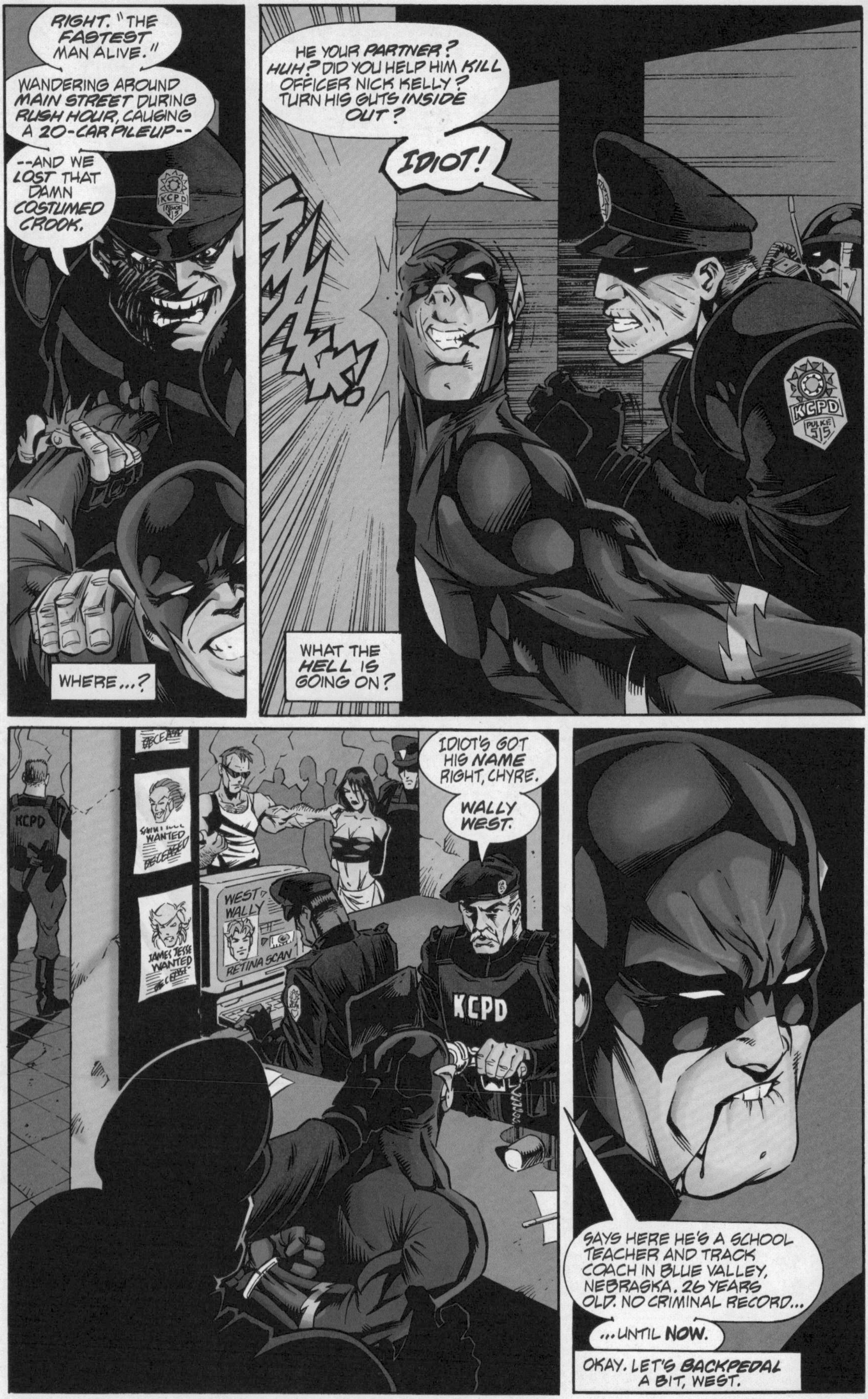
RIGHT. "THE FASTEST MAN ALIVE."
WANDERING AROUND MAIN STREET DURING RUSH HOUR, CAUSING A 20-CAR PILEUP--
--AND WE LOST THAT DAMN COSTUMED CROOK.
WHERE...?
HE YOUR PARTNER? HUH? DID YOU HELP HIM KILL OFFICER NICK KELLY? TURN HIS GUTS INSIDE OUT?
IDIOT!
SMAKK!
WHAT THE HELL IS GOING ON?
KCPD
WANTED
WANTED
IDIOT'S GOT HIS NAME RIGHT, CHYRE.
WALLY WEST.
WEST WALLY
RETINA SCAN
KCPD
SAYS HERE HE'S A SCHOOL TEACHER AND TRACK COACH IN BLUE VALLEY, NEBRASKA. 26 YEARS OLD. NO CRIMINAL RECORD...
...UNTIL NOW.
OKAY. LET'S BACKPEDAL A BIT, WEST.

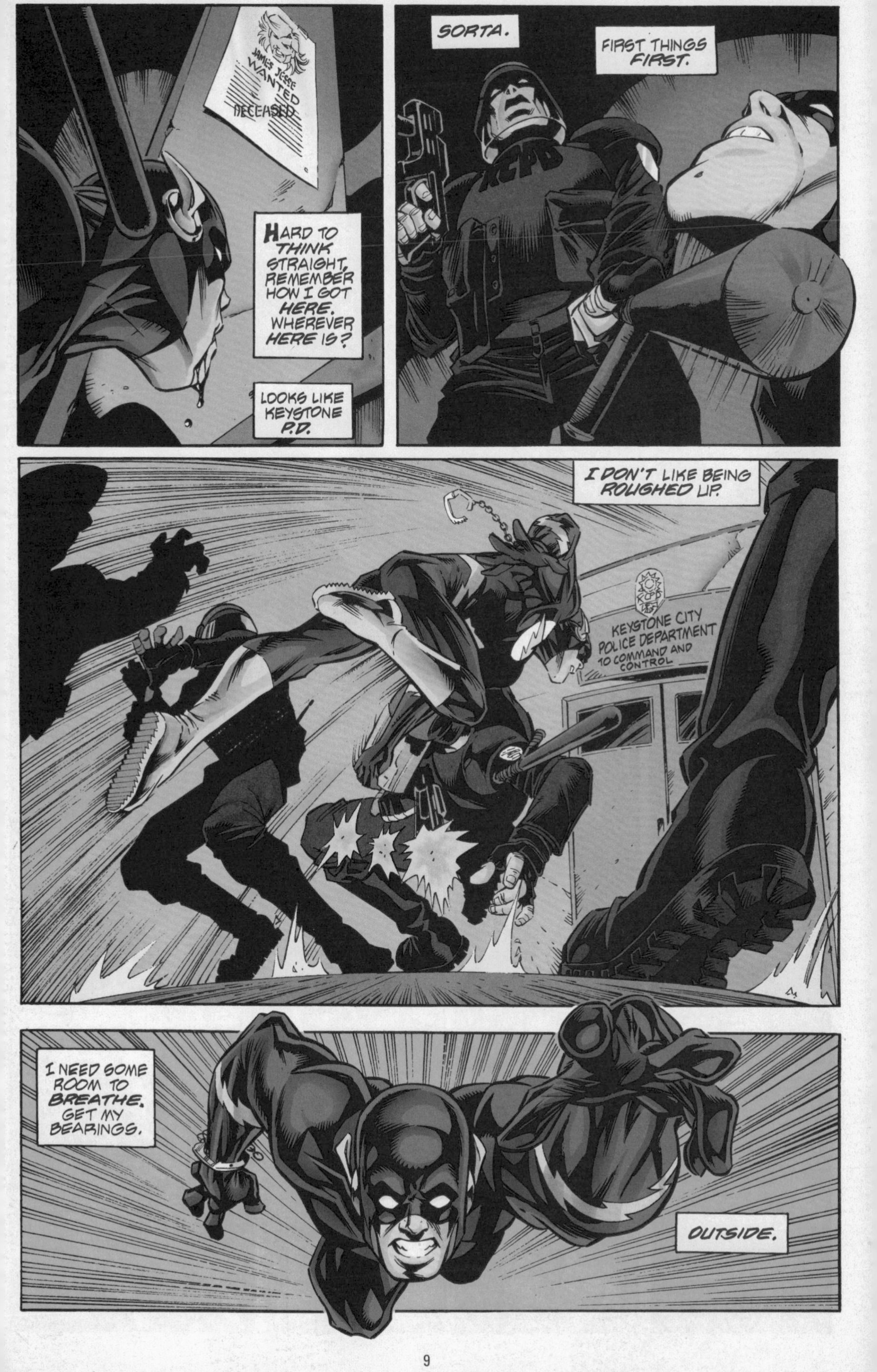
JAMES JESSE
WANTED
DECEASED
HARD TO THINK STRAIGHT, REMEMBER HOW I GOT HERE. WHEREVER HERE IS?
LOOKS LIKE KEYSTONE P.D.
SORTA.
FIRST THINGS FIRST.
KCPD
I DON'T LIKE BEING ROUGHED UP.
KEYSTONE CITY POLICE DEPARTMENT
TO COMMAND AND CONTROL
I NEED SOME ROOM TO BREATHE. GET MY BEARINGS.
OUTSIDE.

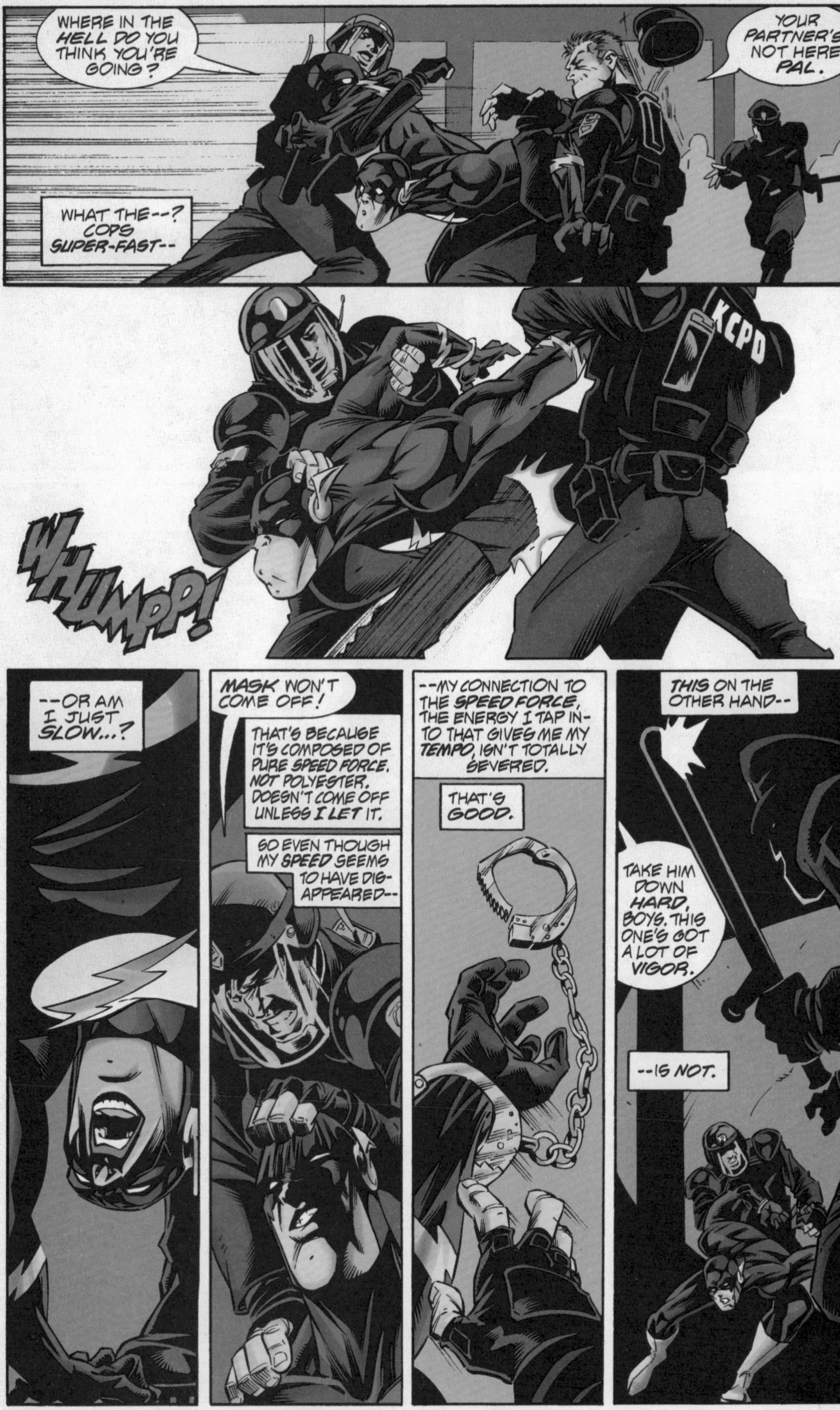
WHERE IN THE HELL DO YOU THINK YOU'RE GOING?
YOUR PARTNER'S NOT HERE, PAL.
WHAT THE--? COPS SUPER-FAST--
WHUMPP!
--OR AM I JUST SLOW...?
MASK WON'T COME OFF!
THAT'S BECAUSE IT'S COMPOSED OF PURE SPEED FORCE. NOT POLYESTER. DOESN'T COME OFF UNLESS I LET IT.
SO EVEN THOUGH MY SPEED SEEMS TO HAVE DISAPPEARED--
--MY CONNECTION TO THE SPEED FORCE, THE ENERGY I TAP INTO THAT GIVES ME MY TEMPO, ISN'T TOTALLY SEVERED.
THAT'S GOOD.
THIS ON THE OTHER HAND--
TAKE HIM DOWN HARD, BOYS. THIS ONE'S GOT A LOT OF VIGOR.
--IS NOT.

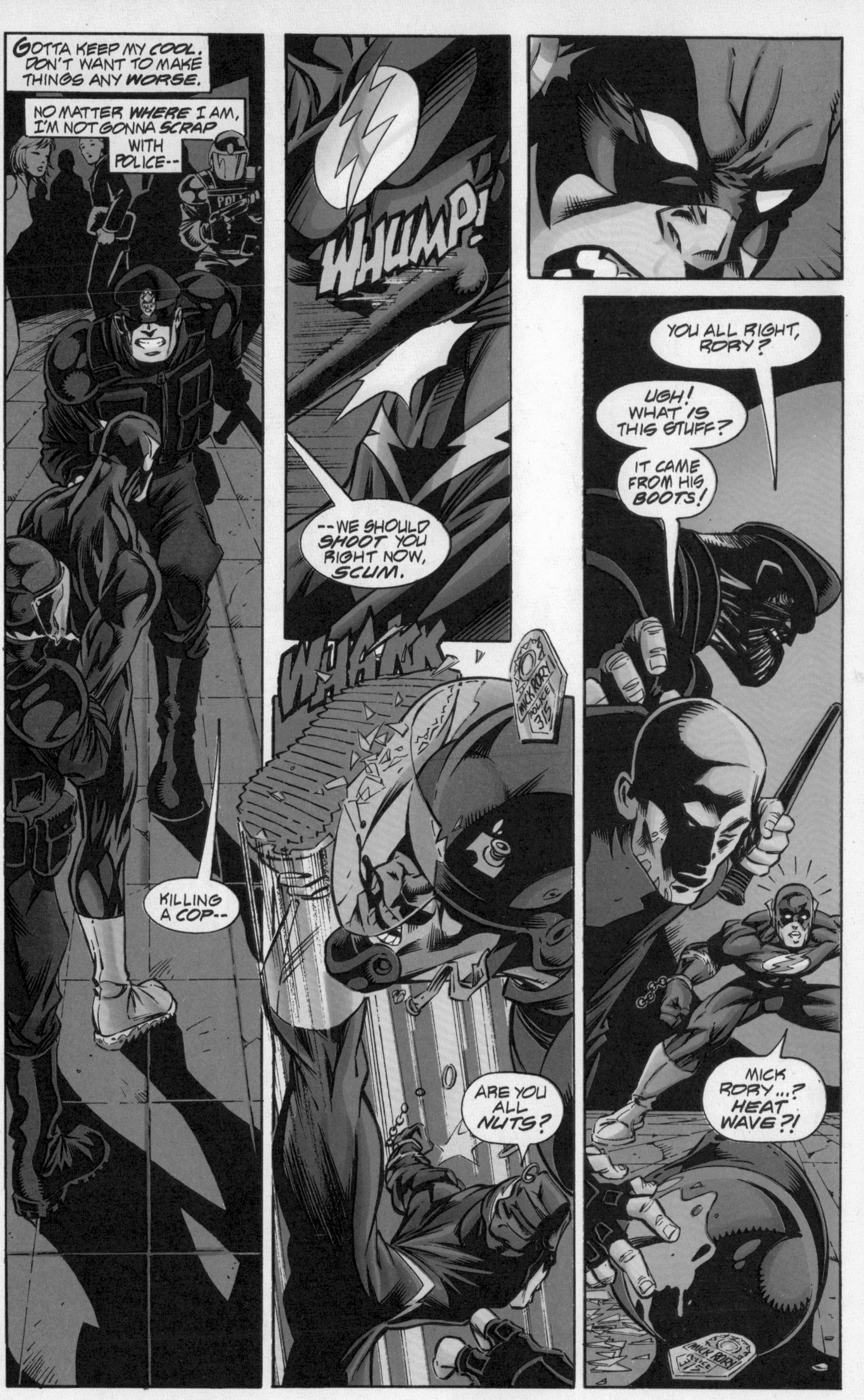
GOTTA KEEP MY COOL. DON'T WANT TO MAKE THINGS ANY WORSE.
NO MATTER WHERE I AM, I'M NOT GONNA SCRAP WITH POLICE--
KILLING A COP--
--WE SHOULD SHOOT YOU RIGHT NOW, SCUM.
WHUMP!
WHAKK
MICK RORY POLICE 315
ARE YOU ALL NUTS?
YOU ALL RIGHT, RORY?
UGH! WHAT IS THIS STUFF?
IT CAME FROM HIS BOOTS!
MICK RORY...? HEAT WAVE?!

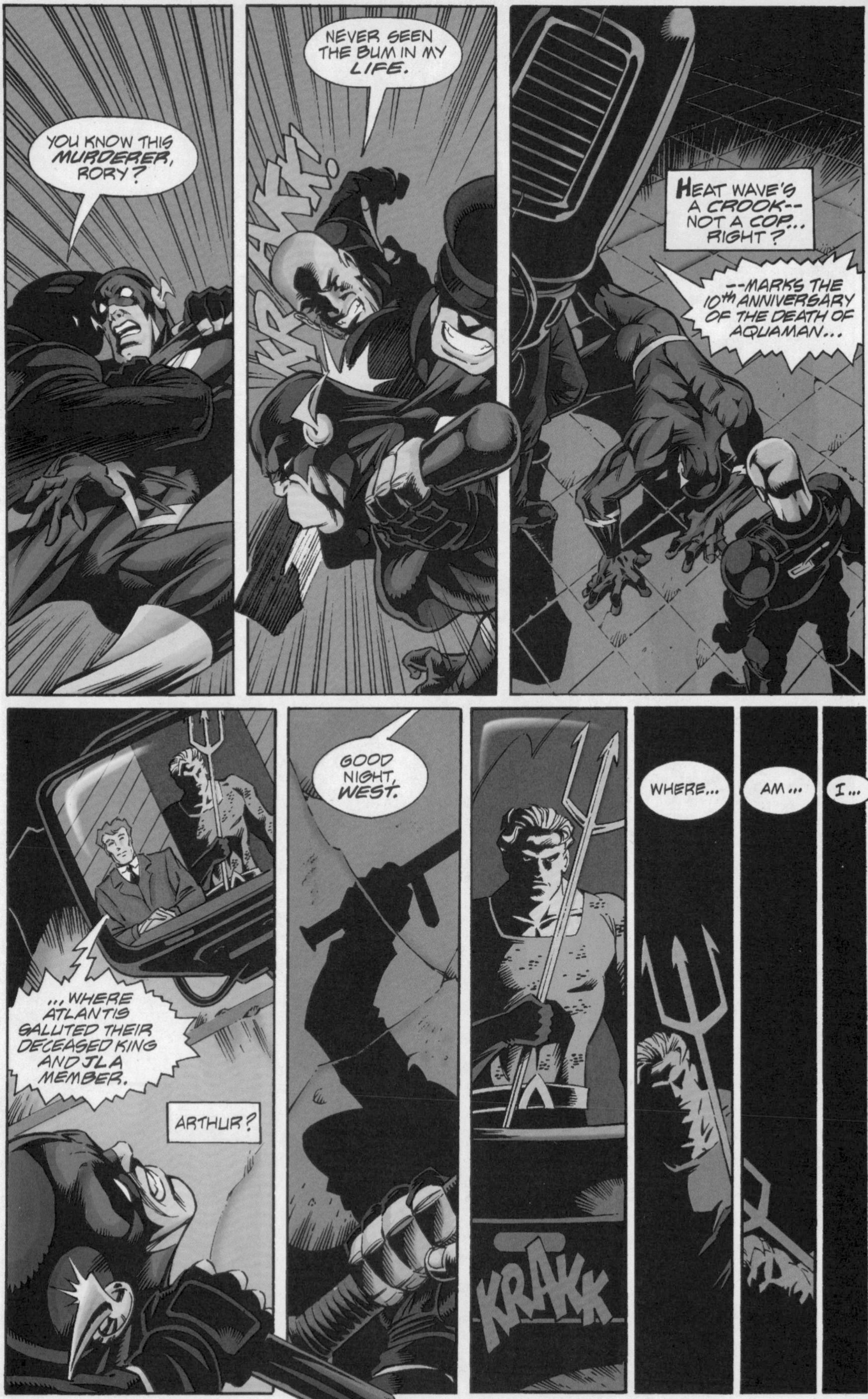

YOU KNOW THIS MURDERER, RORY?
NEVER SEEN THE BUM IN MY LIFE.
KRAKK!
HEAT WAVE'S A CROOK-- NOT A COP... RIGHT?
--MARKS THE 10th ANNIVERSARY OF THE DEATH OF AQUAMAN...
..., WHERE ATLANTIS SALUTED THEIR DECEASED KING AND JLA MEMBER.
ARTHUR?
GOOD NIGHT, WEST.
KRAKK
WHERE...
AM...
I...

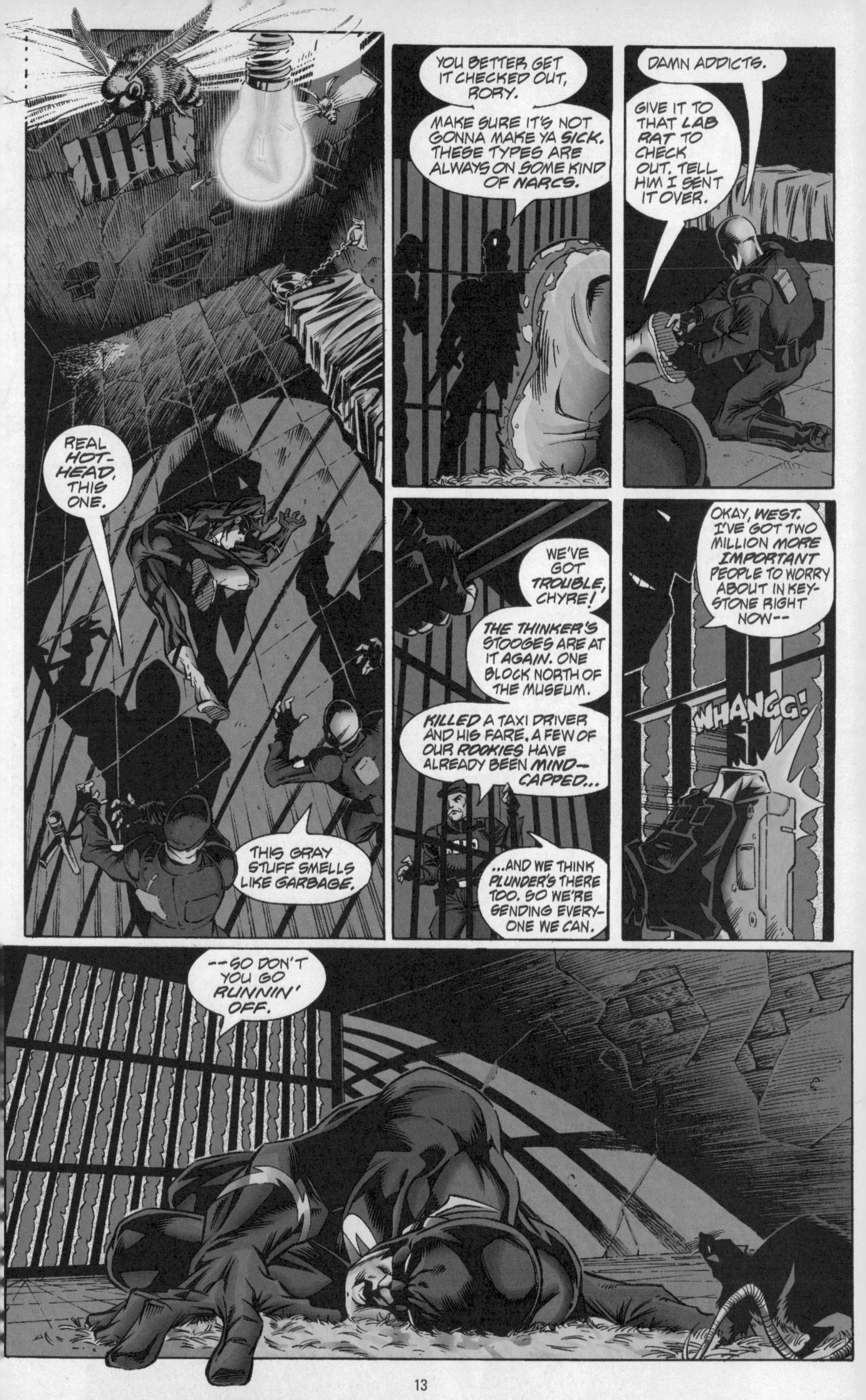
REAL HOT-HEAD, THIS ONE.
THIS GRAY STUFF SMELLS LIKE GARBAGE.
YOU BETTER GET IT CHECKED OUT, RORY.
MAKE SURE IT'S NOT GONNA MAKE YA SICK. THESE TYPES ARE ALWAYS ON SOME KIND OF NARCS.
DAMN ADDICTS.
GIVE IT TO THAT LAB RAT TO CHECK OUT. TELL HIM I SENT IT OVER.
WE'VE GOT TROUBLE, CHYRE!
THE THINKER'S STOOGES ARE AT IT AGAIN. ONE BLOCK NORTH OF THE MUSEUM.
KILLED A TAXI DRIVER AND HIS FARE. A FEW OF OUR ROOKIES HAVE ALREADY BEEN MIND-CAPPED...
...AND WE THINK PLUNDER'S THERE TOO. SO WE'RE SENDING EVERY-ONE WE CAN.
OKAY, WEST. I'VE GOT TWO MILLION MORE IMPORTANT PEOPLE TO WORRY ABOUT IN KEY-STONE RIGHT NOW--
WHANGG!
--SO DON'T YOU GO RUNNIN' OFF.

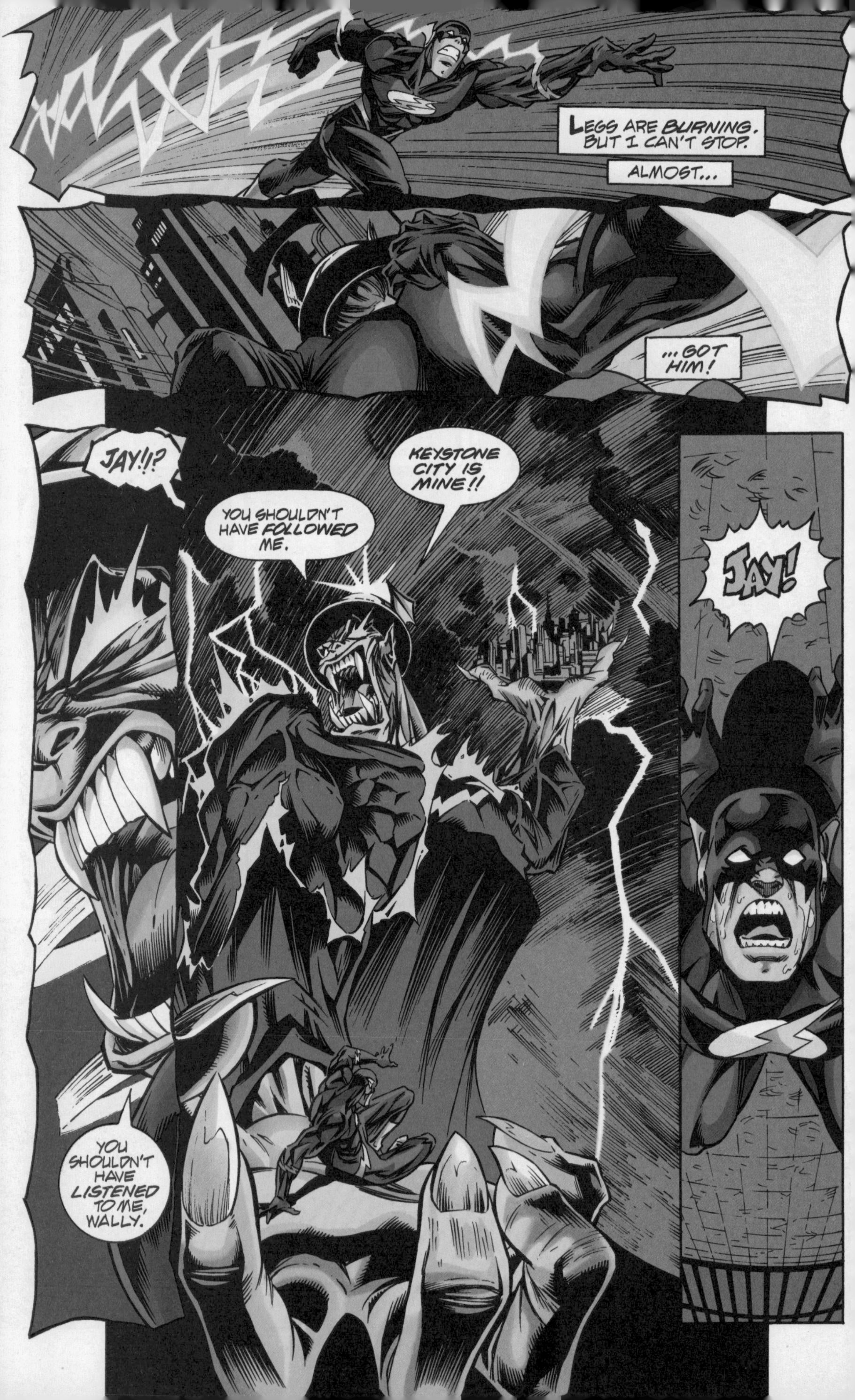
LEGS ARE BURNING. BUT I CAN'T STOP.
ALMOST...
...GOT HIM!
JAY!!?
KEYSTONE CITY IS MINE!!
YOU SHOULDN'T HAVE FOLLOWED ME.
JAY!
YOU SHOULDN'T HAVE LISTENED TO ME, WALLY.

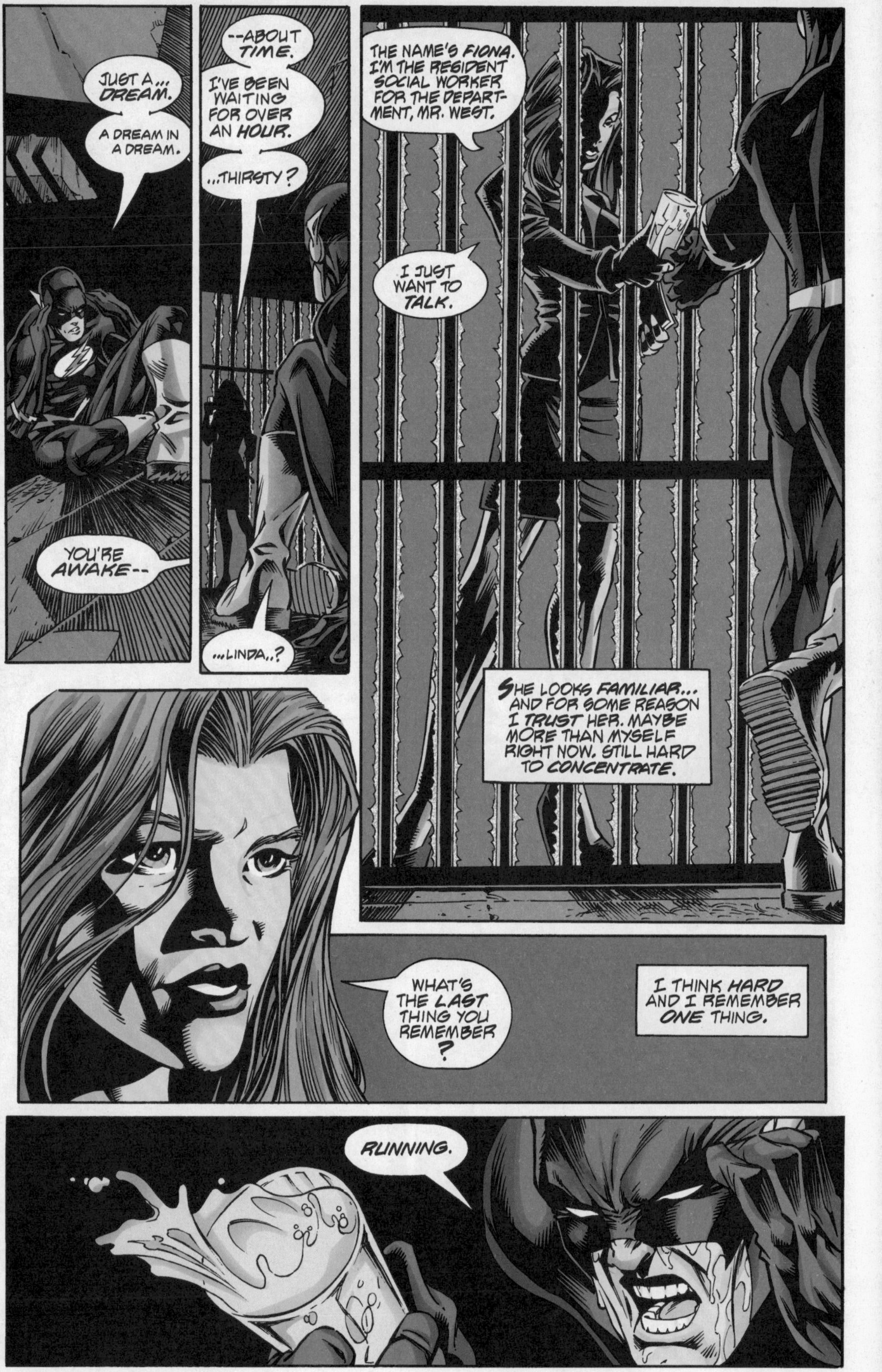
JUST A... DREAM.
A DREAM IN A DREAM.
YOU'RE AWAKE--
--ABOUT TIME.
I'VE BEEN WAITING FOR OVER AN HOUR.
...THIRSTY?
...LINDA..?
THE NAME'S FIONA. I'M THE RESIDENT SOCIAL WORKER FOR THE DEPARTMENT, MR. WEST.
I JUST WANT TO TALK.
SHE LOOKS FAMILIAR... AND FOR SOME REASON I TRUST HER. MAYBE MORE THAN MYSELF RIGHT NOW. STILL HARD TO CONCENTRATE.
WHAT'S THE LAST THING YOU REMEMBER?
I THINK HARD AND I REMEMBER ONE THING.
RUNNING.

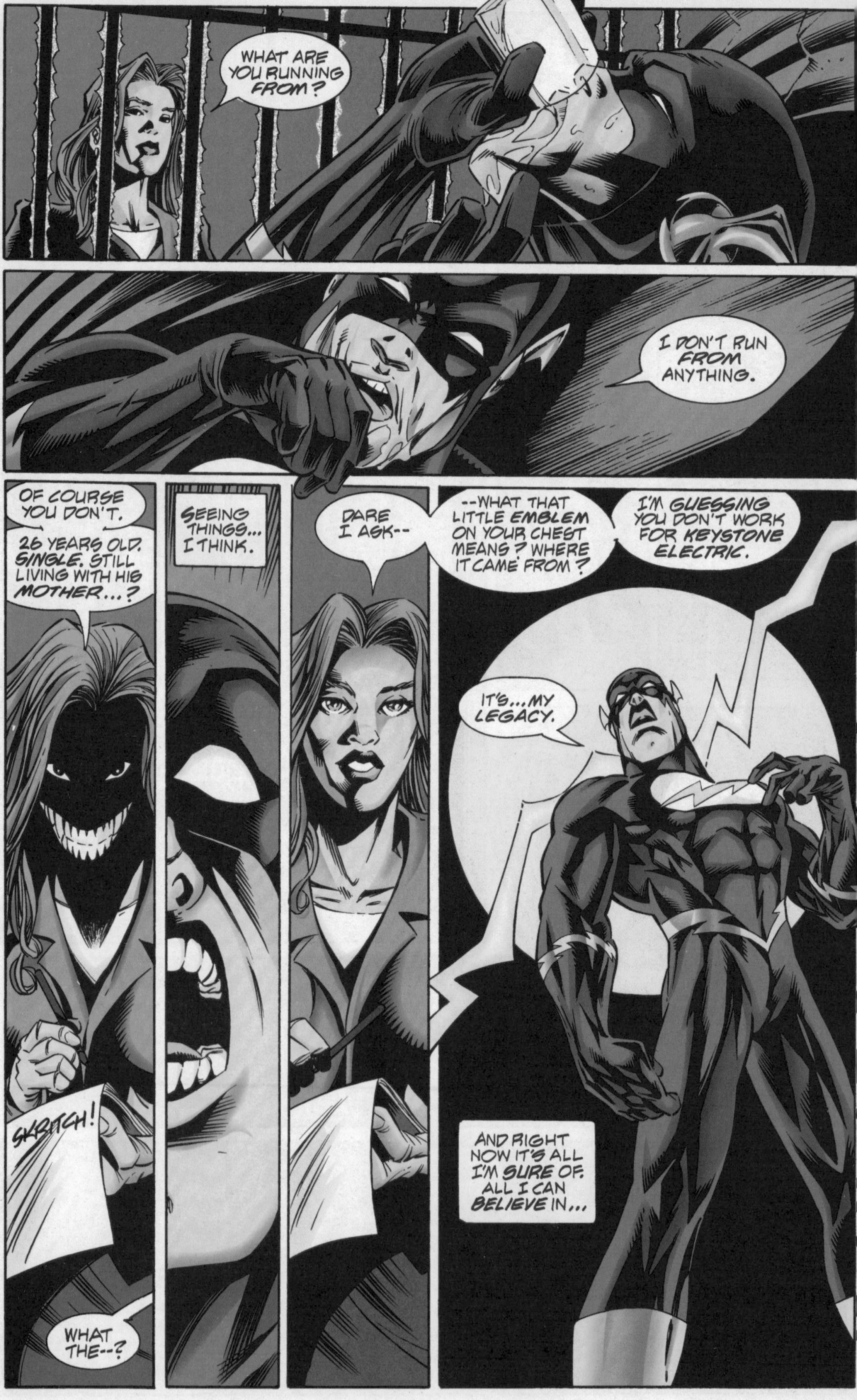
WHAT ARE YOU RUNNING FROM?
I DON'T RUN FROM ANYTHING.
OF COURSE YOU DON'T.
26 YEARS OLD. SINGLE. STILL LIVING WITH HIS MOTHER...?
SKRITCH!
WHAT THE--?
SEEING THINGS... I THINK.
DARE I ASK--
--WHAT THAT LITTLE EMBLEM ON YOUR CHEST MEANS? WHERE IT CAME FROM?
I'M GUESSING YOU DON'T WORK FOR KEYSTONE ELECTRIC.
IT'S... MY LEGACY.
AND RIGHT NOW IT'S ALL I'M SURE OF. ALL I CAN BELIEVE IN...

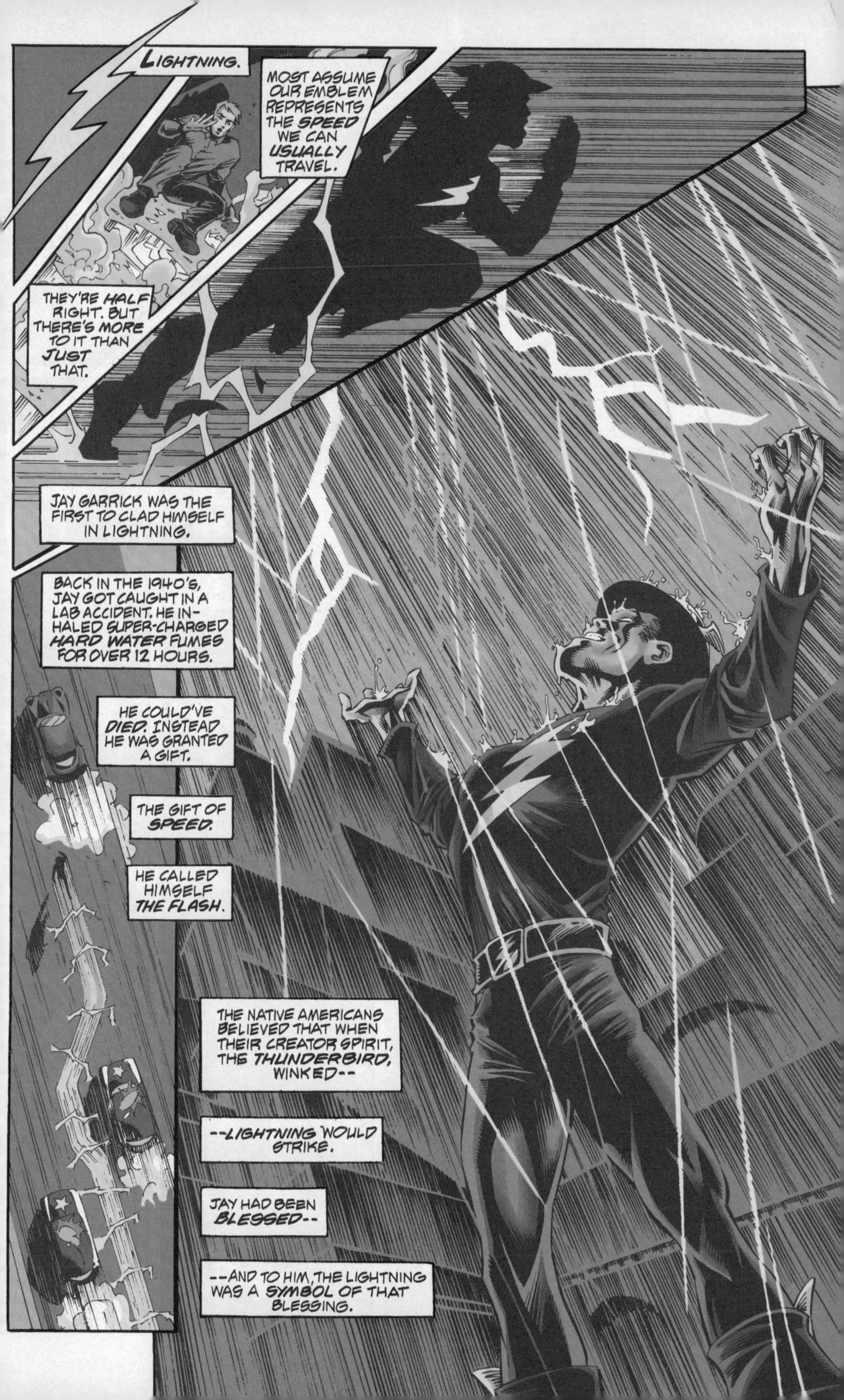
LIGHTNING.
MOST ASSUME OUR EMBLEM REPRESENTS THE SPEED WE CAN USUALLY TRAVEL.
THEY'RE HALF RIGHT. BUT THERE'S MORE TO IT THAN JUST THAT.
JAY GARRICK WAS THE FIRST TO CLAD HIMSELF IN LIGHTNING.
BACK IN THE 1940'S, JAY GOT CAUGHT IN A LAB ACCIDENT. HE IN-HALED SUPER-CHARGED HARD WATER FUMES FOR OVER 12 HOURS.
HE COULD'VE DIED. INSTEAD HE WAS GRANTED A GIFT.
THE GIFT OF SPEED.
HE CALLED HIMSELF THE FLASH.
THE NATIVE AMERICANS BELIEVED THAT WHEN THEIR CREATOR SPIRIT, THE THUNDERBIRD, WINKED--
--LIGHTNING WOULD STRIKE.
JAY HAD BEEN BLESSED--
--AND TO HIM, THE LIGHTNING WAS A SYMBOL OF THAT BLESSING.

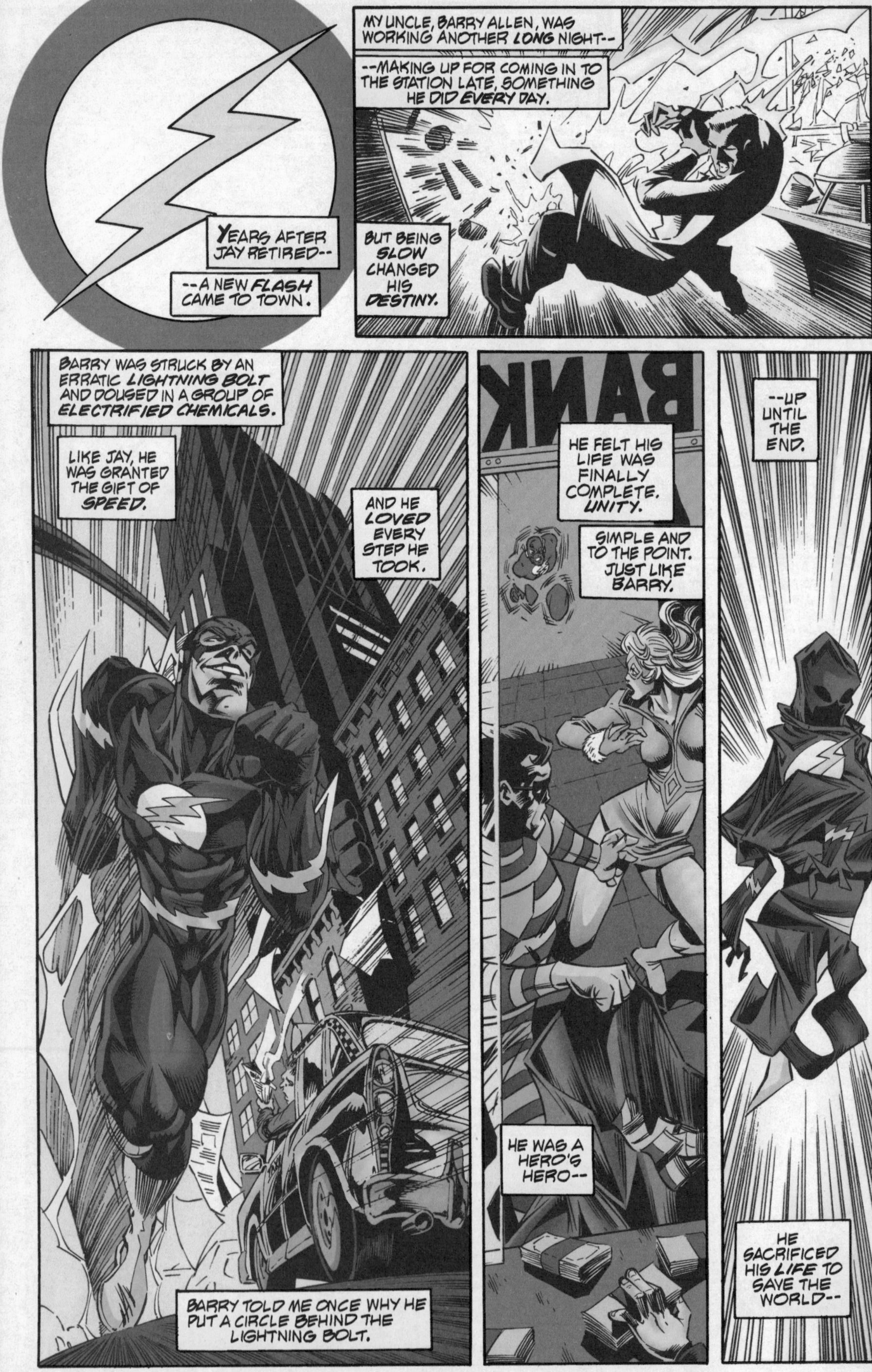
YEARS AFTER JAY RETIRED--
--A NEW FLASH CAME TO TOWN.
MY UNCLE, BARRY ALLEN, WAS WORKING ANOTHER LONG NIGHT--
--MAKING UP FOR COMING IN TO THE STATION LATE, SOMETHING HE DID EVERY DAY.
BUT BEING SLOW CHANGED HIS DESTINY.
BARRY WAS STRUCK BY AN ERRATIC LIGHTNING BOLT AND DOUSED IN A GROUP OF ELECTRIFIED CHEMICALS.
LIKE JAY, HE WAS GRANTED THE GIFT OF SPEED.
AND HE LOVED EVERY STEP HE TOOK.
BARRY TOLD ME ONCE WHY HE PUT A CIRCLE BEHIND THE LIGHTNING BOLT.
BANK
HE FELT HIS LIFE WAS FINALLY COMPLETE. UNITY.
SIMPLE AND TO THE POINT. JUST LIKE BARRY.
HE WAS A HERO'S HERO--
--UP UNTIL THE END.
HE SACRIFICED HIS LIFE TO SAVE THE WORLD--

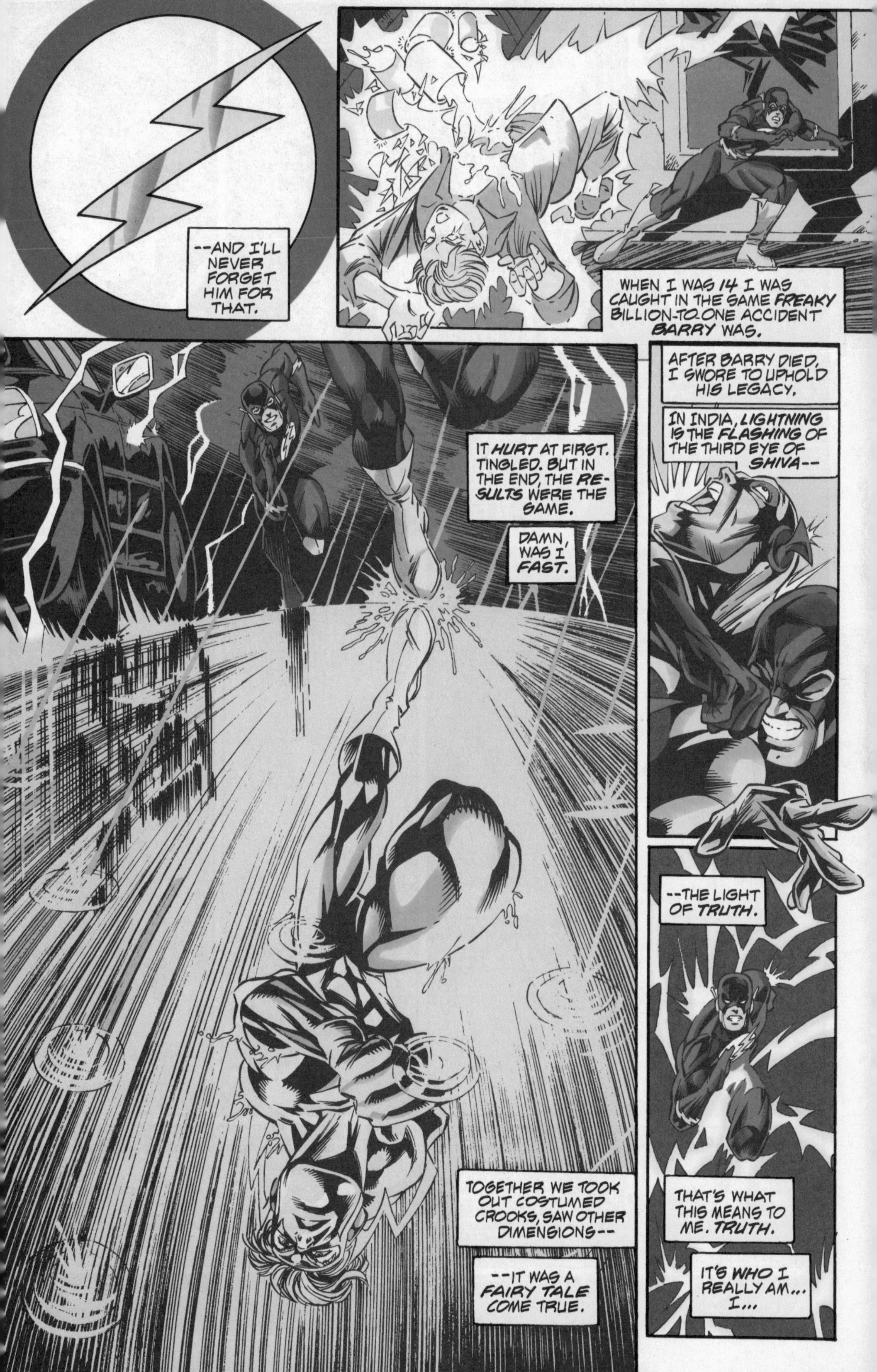
--AND I'LL NEVER FORGET HIM FOR THAT.
WHEN I WAS 14 I WAS CAUGHT IN THE SAME FREAKY BILLION-TO-ONE ACCIDENT BARRY WAS.
IT HURT AT FIRST. TINGLED. BUT IN THE END, THE RESULTS WERE THE SAME.
DAMN, WAS I FAST.
TOGETHER WE TOOK OUT COSTUMED CROOKS, SAW OTHER DIMENSIONS--
--IT WAS A FAIRY TALE COME TRUE.
AFTER BARRY DIED, I SWORE TO UPHOLD HIS LEGACY.
IN INDIA, LIGHTNING IS THE FLASHING OF THE THIRD EYE OF SHIVA--
--THE LIGHT OF TRUTH.
THAT'S WHAT THIS MEANS TO ME. TRUTH.
IT'S WHO I REALLY AM... I...

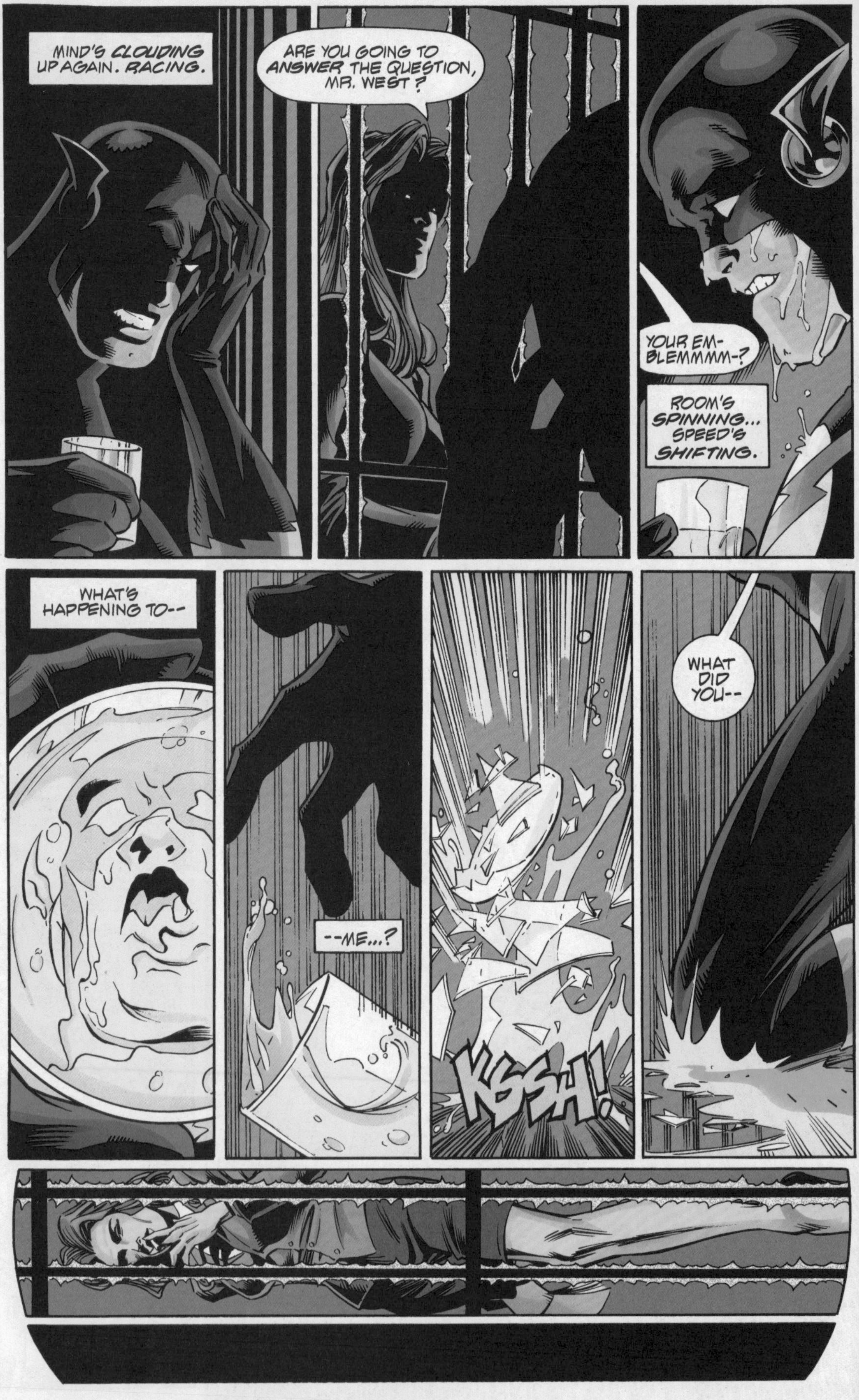

MIND'S CLOUDING UP AGAIN. RACING.
ARE YOU GOING TO ANSWER THE QUESTION, MR. WEST?
YOUR EM-BLEMMMM-?
ROOM'S SPINNING... SPEED'S SHIFTING.
WHAT'S HAPPENING TO--
--ME...?
KSSH!
WHAT DID YOU--

JUST A HEAVY *TRUTH SERUM* AND *TRANQUILIZER.*

YOUR METABOLISM IS BREAKING IT DOWN *FASTER* THAN I'D HOPED. IT MAY BE *TWISSSSSTING* YOUR PERCEPTIONS A BIT.

...A *BIT?*

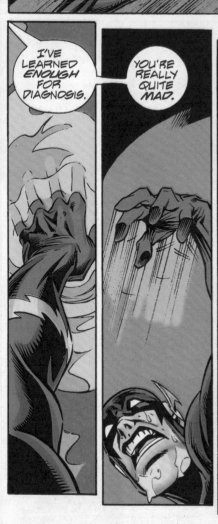

I'VE LEARNED *ENOUGH* FOR *DIAGNOSIS.*

YOU'RE REALLY QUITE *MAD.*

NO. I'M...I'M...

YOU'RE A *SCHOOL TEACHER,* MR. WEST.

A *FELON.*

YOU HAVE *NO* IDEA OF *WHERE* YOU ARE OR WHERE *YOU'RE GOING.*

YOU NEED *HELP.*

BUT FOR A *LITTLE* REASSURANCE, LET ME CHECK--

SCHOOL TEACHER? SINGLE? SHE'S WRONG...

...I'VE BEEN IN THE *SUPERHERO* BUSINESS WAY TOO LONG TO SECOND-GUESS MYSELF.

THAT'S KYLE'S JOB.

-- FOR SOMETHING I NEVER LEAVE *HOME* WITHOUT.

THERE IT IS. PROOF I'M *NOT* A FOOT SHORT OF A YARD.

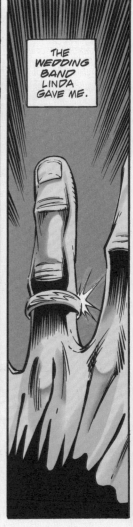

THE WEDDING BAND LINDA GAVE ME.

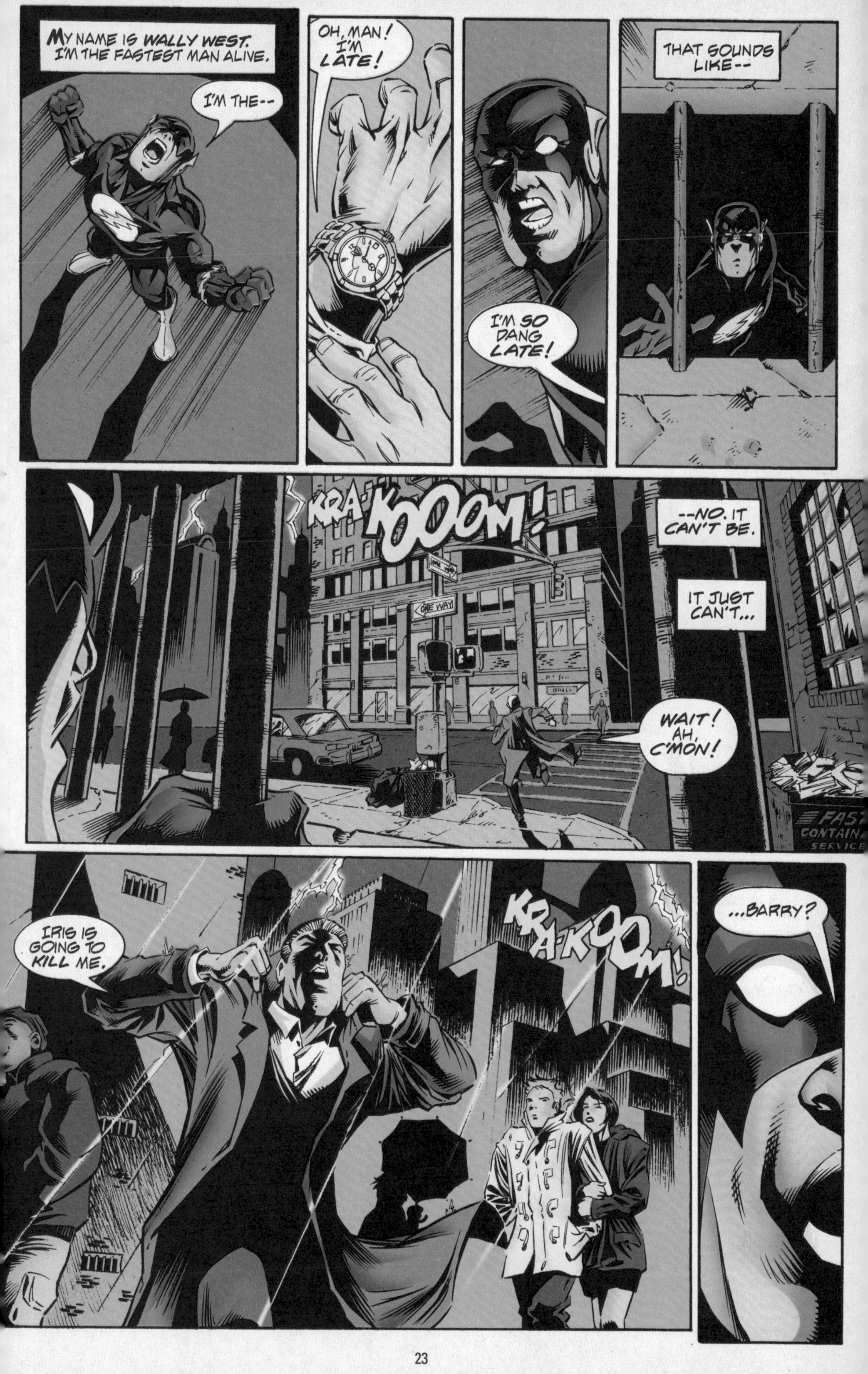
MY NAME IS WALLY WEST. I'M THE FASTEST MAN ALIVE.
I'M THE--
OH, MAN! I'M LATE!
I'M SO DANG LATE!
THAT SOUNDS LIKE--
KRA-KOOOM!
--NO. IT CAN'T BE.
IT JUST CAN'T...
WAIT! AH, C'MON!
ONE WAY
FAST CONTAIN SERVICE
IRIS IS GOING TO KILL ME.
KRA-KOOOM!
...BARRY?

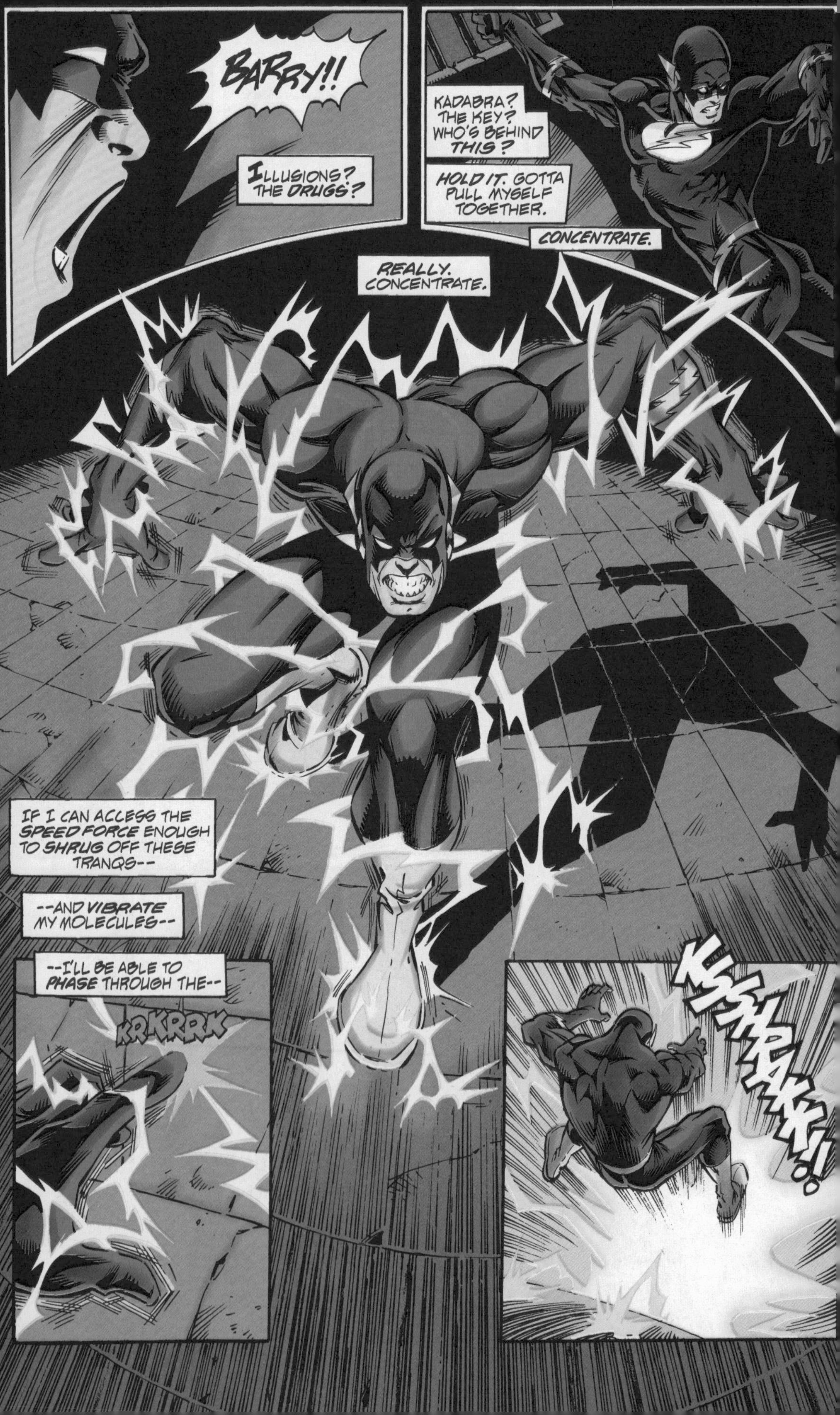
BARRY!!
ILLUSIONS? THE DRUGS?
KADABRA? THE KEY? WHO'S BEHIND THIS?
HOLD IT. GOTTA PULL MYSELF TOGETHER.
CONCENTRATE.
REALLY. CONCENTRATE.
IF I CAN ACCESS THE SPEED FORCE ENOUGH TO SHRUG OFF THESE TRANQS--
--AND VIBRATE MY MOLECULES--
--I'LL BE ABLE TO PHASE THROUGH THE--
KRKRRK
KUSHRAKK!!

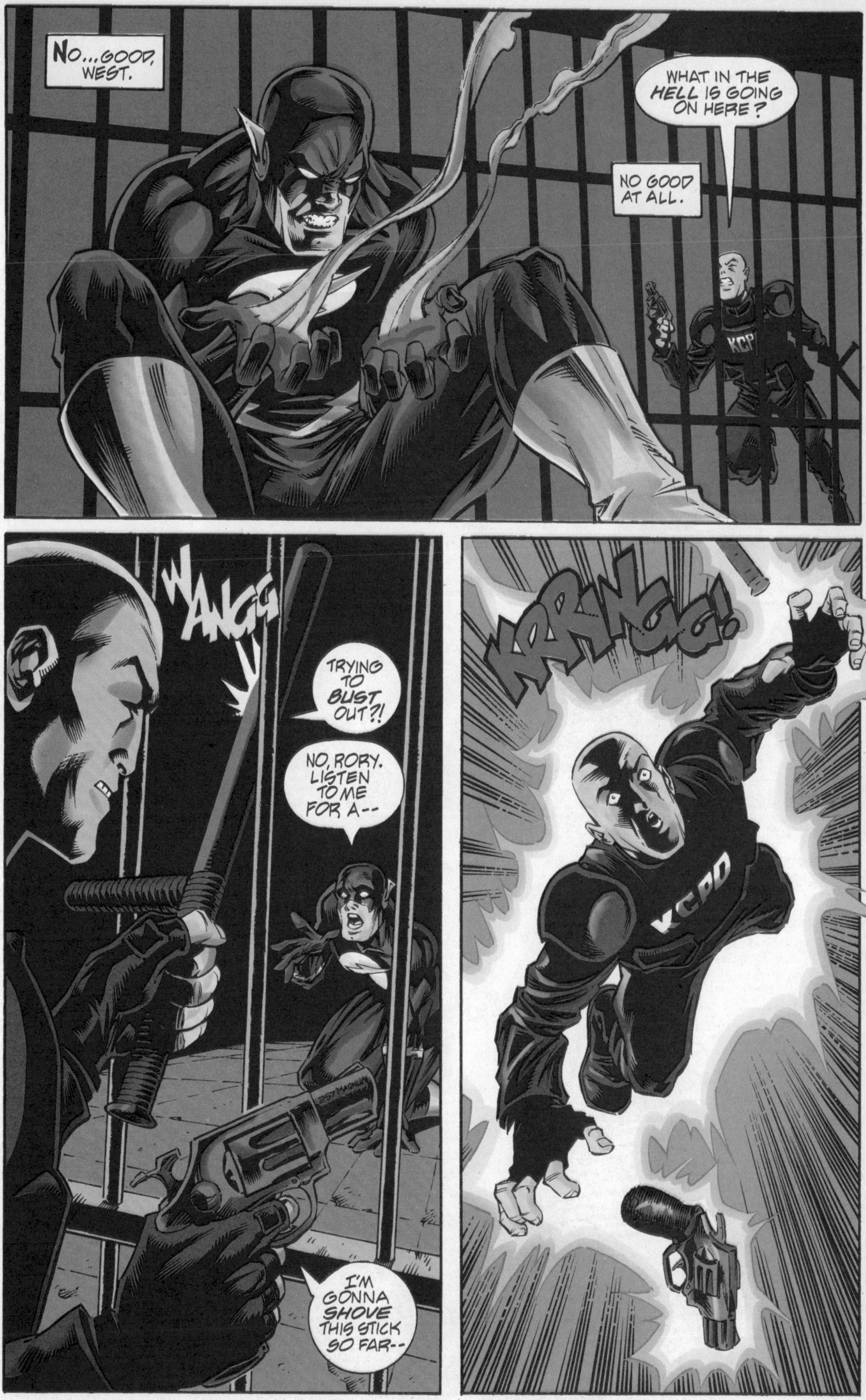
NO...GOOD, WEST.
WHAT IN THE HELL IS GOING ON HERE?
NO GOOD AT ALL.
WANGG
TRYING TO BUST OUT?!
NO, RORY. LISTEN TO ME FOR A--
I'M GONNA SHOVE THIS STICK SO FAR--
KRANGG!

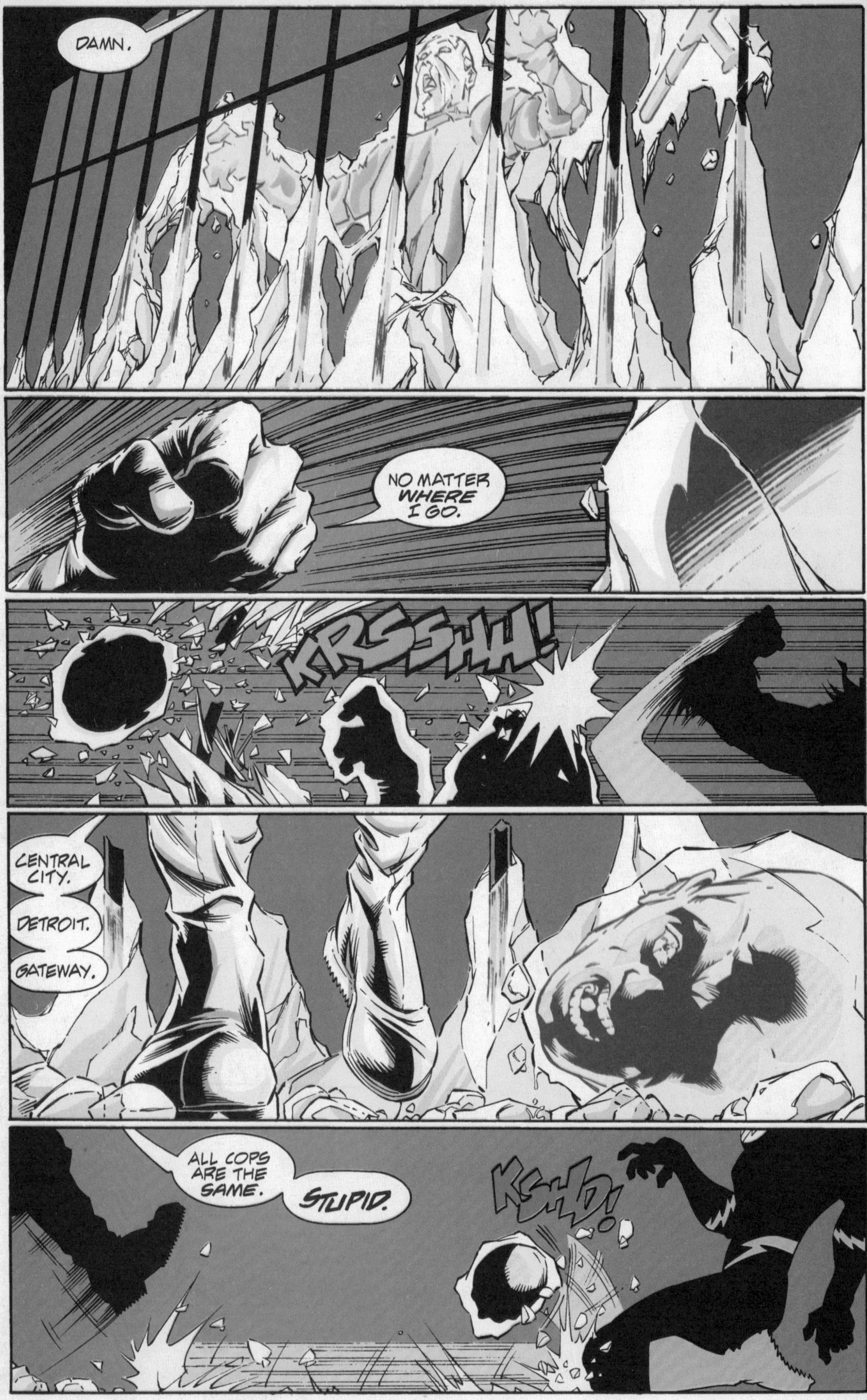
DAMN.
NO MATTER WHERE I GO.
KRSSHH!
CENTRAL CITY.
DETROIT.
GATEWAY.
ALL COPS ARE THE SAME.
STUPID.
KSHD!

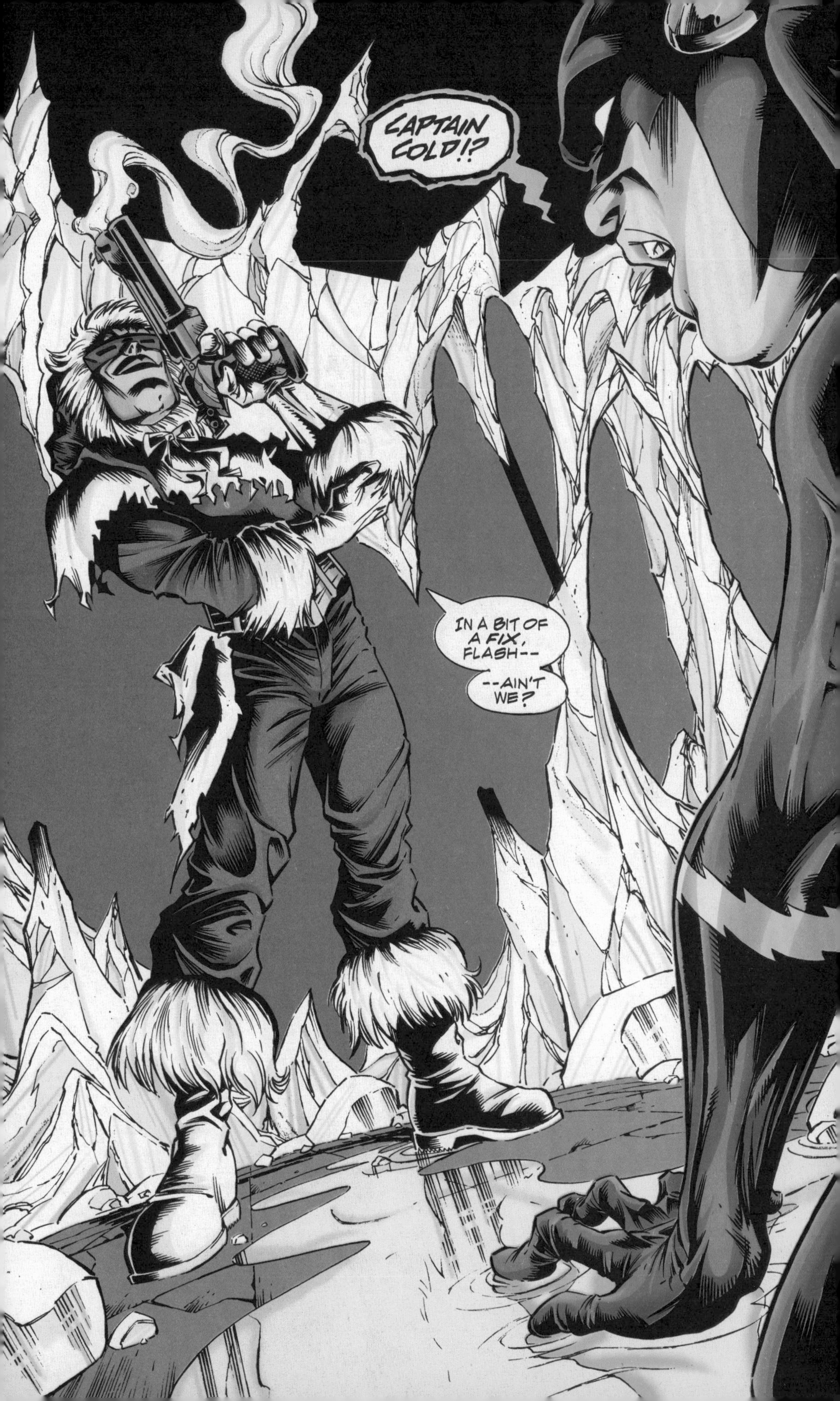
CAPTAIN COLD!?
IN A BIT OF A FIX, FLASH--
--AIN'T WE?

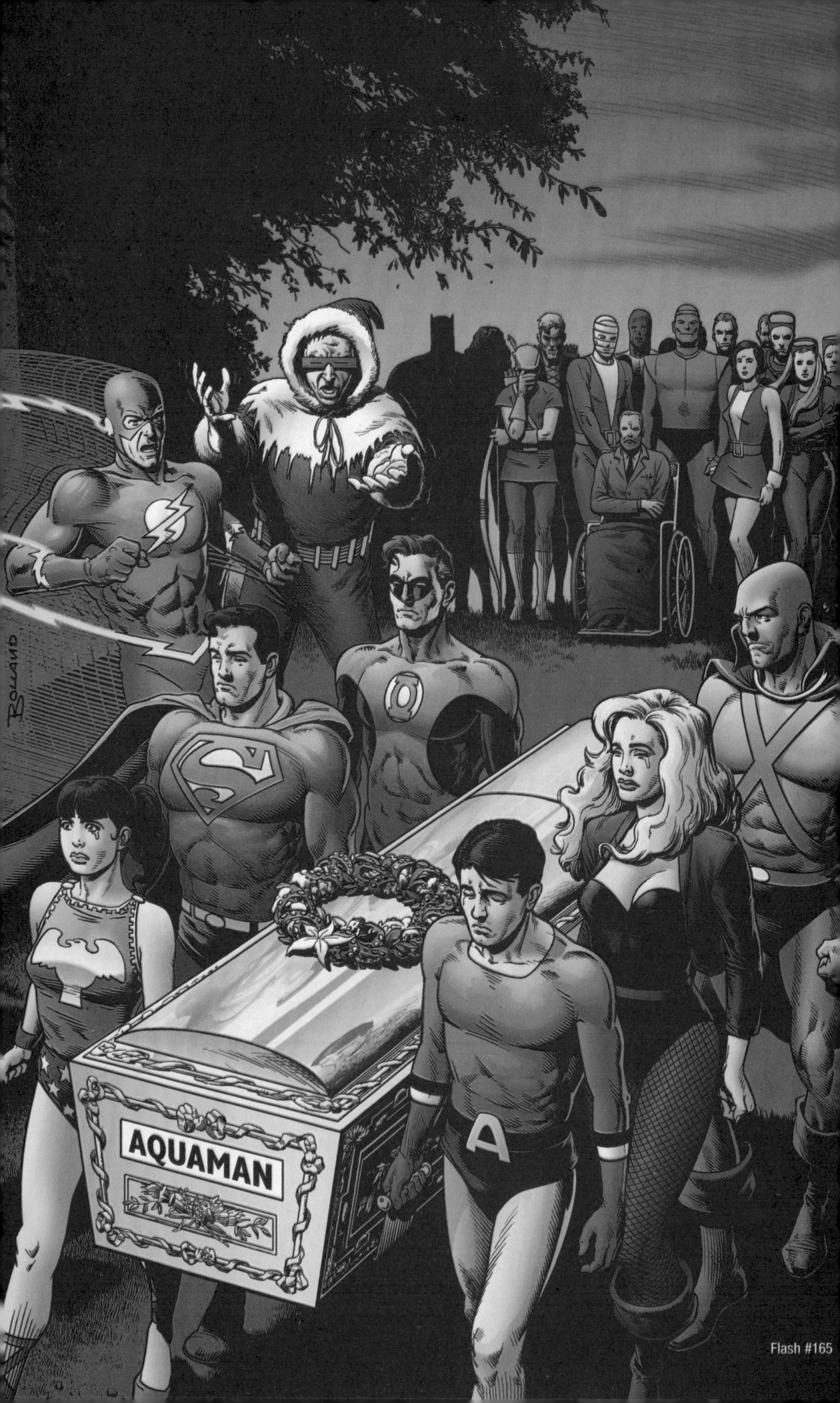
BOLLAND
AQUAMAN

Flash #165

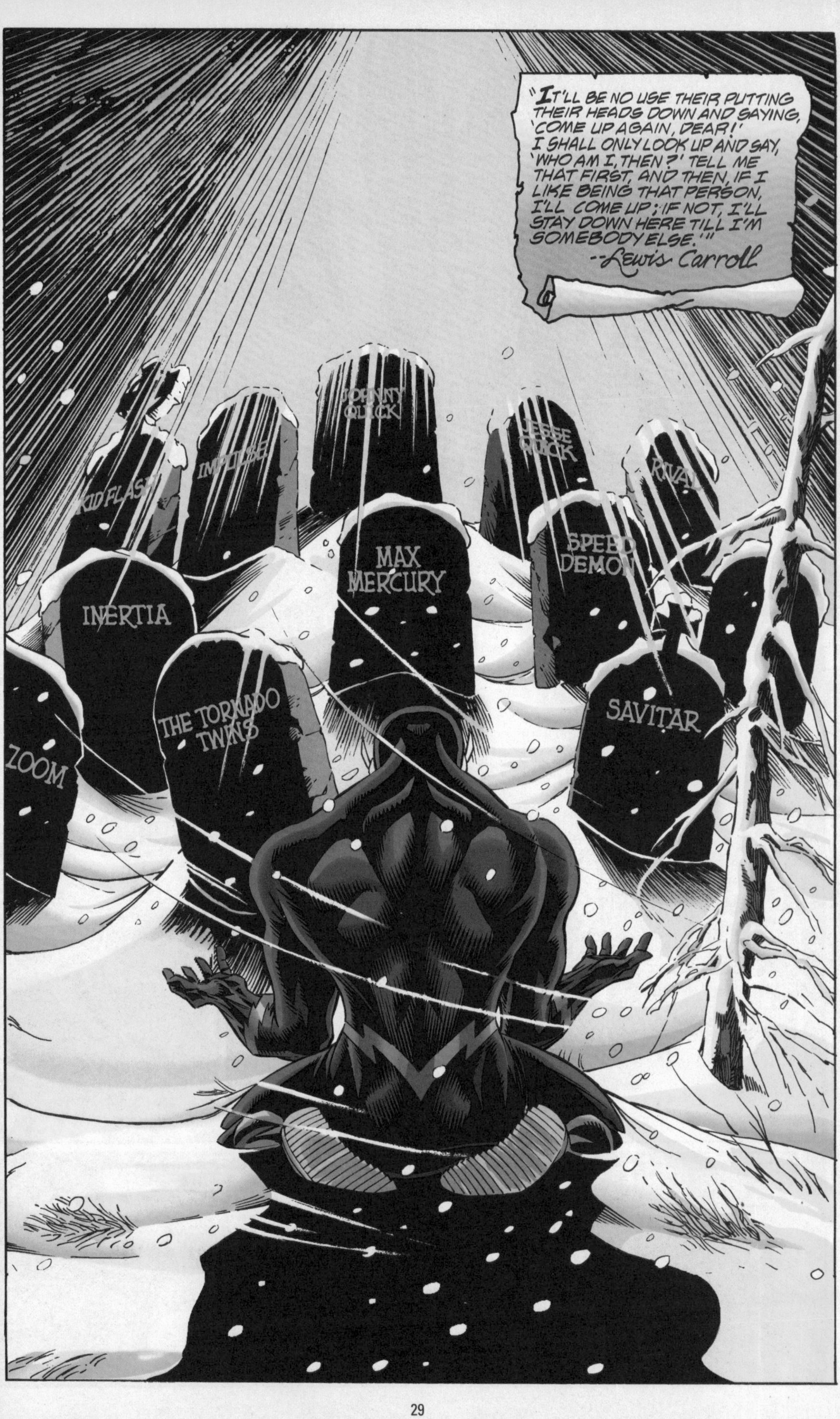
"IT'LL BE NO USE THEIR PUTTING THEIR HEADS DOWN AND SAYING, 'COME UP AGAIN, DEAR!' I SHALL ONLY LOOK UP AND SAY, 'WHO AM I, THEN?' TELL ME THAT FIRST, AND THEN, IF I LIKE BEING THAT PERSON, I'LL COME UP; IF NOT, I'LL STAY DOWN HERE TILL I'M SOMEBODY ELSE.'"
--Lewis Carroll
JOHNNY QUICK
IMPULSE
KID FLASH
JESSE QUICK
RIVAL
MAX MERCURY
SPEED DEMON
INERTIA
THE TORNADO TWINS
SAVITAR
ZOOM

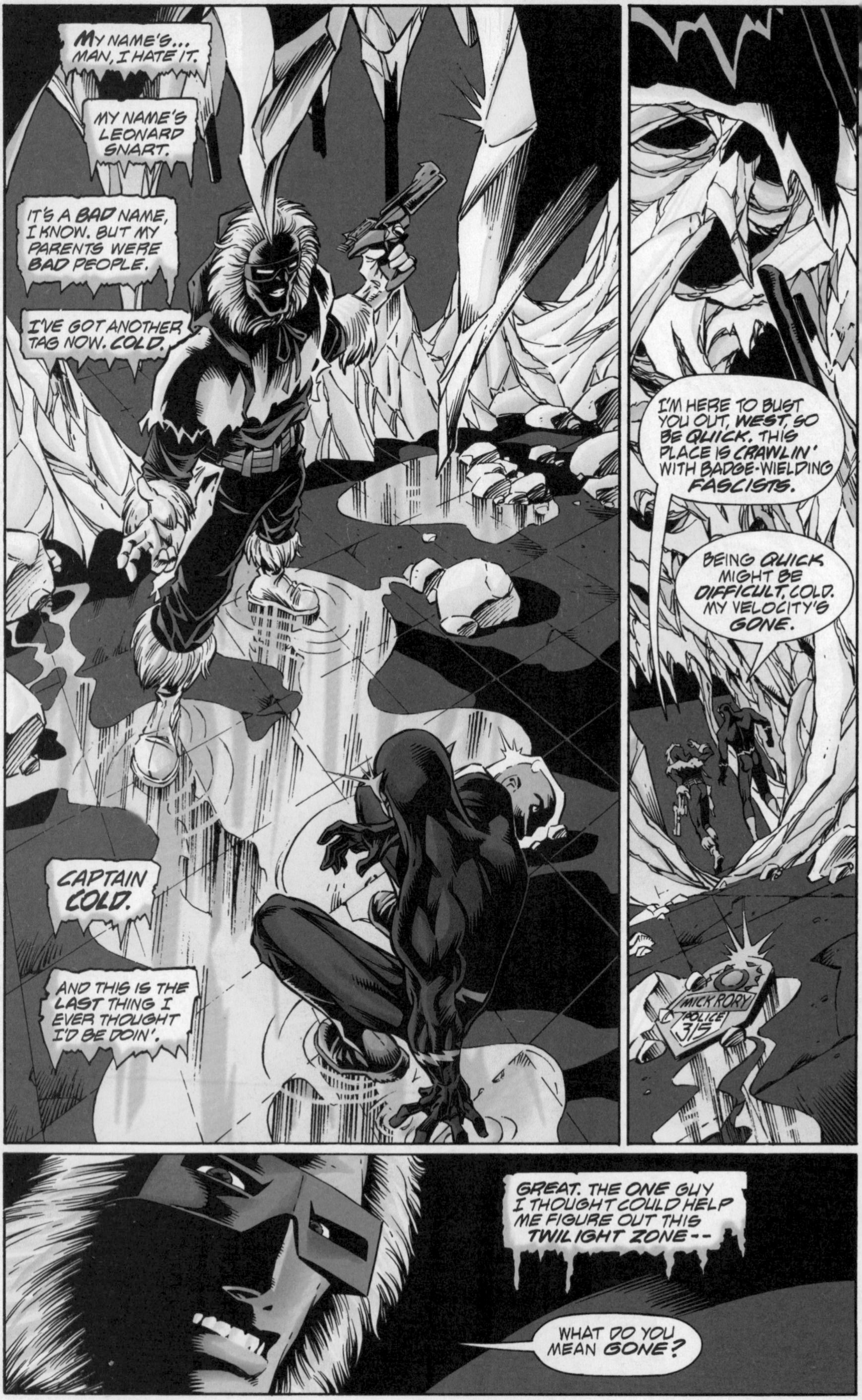
MY NAME'S... MAN, I HATE IT.
MY NAME'S LEONARD SNART.
IT'S A BAD NAME, I KNOW. BUT MY PARENTS WERE BAD PEOPLE.
I'VE GOT ANOTHER TAG NOW. COLD.
CAPTAIN COLD.
AND THIS IS THE LAST THING I EVER THOUGHT I'D BE DOIN'.
I'M HERE TO BUST YOU OUT, WEST, SO BE QUICK. THIS PLACE IS CRAWLIN' WITH BADGE-WIELDING FASCISTS.
BEING QUICK MIGHT BE DIFFICULT, COLD. MY VELOCITY'S GONE.
MICK RORY
POLICE
315
GREAT. THE ONE GUY I THOUGHT COULD HELP ME FIGURE OUT THIS TWILIGHT ZONE--
WHAT DO YOU MEAN GONE?

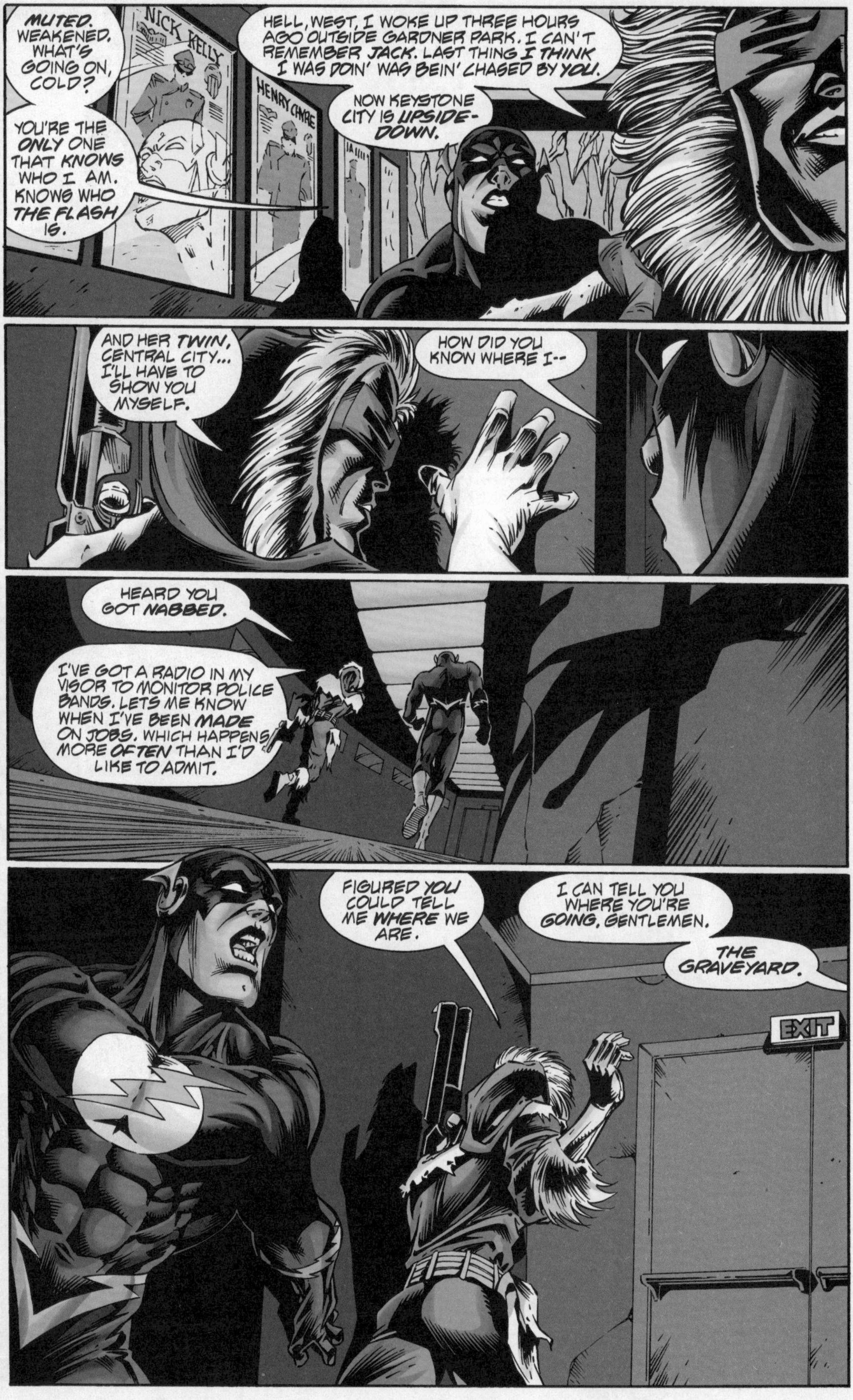
NICK KELLY
MUTED. WEAKENED. WHAT'S GOING ON, COLD?
HELL, WEST, I WOKE UP THREE HOURS AGO OUTSIDE GARDNER PARK. I CAN'T REMEMBER JACK. LAST THING I THINK I WAS DOIN' WAS BEIN' CHASED BY YOU.
NOW KEYSTONE CITY IS UPSIDE-DOWN.
YOU'RE THE ONLY ONE THAT KNOWS WHO I AM. KNOWS WHO THE FLASH IS.
AND HER TWIN, CENTRAL CITY... I'LL HAVE TO SHOW YOU MYSELF.
HOW DID YOU KNOW WHERE I--
HEARD YOU GOT NABBED.
I'VE GOT A RADIO IN MY VISOR TO MONITOR POLICE BANDS. LETS ME KNOW WHEN I'VE BEEN MADE ON JOBS. WHICH HAPPENS MORE OFTEN THAN I'D LIKE TO ADMIT.
FIGURED YOU COULD TELL ME WHERE WE ARE.
I CAN TELL YOU WHERE YOU'RE GOING, GENTLEMEN.
THE GRAVEYARD.
EXIT

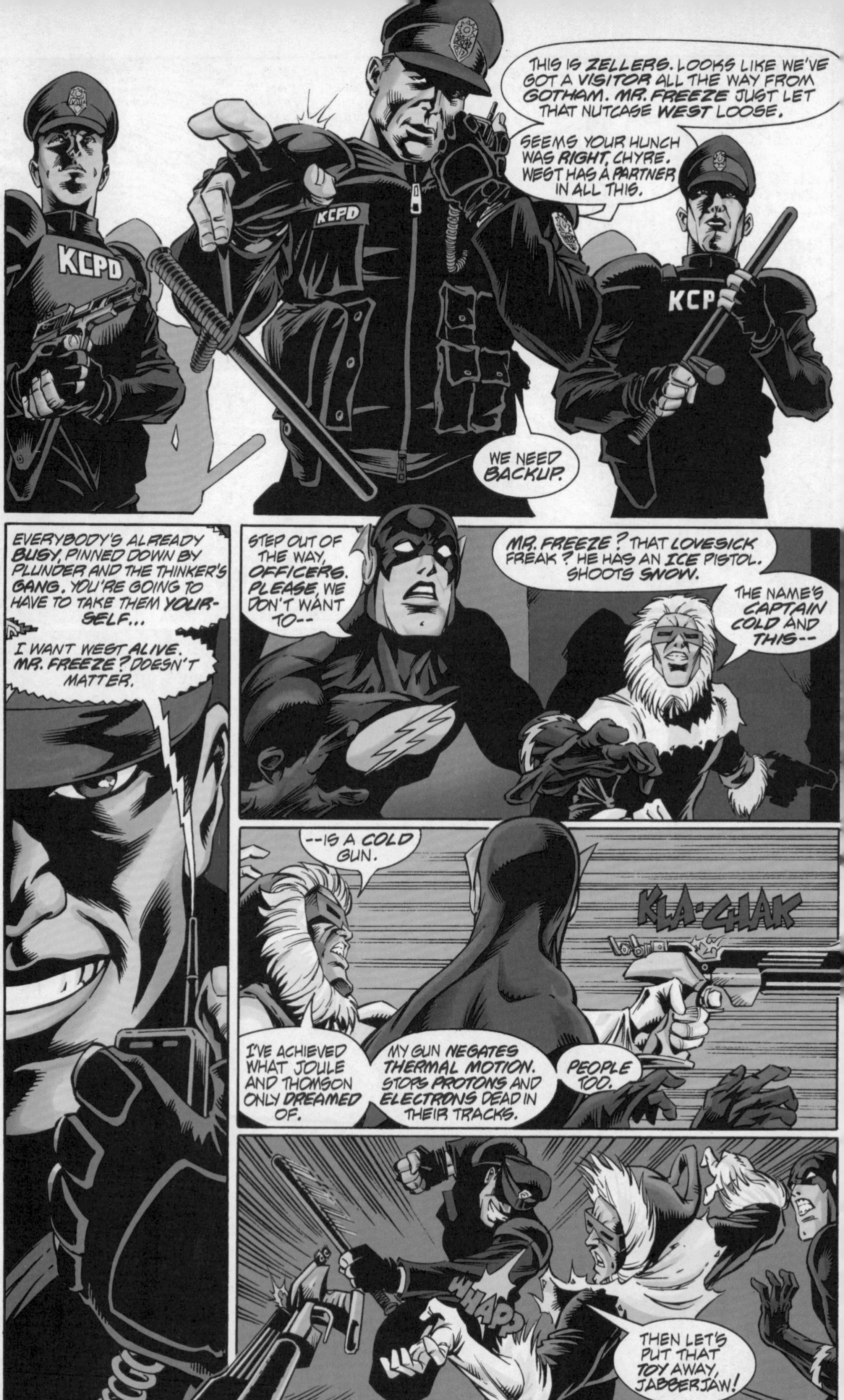
THIS IS ZELLERS. LOOKS LIKE WE'VE GOT A VISITOR ALL THE WAY FROM GOTHAM. MR. FREEZE JUST LET THAT NUTCASE WEST LOOSE.
SEEMS YOUR HUNCH WAS RIGHT, CHYRE. WEST HAS A PARTNER IN ALL THIS.
KCPD
KCPD
KCPD
WE NEED BACKUP.
EVERYBODY'S ALREADY BUSY, PINNED DOWN BY PLUNDER AND THE THINKER'S GANG. YOU'RE GOING TO HAVE TO TAKE THEM YOURSELF...
I WANT WEST ALIVE. MR. FREEZE? DOESN'T MATTER.
STEP OUT OF THE WAY, OFFICERS. PLEASE, WE DON'T WANT TO--
MR. FREEZE? THAT LOVESICK FREAK? HE HAS AN ICE PISTOL. SHOOTS SNOW.
THE NAME'S CAPTAIN COLD AND THIS--
--IS A COLD GUN.
KLA-CHAK
I'VE ACHIEVED WHAT JOULE AND THOMSON ONLY DREAMED OF.
MY GUN NEGATES THERMAL MOTION. STOPS PROTONS AND ELECTRONS DEAD IN THEIR TRACKS.
PEOPLE TOO.
WHAP
THEN LET'S PUT THAT TOY AWAY, JABBERJAW!

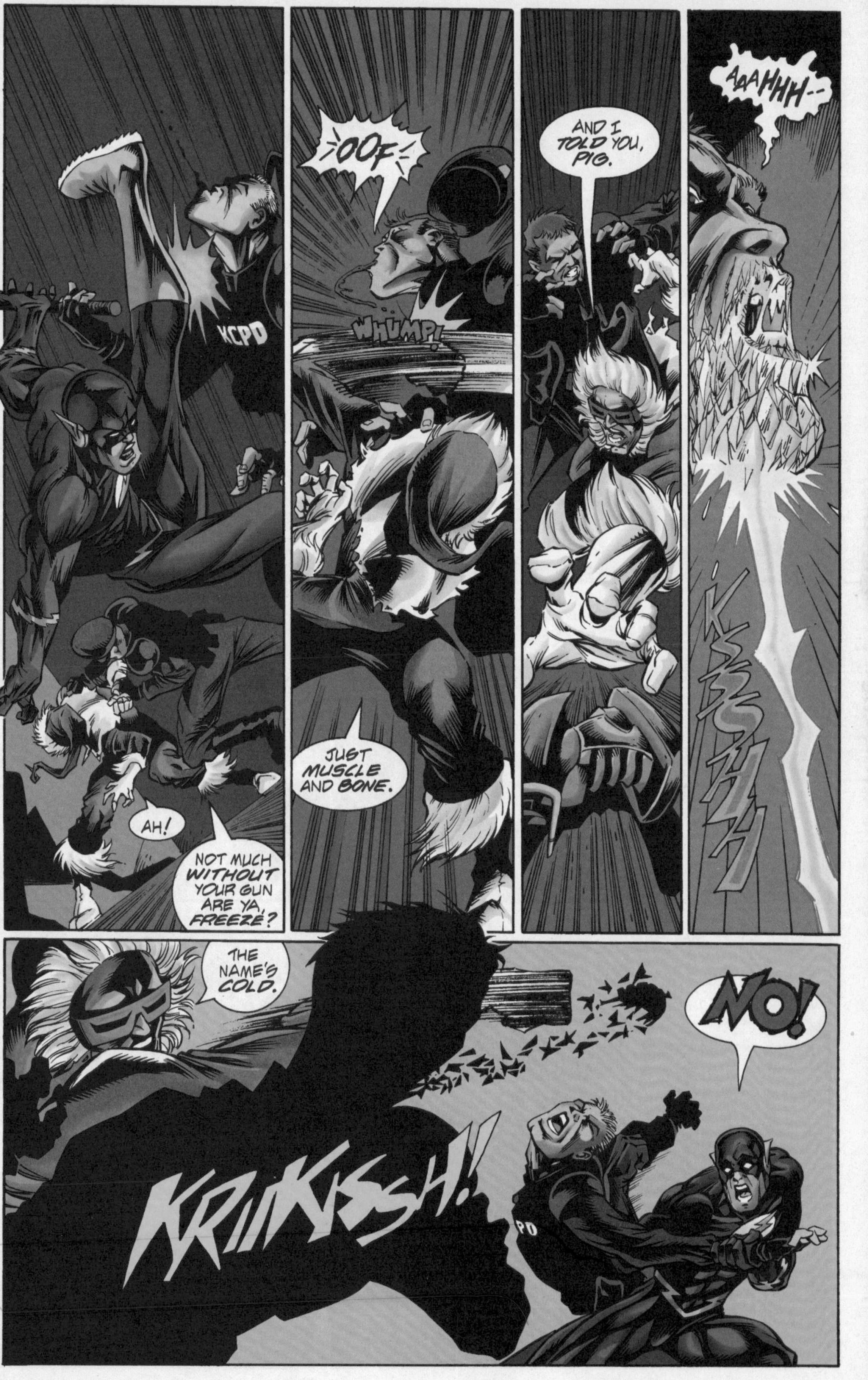
KCPD
AH!
NOT MUCH WITHOUT YOUR GUN ARE YA, FREEZE?
OOF
WHUMP!
JUST MUSCLE AND BONE.
AND I TOLD YOU, PIG.
AAAHHH--
KSSSHHH
THE NAME'S COLD.
NO!
KRIIKSSH!!
PD

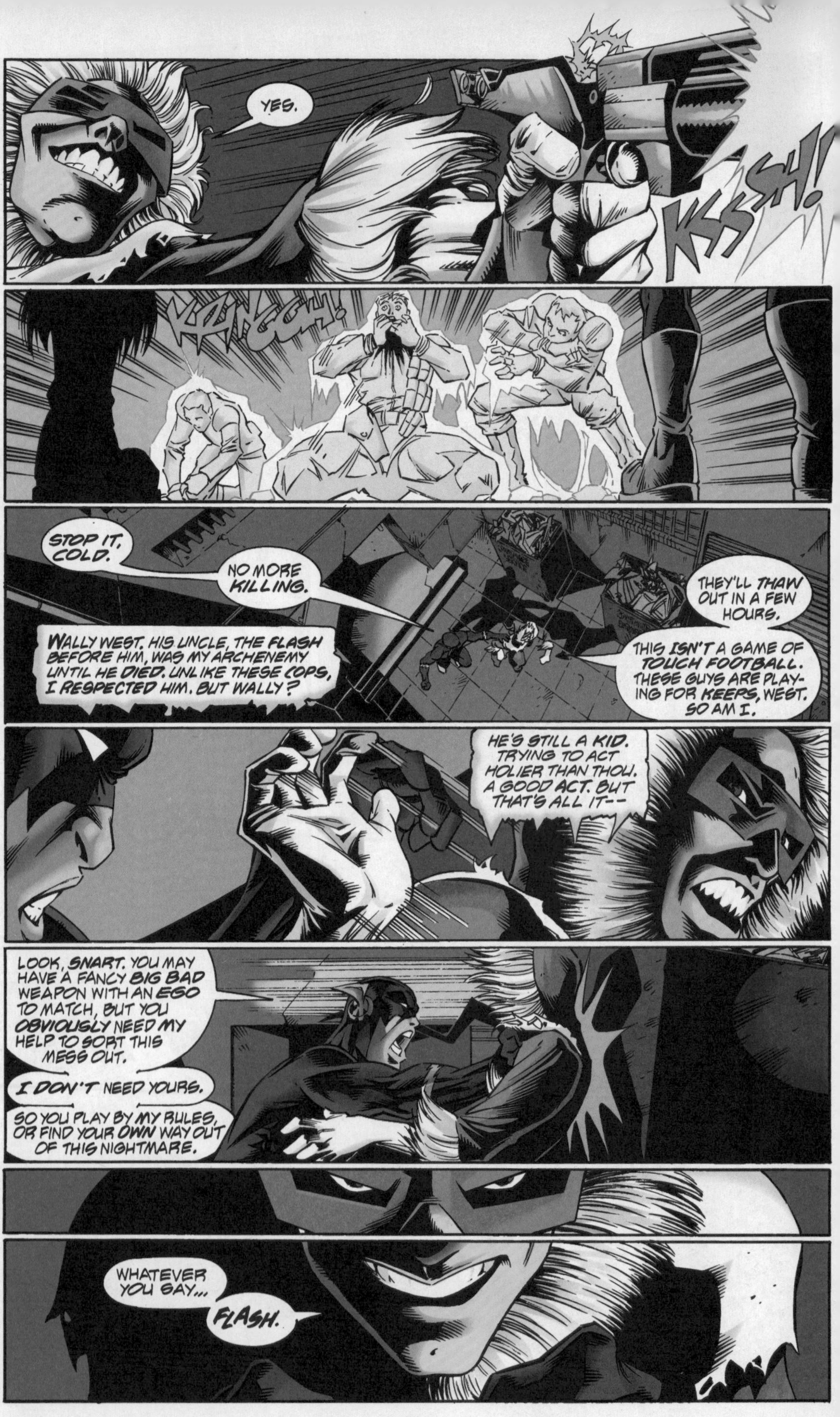
YES.
KSSSH!
KRNGGH!
STOP IT, COLD.
NO MORE KILLING.
WALLY WEST. HIS UNCLE, THE FLASH BEFORE HIM, WAS MY ARCHENEMY UNTIL HE DIED. UNLIKE THESE COPS, I RESPECTED HIM. BUT WALLY?
THEY'LL THAW OUT IN A FEW HOURS.
THIS ISN'T A GAME OF TOUCH FOOTBALL. THESE GUYS ARE PLAYING FOR KEEPS, WEST. SO AM I.
HE'S STILL A KID. TRYING TO ACT HOLIER THAN THOU. A GOOD ACT. BUT THAT'S ALL IT--
LOOK, SNART. YOU MAY HAVE A FANCY BIG BAD WEAPON WITH AN EGO TO MATCH, BUT YOU OBVIOUSLY NEED MY HELP TO SORT THIS MESS OUT.
I DON'T NEED YOURS.
SO YOU PLAY BY MY RULES, OR FIND YOUR OWN WAY OUT OF THIS NIGHTMARE.
WHATEVER YOU SAY...
FLASH.

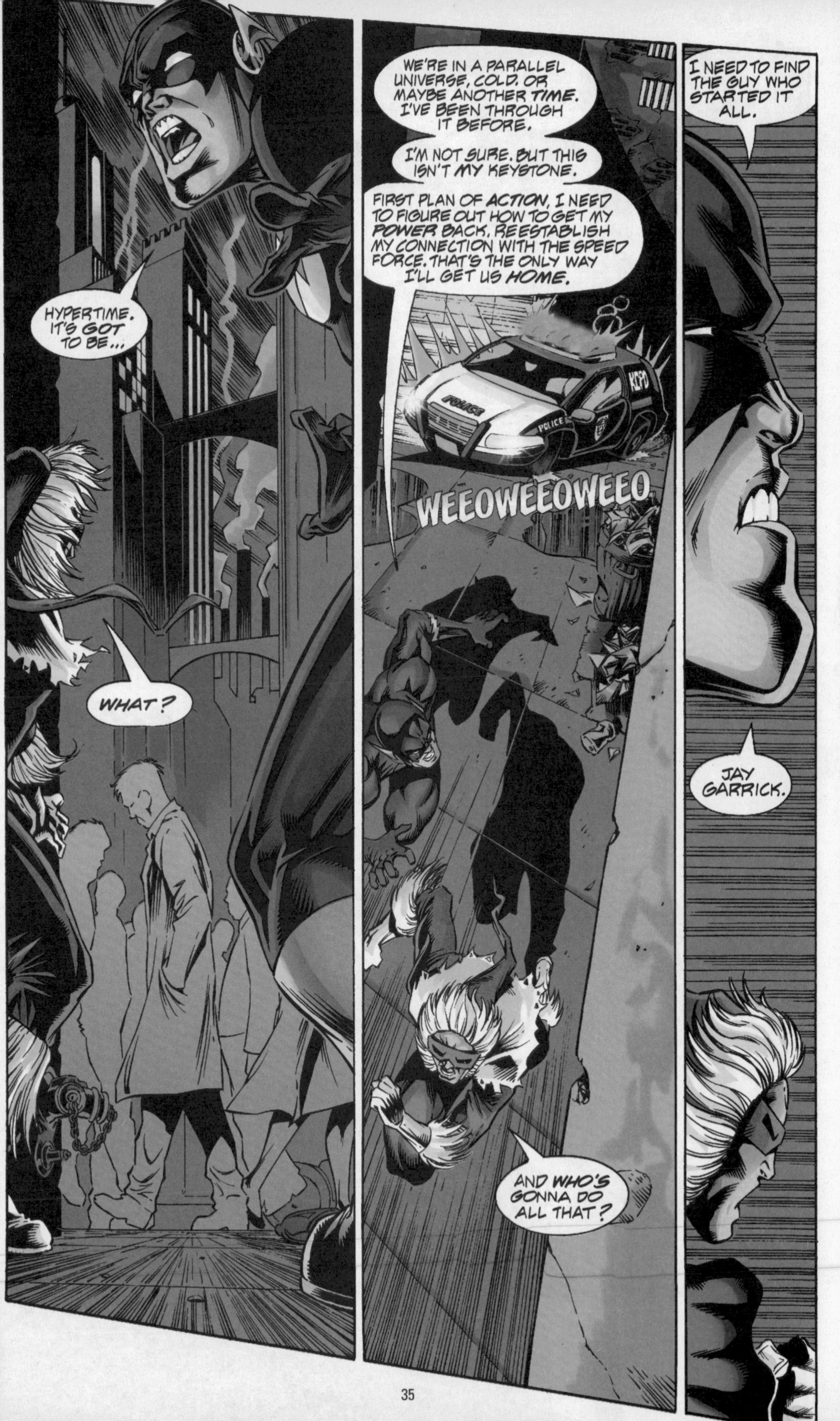
HYPERTIME. IT'S GOT TO BE...
WHAT?
WE'RE IN A PARALLEL UNIVERSE, COLD. OR MAYBE ANOTHER TIME. I'VE BEEN THROUGH IT BEFORE.
I'M NOT SURE. BUT THIS ISN'T MY KEYSTONE.
FIRST PLAN OF ACTION, I NEED TO FIGURE OUT HOW TO GET MY POWER BACK. REESTABLISH MY CONNECTION WITH THE SPEED FORCE. THAT'S THE ONLY WAY I'LL GET US HOME.
KCPD
POLICE
WEEOWEEOWEEO
AND WHO'S GONNA DO ALL THAT?
I NEED TO FIND THE GUY WHO STARTED IT ALL.
JAY GARRICK.

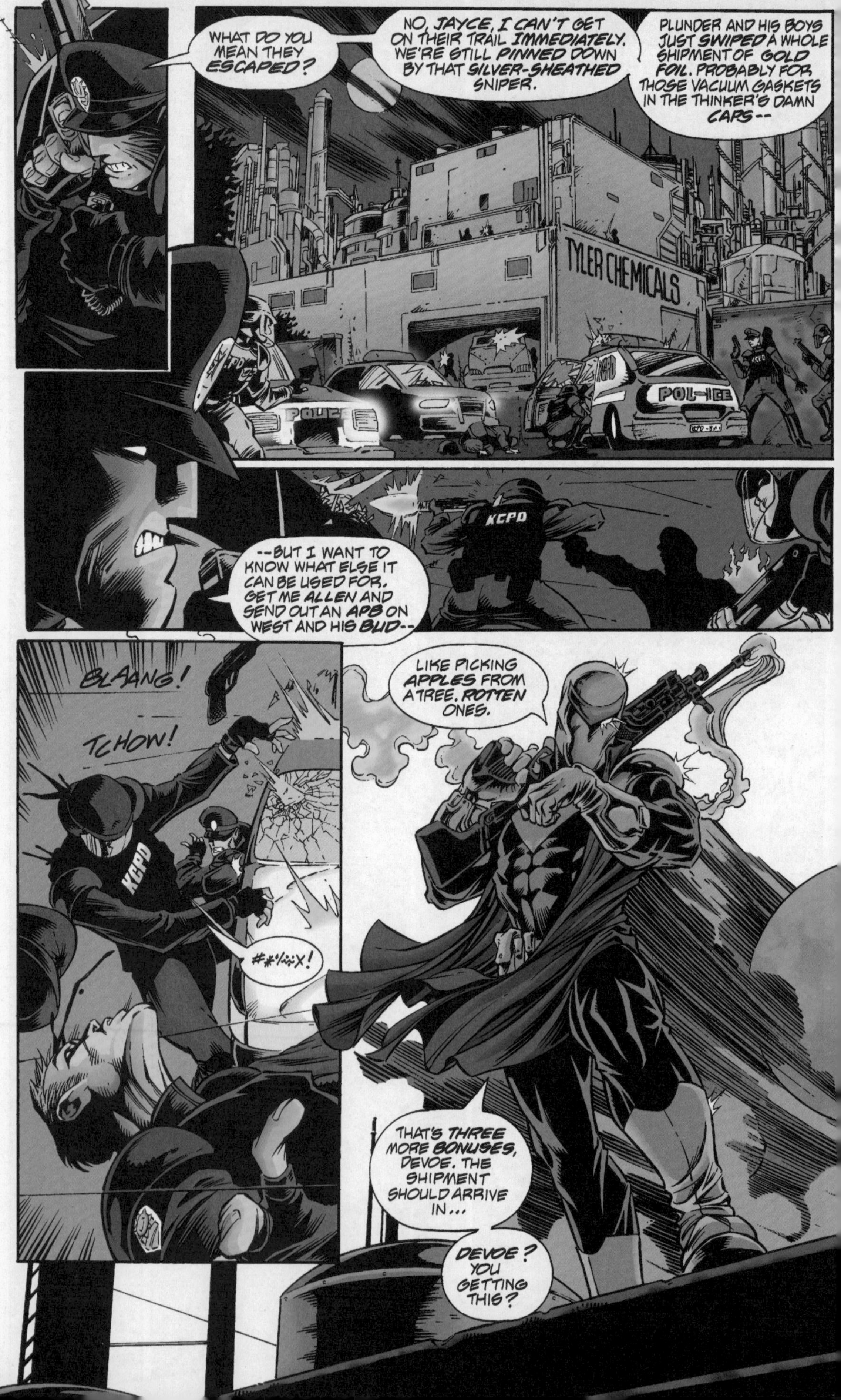

WHAT DO YOU MEAN THEY ESCAPED?
NO, JAYCE, I CAN'T GET ON THEIR TRAIL IMMEDIATELY. WE'RE STILL PINNED DOWN BY THAT SILVER-SHEATHED SNIPER.
PLUNDER AND HIS BOYS JUST SWIPED A WHOLE SHIPMENT OF GOLD FOIL. PROBABLY FOR THOSE VACUUM GASKETS IN THE THINKER'S DAMN CAPS--
TYLER CHEMICALS
POL-ICE
KCPD
--BUT I WANT TO KNOW WHAT ELSE IT CAN BE USED FOR. GET ME ALLEN AND SEND OUT AN APB ON WEST AND HIS BUD--
BLAANG!
TCHOW!
KCPD
#*%X!
LIKE PICKING APPLES FROM A TREE. ROTTEN ONES.
THAT'S THREE MORE BONUSES, DEVOE. THE SHIPMENT SHOULD ARRIVE IN...
DEVOE? YOU GETTING THIS?

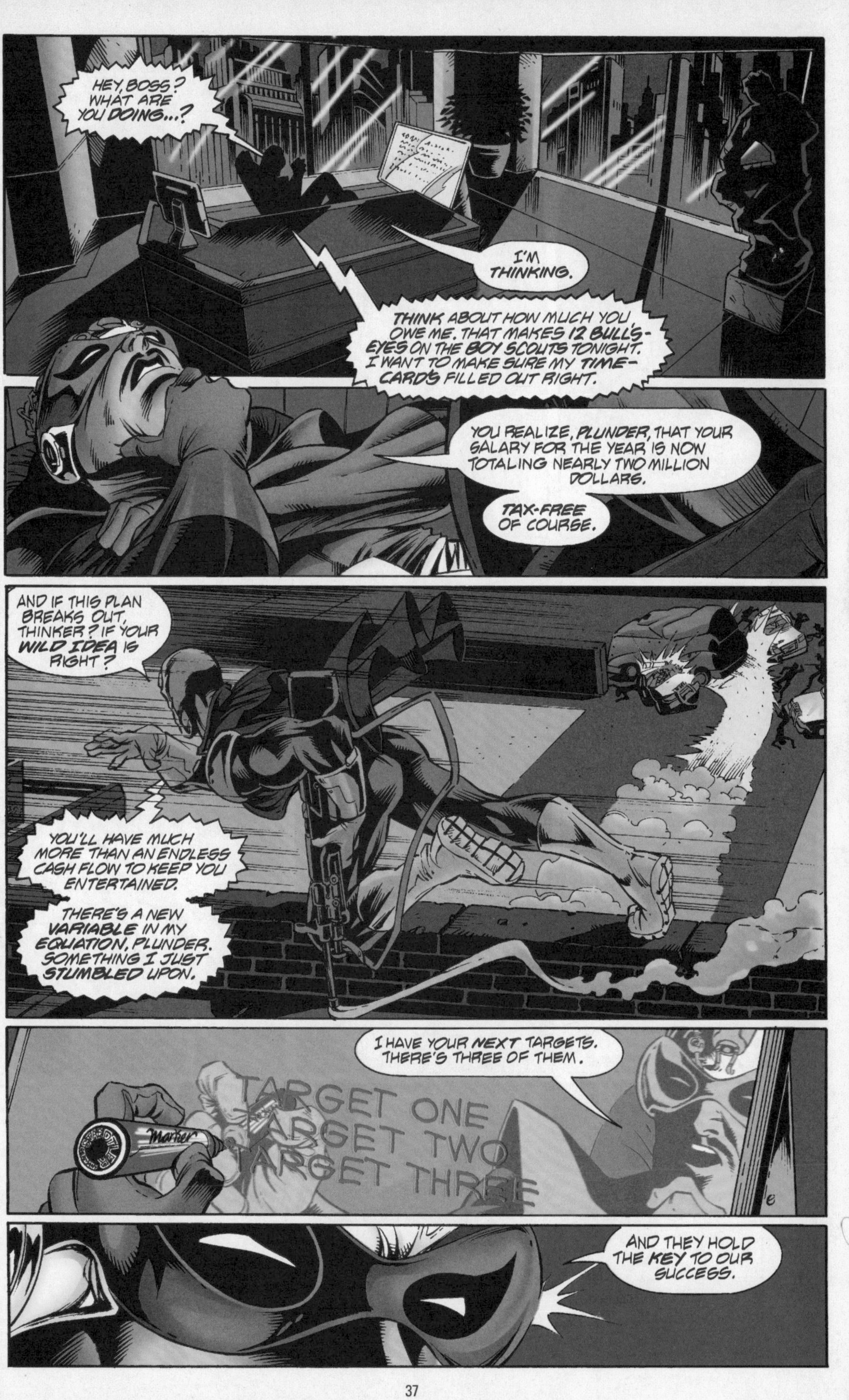
HEY, BOSS? WHAT ARE YOU DOING...?
I'M THINKING.
THINK ABOUT HOW MUCH YOU OWE ME. THAT MAKES 12 BULL'S-EYES ON THE BOY SCOUTS TONIGHT. I WANT TO MAKE SURE MY TIME-CARD'S FILLED OUT RIGHT.
YOU REALIZE, PLUNDER, THAT YOUR SALARY FOR THE YEAR IS NOW TOTALING NEARLY TWO MILLION DOLLARS.
TAX-FREE OF COURSE.
AND IF THIS PLAN BREAKS OUT, THINKER? IF YOUR WILD IDEA IS RIGHT?
YOU'LL HAVE MUCH MORE THAN AN ENDLESS CASH FLOW TO KEEP YOU ENTERTAINED.
THERE'S A NEW VARIABLE IN MY EQUATION, PLUNDER. SOMETHING I JUST STUMBLED UPON.
I HAVE YOUR NEXT TARGETS. THERE'S THREE OF THEM.
TARGET ONE
TARGET TWO
TARGET THREE
Marker
AND THEY HOLD THE KEY TO OUR SUCCESS.

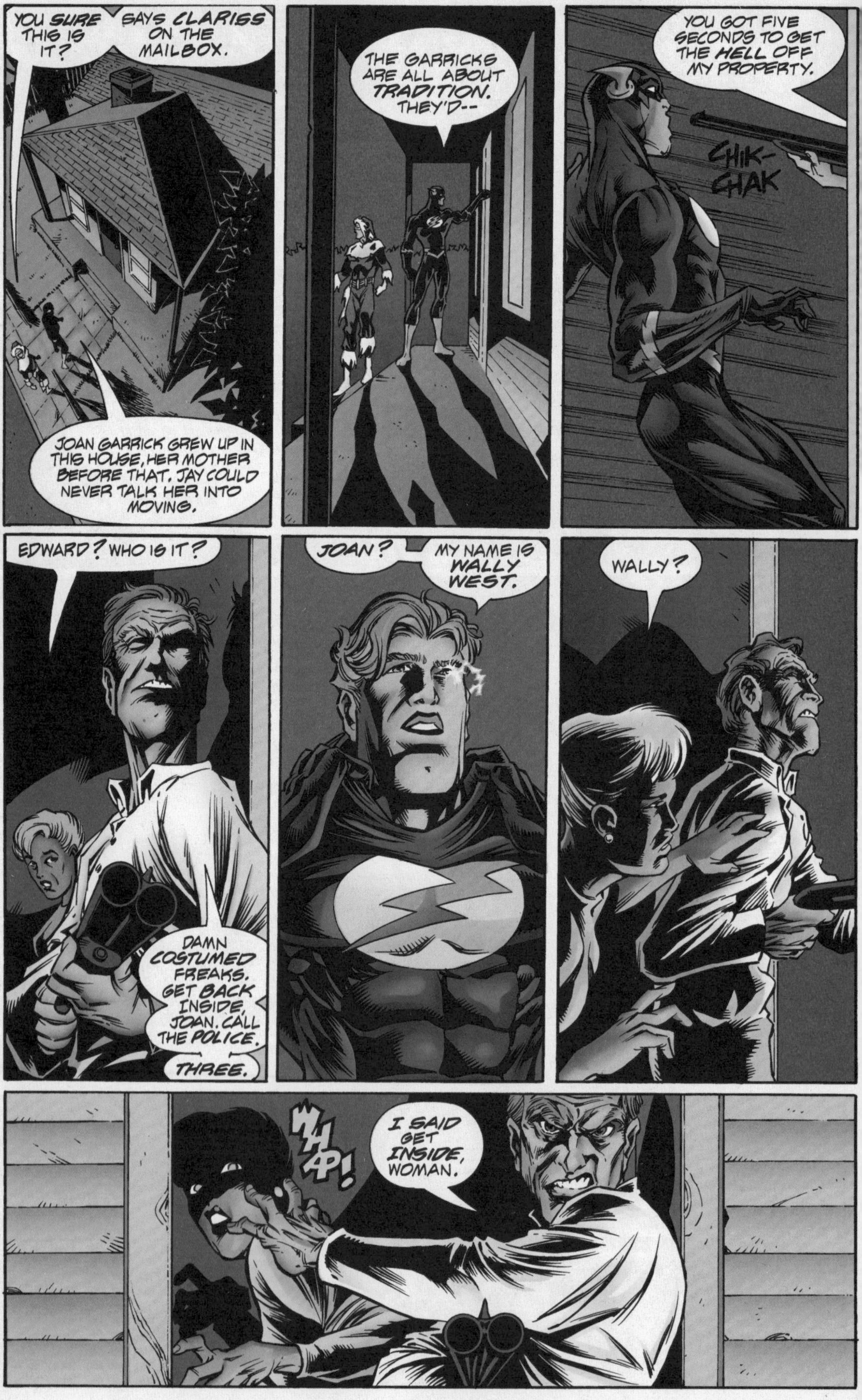
YOU SURE THIS IS IT?
SAYS CLARISS ON THE MAILBOX.
JOAN GARRICK GREW UP IN THIS HOUSE, HER MOTHER BEFORE THAT. JAY COULD NEVER TALK HER INTO MOVING.
THE GARRICKS ARE ALL ABOUT TRADITION. THEY'D--
YOU GOT FIVE SECONDS TO GET THE HELL OFF MY PROPERTY.
CHIK-CHAK
EDWARD? WHO IS IT?
DAMN COSTUMED FREAKS. GET BACK INSIDE, JOAN. CALL THE POLICE.
THREE.
JOAN?
MY NAME IS WALLY WEST.
WALLY?
WHAP!
I SAID GET INSIDE, WOMAN.

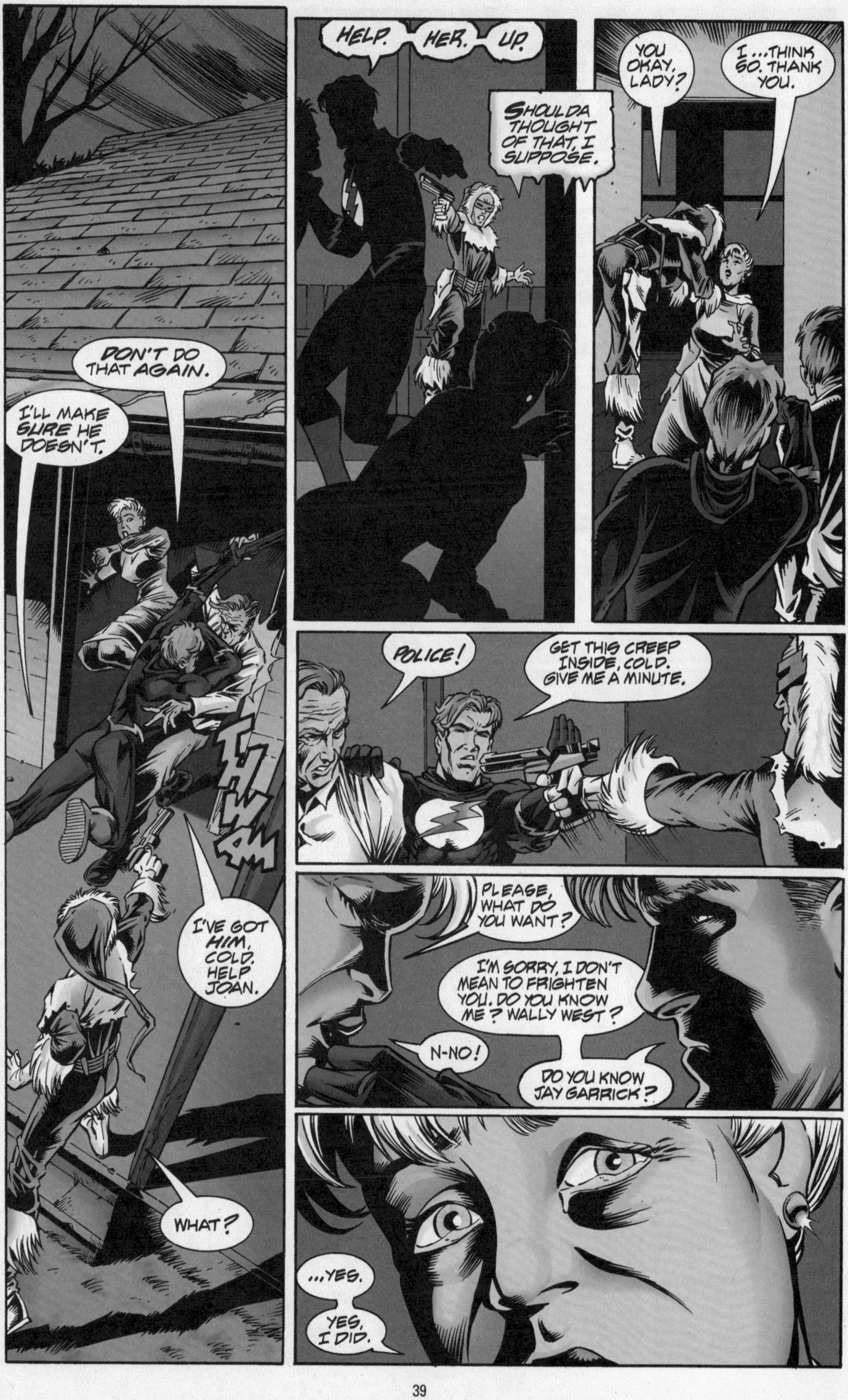
DON'T DO THAT AGAIN.
I'LL MAKE SURE HE DOESN'T.
THWAM
I'VE GOT HIM, COLD. HELP JOAN.
WHAT?
HELP. HER. UP.
SHOULDA THOUGHT OF THAT, I SUPPOSE.
YOU OKAY, LADY?
I...THINK SO. THANK YOU.
POLICE!
GET THIS CREEP INSIDE, COLD. GIVE ME A MINUTE.
PLEASE, WHAT DO YOU WANT?
I'M SORRY, I DON'T MEAN TO FRIGHTEN YOU. DO YOU KNOW ME? WALLY WEST?
N-NO!
DO YOU KNOW JAY GARRICK?
...YES.
YES, I DID.

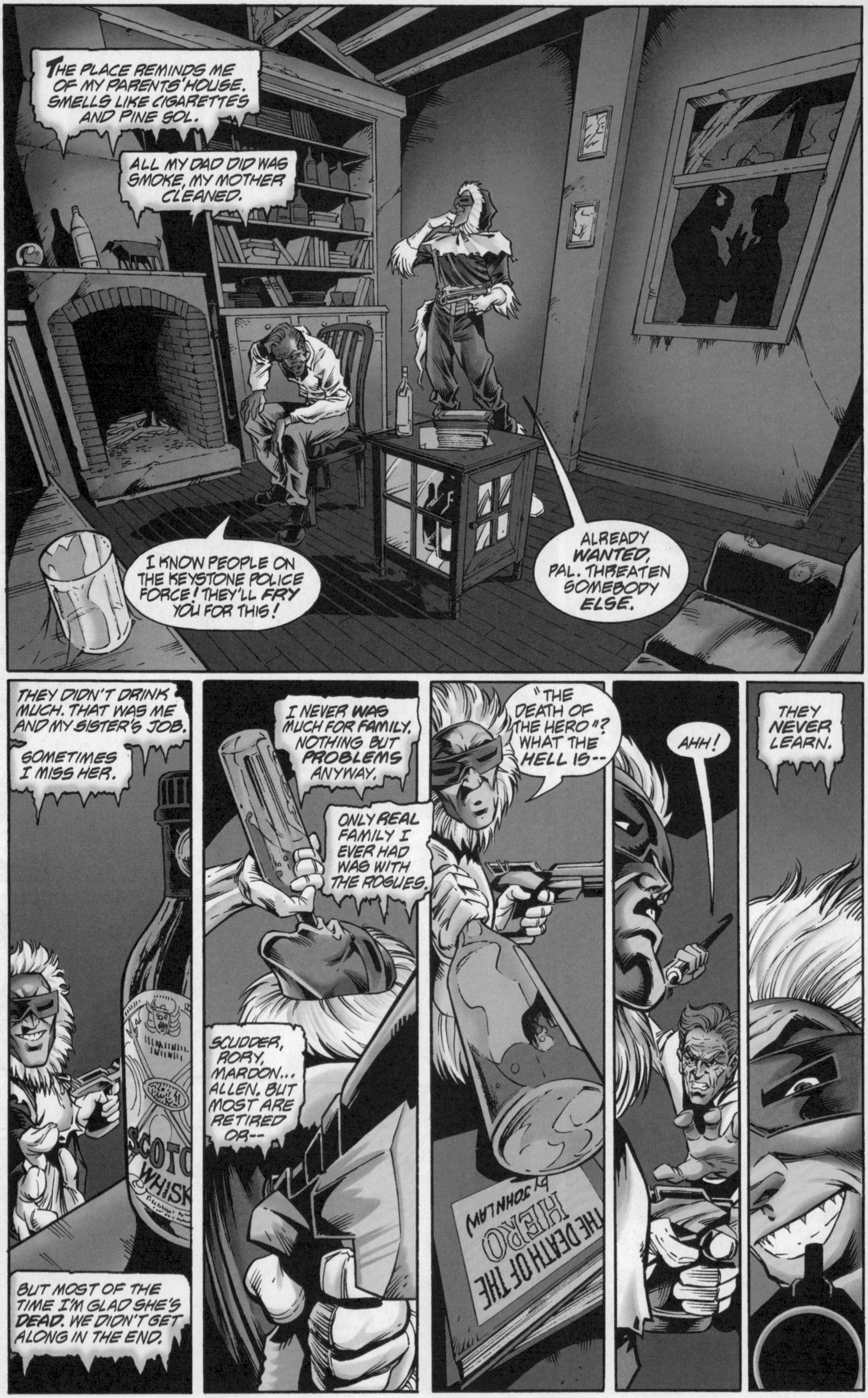
THE PLACE REMINDS ME OF MY PARENTS' HOUSE. SMELLS LIKE CIGARETTES AND PINE SOL.
ALL MY DAD DID WAS SMOKE, MY MOTHER CLEANED.
I KNOW PEOPLE ON THE KEYSTONE POLICE FORCE! THEY'LL FRY YOU FOR THIS!
ALREADY WANTED, PAL. THREATEN SOMEBODY ELSE.
THEY DIDN'T DRINK MUCH. THAT WAS ME AND MY SISTER'S JOB.
SOMETIMES I MISS HER.
SCOTCH WHISKY
BUT MOST OF THE TIME I'M GLAD SHE'S DEAD. WE DIDN'T GET ALONG IN THE END.
I NEVER WAS MUCH FOR FAMILY. NOTHING BUT PROBLEMS ANYWAY.
ONLY REAL FAMILY I EVER HAD WAS WITH THE ROGUES.
SCUDDER, RORY, MARDON... ALLEN. BUT MOST ARE RETIRED OR--
"THE DEATH OF THE HERO"? WHAT THE HELL IS--
THE DEATH OF THE HERO by JOHN LAW
AHH!
THEY NEVER LEARN.

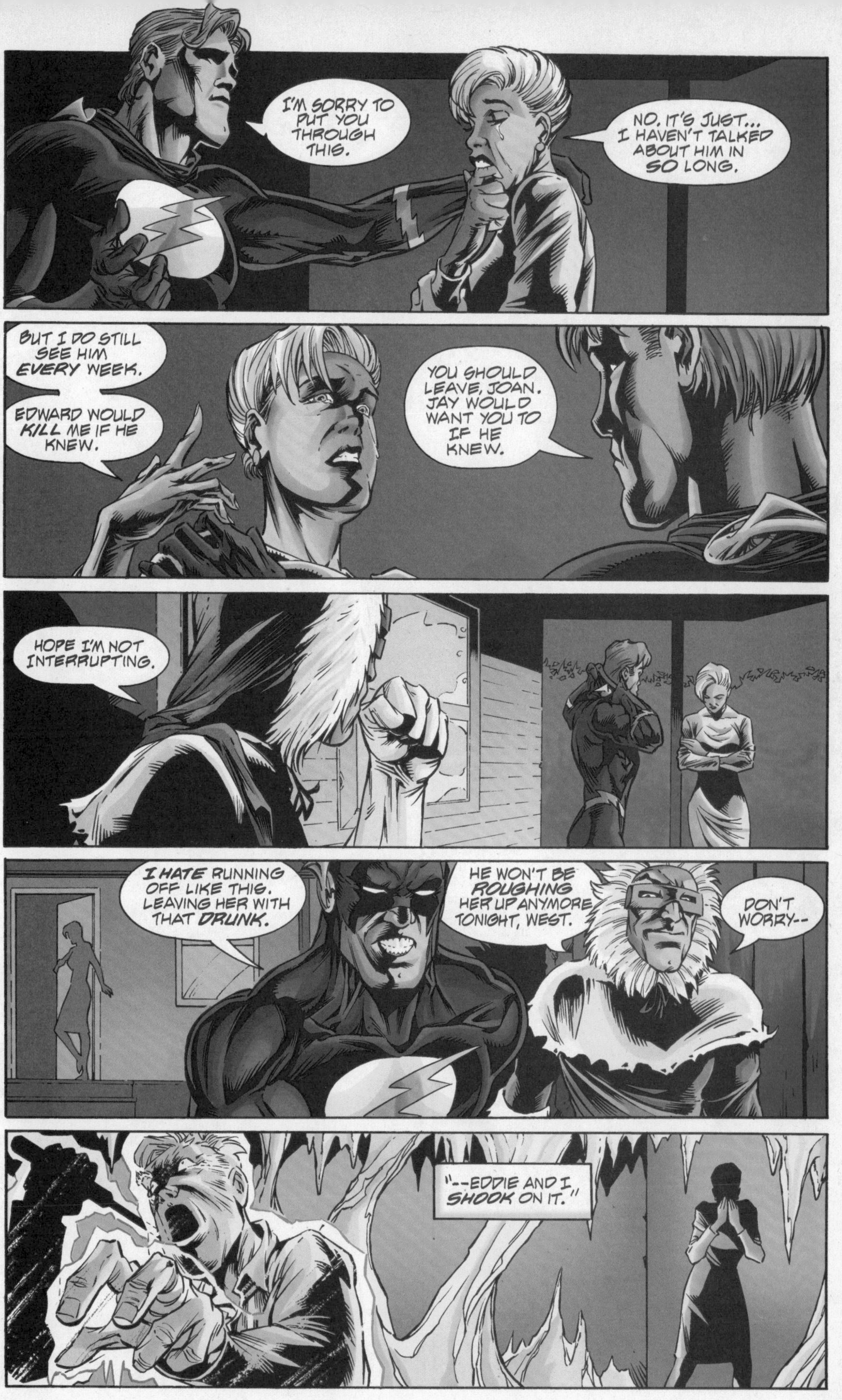
I'M SORRY TO PUT YOU THROUGH THIS.
NO. IT'S JUST... I HAVEN'T TALKED ABOUT HIM IN SO LONG.
BUT I DO STILL SEE HIM EVERY WEEK.
EDWARD WOULD KILL ME IF HE KNEW.
YOU SHOULD LEAVE, JOAN. JAY WOULD WANT YOU TO IF HE KNEW.
HOPE I'M NOT INTERRUPTING.
I HATE RUNNING OFF LIKE THIS. LEAVING HER WITH THAT DRUNK.
HE WON'T BE ROUGHING HER UP ANYMORE TONIGHT, WEST.
DON'T WORRY--
"--EDDIE AND I SHOOK ON IT."

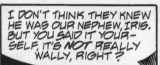

WHY DIDN'T THEY TELL YOU? IT'S SO STRANGE.

I DON'T THINK THEY KNEW HE WAS OUR NEPHEW, IRIS. BUT YOU SAID IT YOUR-SELF, IT'S *NOT* REALLY WALLY, RIGHT?

I JUST TALKED TO HIM. HE'S WITH HIS MOM. STILL TRYING TO HELP PATCH UP HIS PARENTS' RELATION-SHIP. I WISH HE'D WORRY ABOUT FINDING ONE OF HIS *OWN.*

HE'S ALWAYS SAYING HE CAN'T *RUN* AWAY FAST ENOUGH TO ESCAPE THE GRAVITATIONAL PULL OF BLUE VALLEY. POOR KID. SO MUCH POTENTIAL.

I'M SURE IT'S A BIG MISTAKE. I'M GOING TO MEET *CHYRE* RIGHT NOW. I JUST GOT SOME LAB RESULTS AND--

POLICE LABORATORY

HURRY HOME, HONEY.

DON'T WAIT UP.

YOU KNOW I WILL.

WONDER WHAT CHYRE'S GOING TO SAY? THIS GREY STUFF THAT WAS ON "WALLY'S" BOOTS--

--WAS POWDERED GLASS.

42

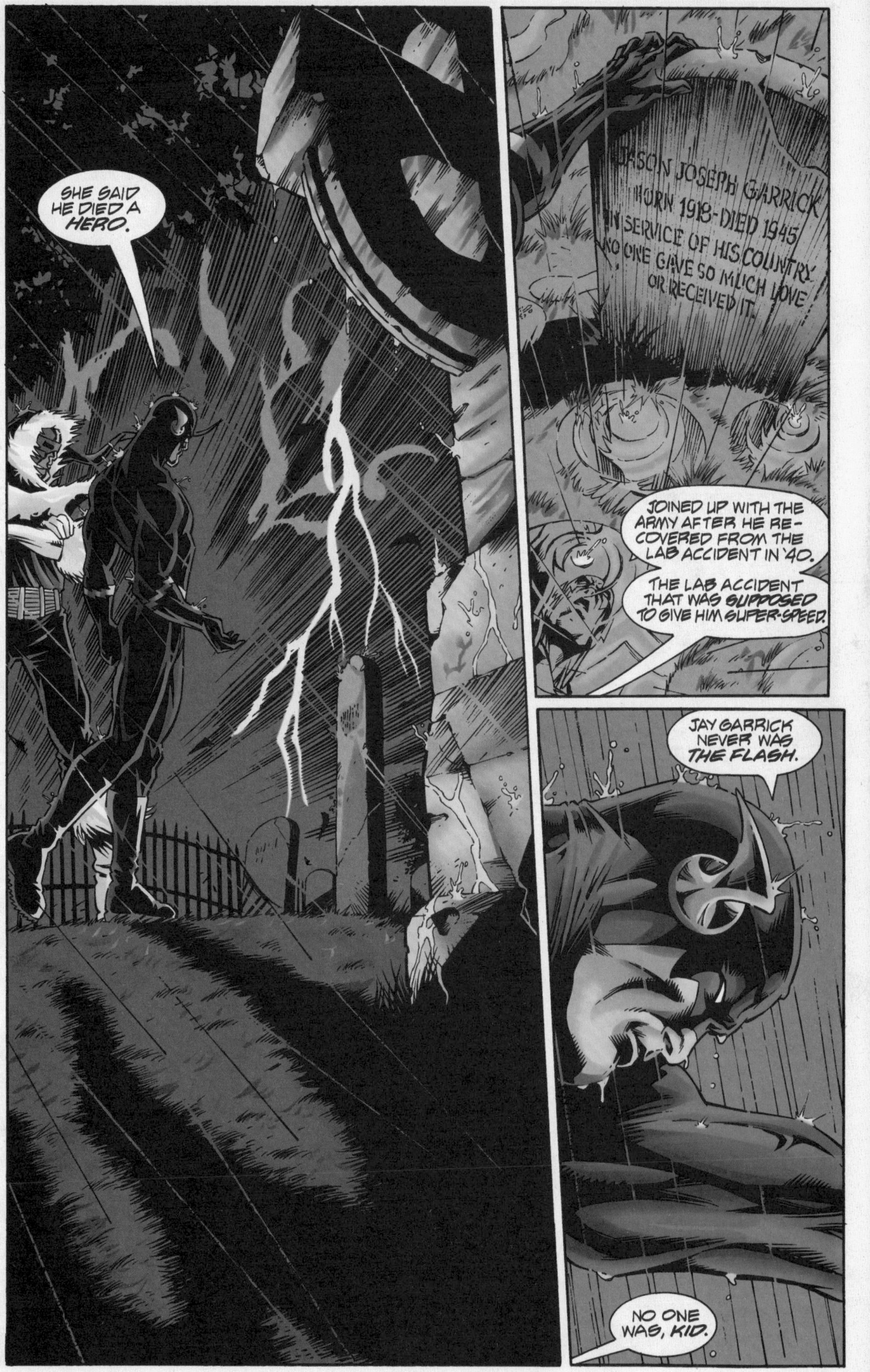

SHE SAID HE DIED A **HERO**.
JASON JOSEPH GARRICK
BORN 1918-DIED 1945
IN SERVICE OF HIS COUNTRY
NO ONE GAVE SO MUCH LOVE
OR RECEIVED IT.
JOINED UP WITH THE ARMY AFTER HE RE-COVERED FROM THE LAB ACCIDENT IN '40.
THE LAB ACCIDENT THAT WAS **SUPPOSED** TO GIVE HIM SUPER-SPEED.
JAY GARRICK NEVER WAS **THE FLASH**.
NO ONE WAS, **KID**.

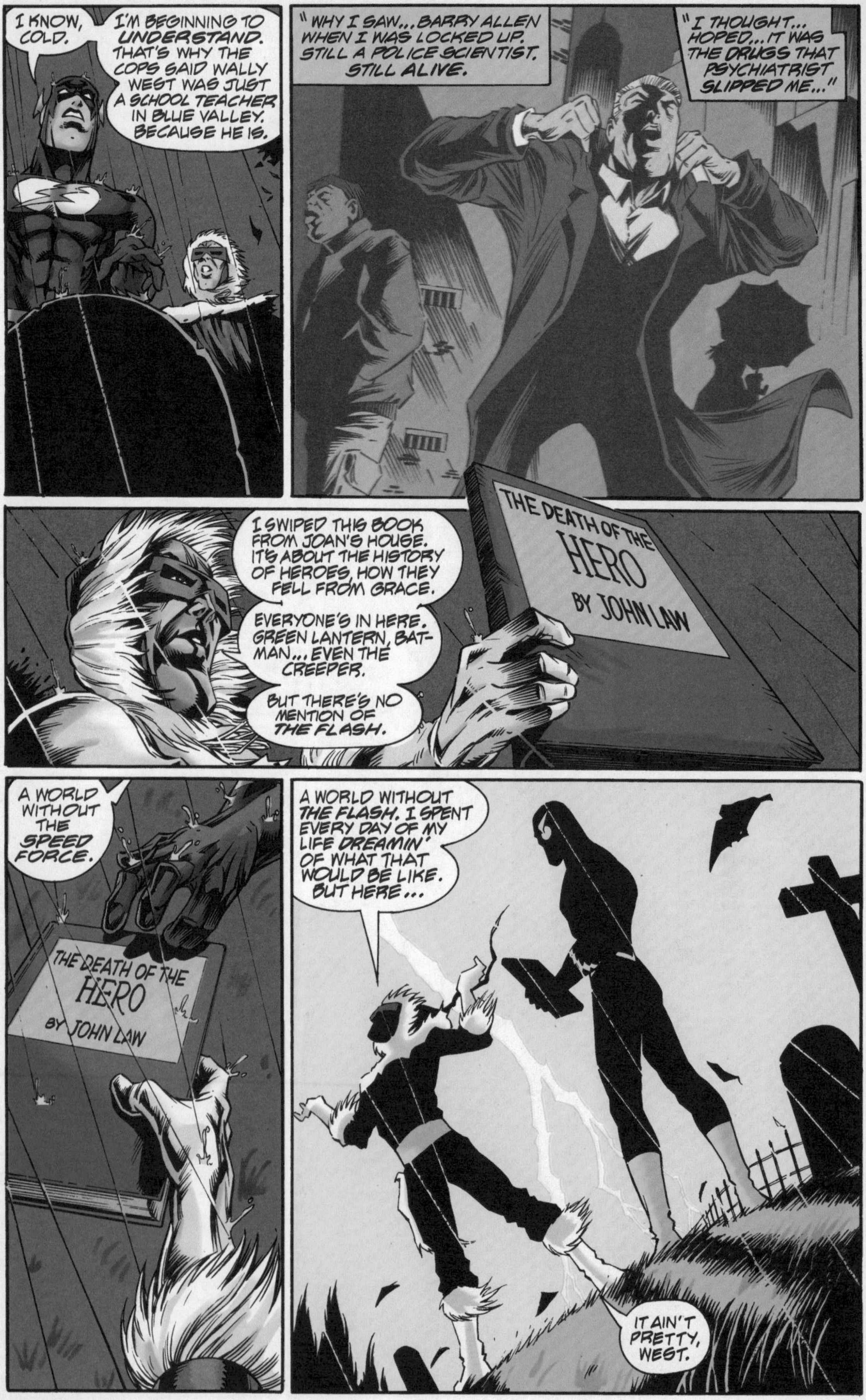
I KNOW, COLD.
I'M BEGINNING TO UNDERSTAND. THAT'S WHY THE COPS SAID WALLY WEST WAS JUST A SCHOOL TEACHER IN BLUE VALLEY. BECAUSE HE IS.
"WHY I SAW... BARRY ALLEN WHEN I WAS LOCKED UP. STILL A POLICE SCIENTIST. STILL ALIVE.
"I THOUGHT... HOPED... IT WAS THE DRUGS THAT PSYCHIATRIST SLIPPED ME..."
I SWIPED THIS BOOK FROM JOAN'S HOUSE. IT'S ABOUT THE HISTORY OF HEROES, HOW THEY FELL FROM GRACE.
EVERYONE'S IN HERE. GREEN LANTERN, BATMAN... EVEN THE CREEPER.
BUT THERE'S NO MENTION OF THE FLASH.
THE DEATH OF THE HERO
BY JOHN LAW
A WORLD WITHOUT THE SPEED FORCE.
THE DEATH OF THE HERO
BY JOHN LAW
A WORLD WITHOUT THE FLASH. I SPENT EVERY DAY OF MY LIFE DREAMIN' OF WHAT THAT WOULD BE LIKE. BUT HERE...
IT AIN'T PRETTY, WEST.

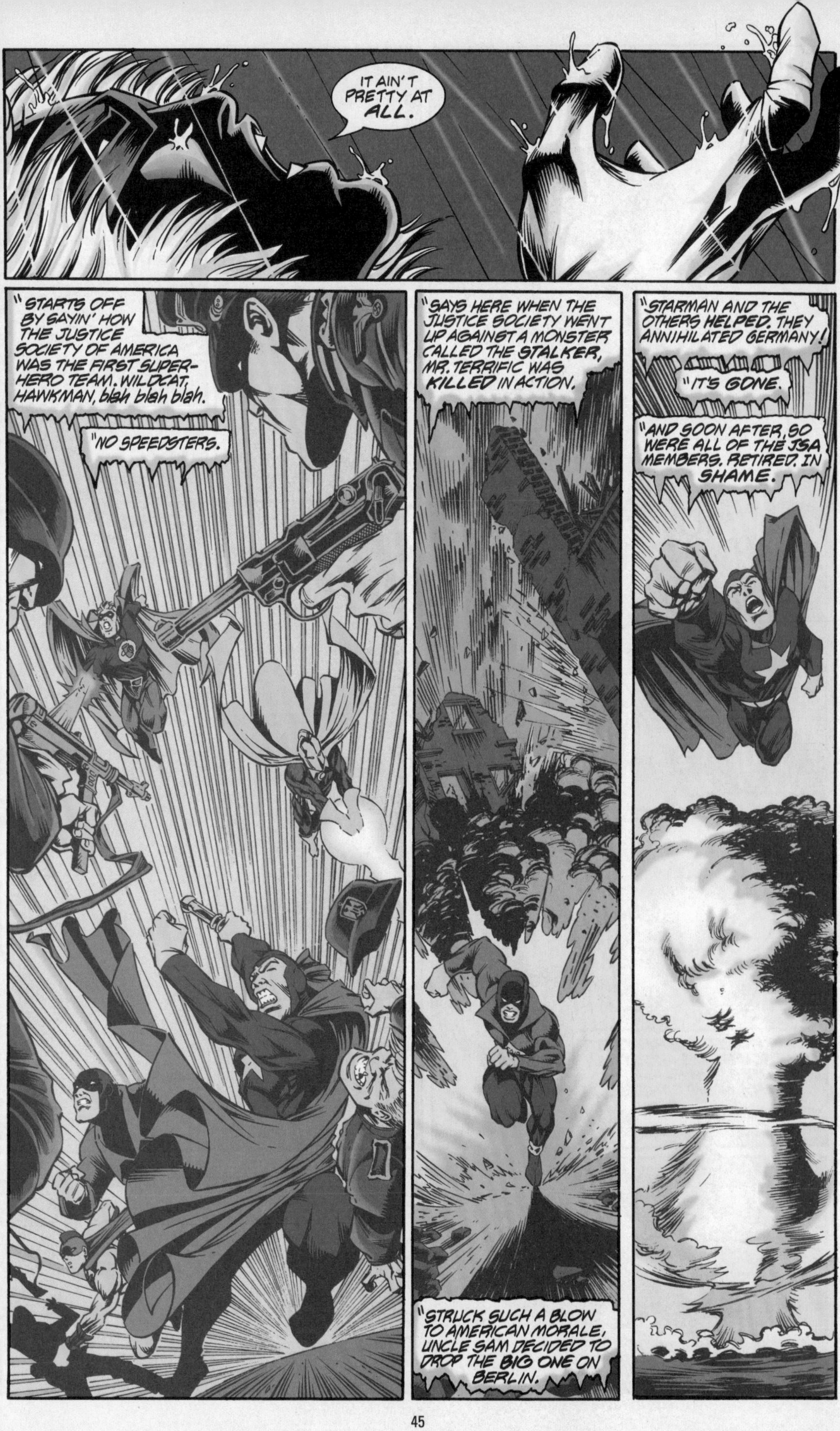

IT AIN'T PRETTY AT ALL.
"STARTS OFF BY SAYIN' HOW THE JUSTICE SOCIETY OF AMERICA WAS THE FIRST SUPER-HERO TEAM. WILDCAT, HAWKMAN, blah blah blah.
"NO SPEEDSTERS.
"SAYS HERE WHEN THE JUSTICE SOCIETY WENT UP AGAINST A MONSTER CALLED THE STALKER, MR. TERRIFIC WAS KILLED IN ACTION.
"STRUCK SUCH A BLOW TO AMERICAN MORALE, UNCLE SAM DECIDED TO DROP THE BIG ONE ON BERLIN.
"STARMAN AND THE OTHERS HELPED. THEY ANNIHILATED GERMANY!
"IT'S GONE.
"AND SOON AFTER, SO WERE ALL OF THE JSA MEMBERS. RETIRED. IN SHAME.

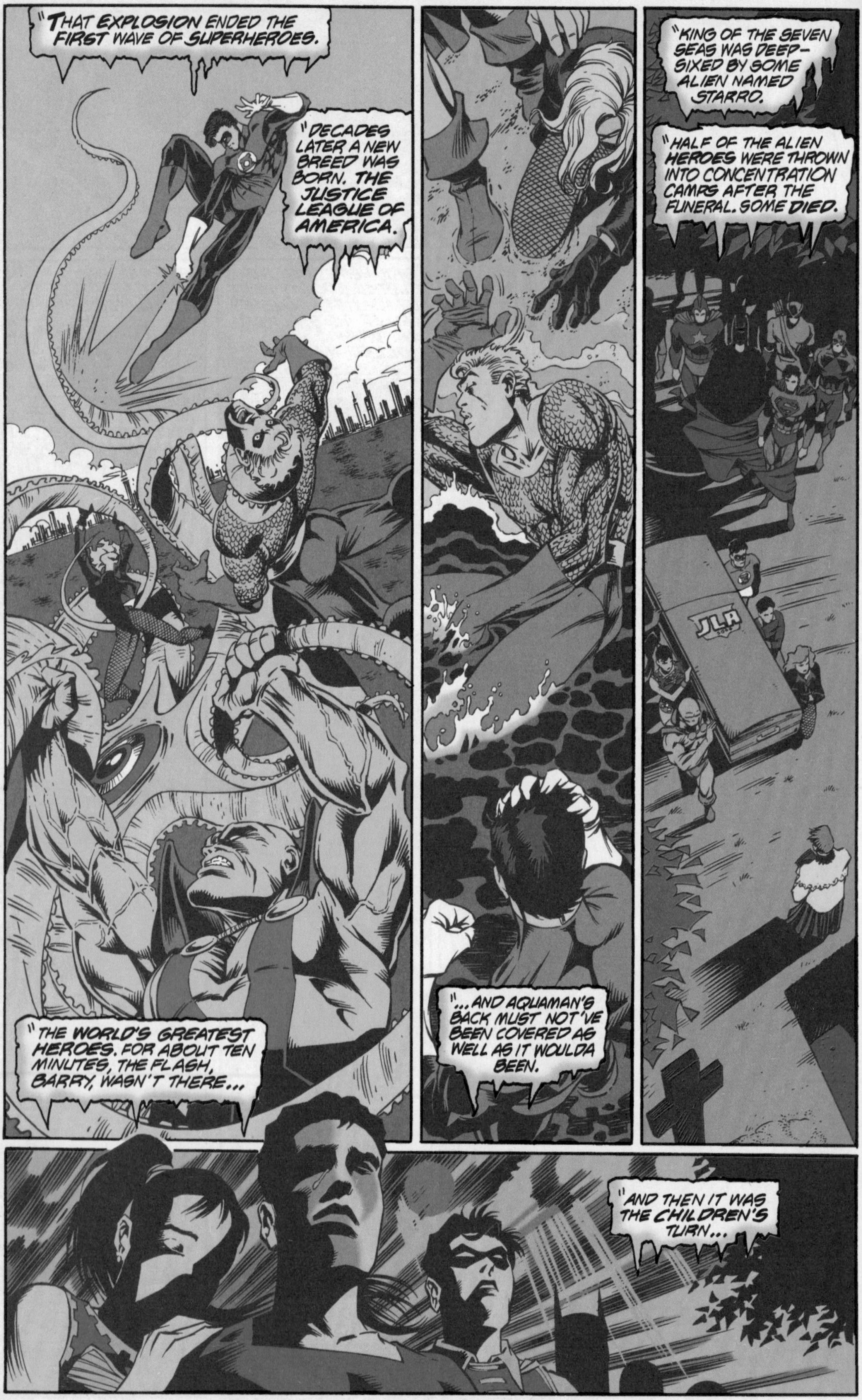
"THAT EXPLOSION ENDED THE FIRST WAVE OF SUPERHEROES.
"DECADES LATER A NEW BREED WAS BORN. THE JUSTICE LEAGUE OF AMERICA.
"THE WORLD'S GREATEST HEROES. FOR ABOUT TEN MINUTES, THE FLASH, BARRY, WASN'T THERE...
"...AND AQUAMAN'S BACK MUST NOT'VE BEEN COVERED AS WELL AS IT WOULDA BEEN.
"KING OF THE SEVEN SEAS WAS DEEP-SIXED BY SOME ALIEN NAMED STARRO.
"HALF OF THE ALIEN HEROES WERE THROWN INTO CONCENTRATION CAMPS AFTER THE FUNERAL. SOME DIED.
JLA
"AND THEN IT WAS THE CHILDREN'S TURN...

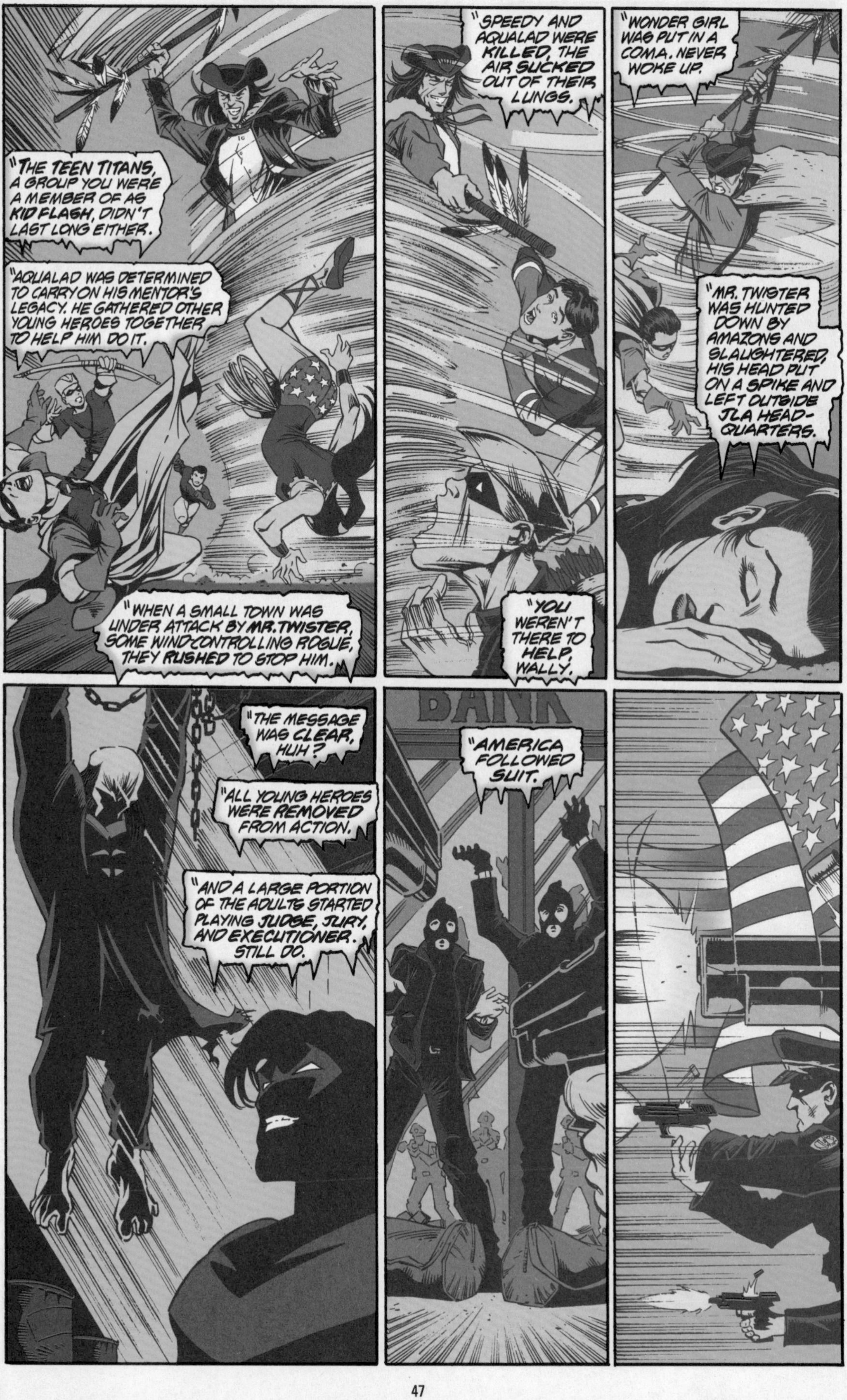
"THE TEEN TITANS, A GROUP YOU WERE A MEMBER OF AS KID FLASH, DIDN'T LAST LONG EITHER.
"AQUALAD WAS DETERMINED TO CARRY ON HIS MENTOR'S LEGACY. HE GATHERED OTHER YOUNG HEROES TOGETHER TO HELP HIM DO IT.
"WHEN A SMALL TOWN WAS UNDER ATTACK BY MR. TWISTER, SOME WIND-CONTROLLING ROGUE, THEY RUSHED TO STOP HIM.
"SPEEDY AND AQUALAD WERE KILLED, THE AIR SUCKED OUT OF THEIR LUNGS.
"YOU WEREN'T THERE TO HELP, WALLY.
"WONDER GIRL WAS PUT IN A COMA. NEVER WOKE UP.
"MR. TWISTER WAS HUNTED DOWN BY AMAZONS AND SLAUGHTERED, HIS HEAD PUT ON A SPIKE AND LEFT OUTSIDE JLA HEAD-QUARTERS.
"THE MESSAGE WAS CLEAR, HUH?
"ALL YOUNG HEROES WERE REMOVED FROM ACTION.
"AND A LARGE PORTION OF THE ADULTS STARTED PLAYING JUDGE, JURY, AND EXECUTIONER. STILL DO.
BANK
"AMERICA FOLLOWED SUIT.

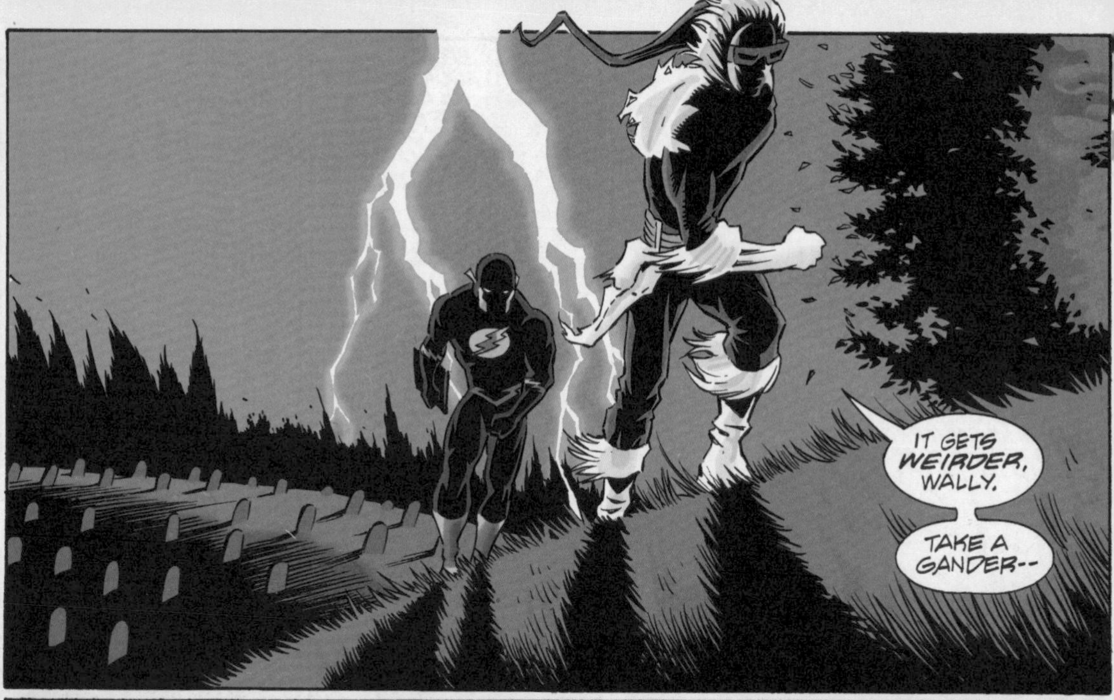
IT GETS WEIRDER, WALLY.
TAKE A GANDER--

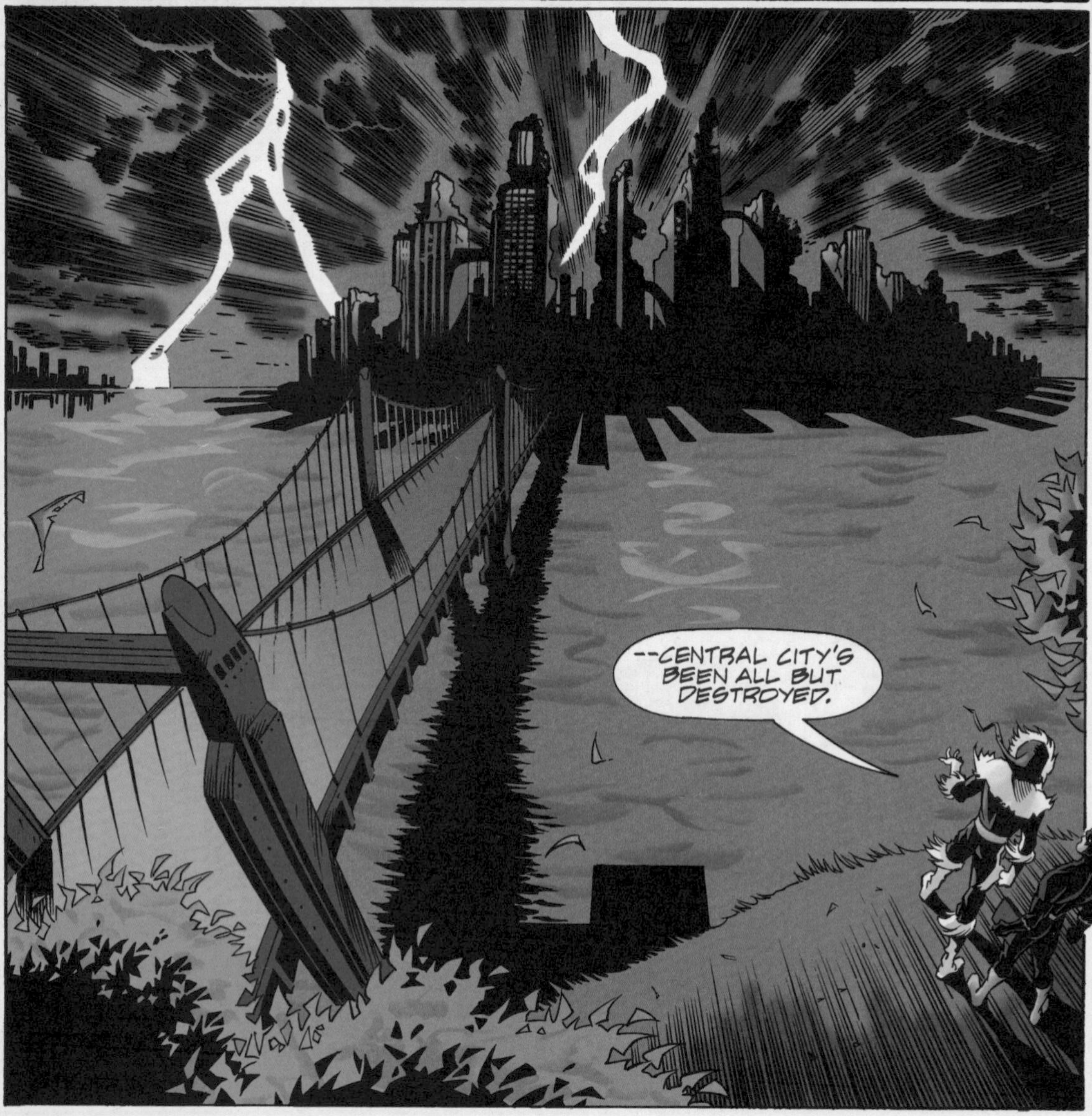
--CENTRAL CITY'S BEEN ALL BUT DESTROYED.

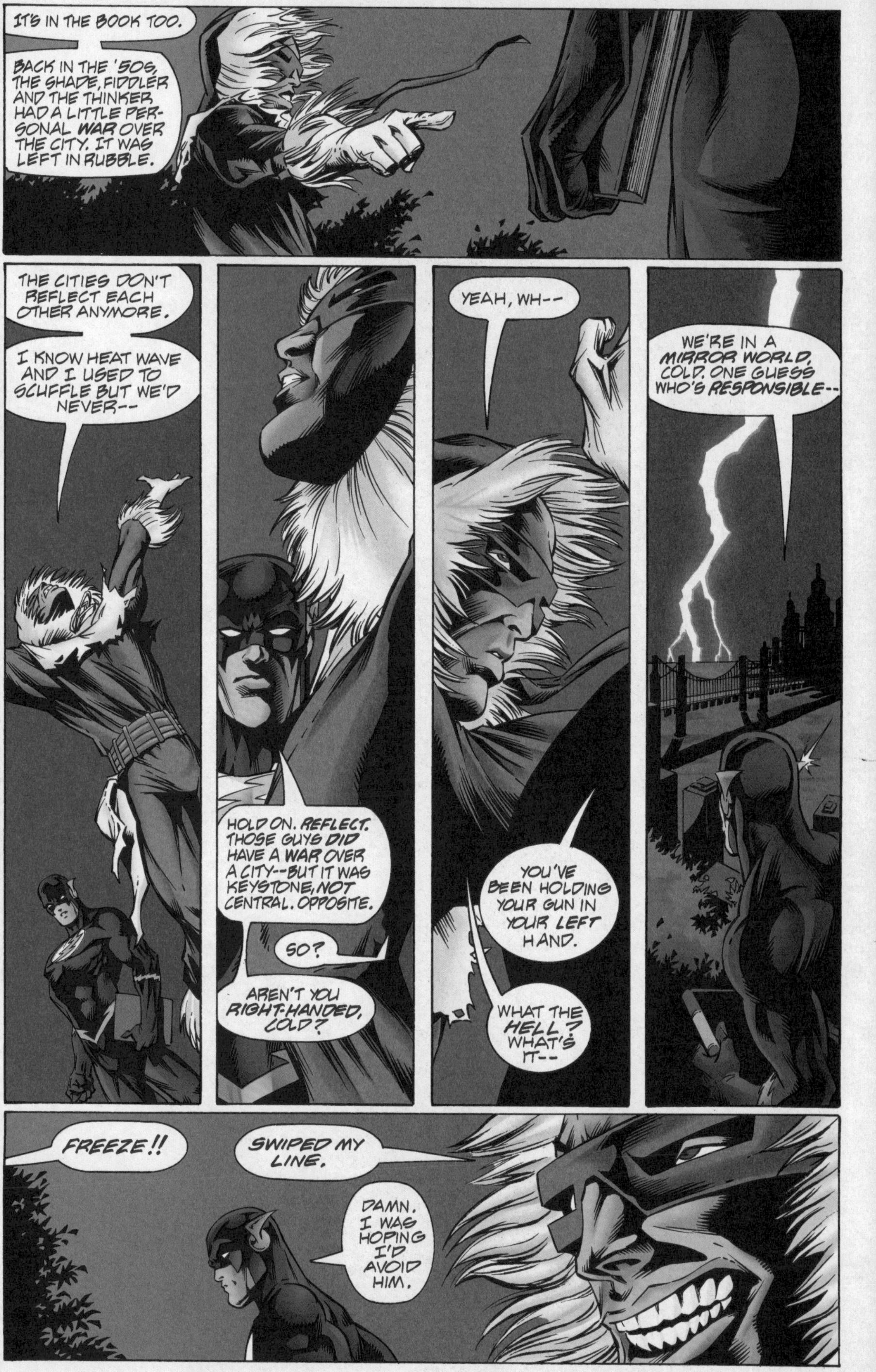
IT'S IN THE BOOK TOO.
BACK IN THE '50S, THE SHADE, FIDDLER AND THE THINKER HAD A LITTLE PERSONAL WAR OVER THE CITY. IT WAS LEFT IN RUBBLE.
THE CITIES DON'T REFLECT EACH OTHER ANYMORE.
I KNOW HEAT WAVE AND I USED TO SCUFFLE BUT WE'D NEVER--
HOLD ON. REFLECT. THOSE GUYS DID HAVE A WAR OVER A CITY--BUT IT WAS KEYSTONE, NOT CENTRAL. OPPOSITE.
SO?
AREN'T YOU RIGHT-HANDED, COLD?
YEAH, WH--
YOU'VE BEEN HOLDING YOUR GUN IN YOUR LEFT HAND.
WHAT THE HELL? WHAT'S IT--
WE'RE IN A MIRROR WORLD, COLD. ONE GUESS WHO'S RESPONSIBLE--
FREEZE!!
SWIPED MY LINE.
DAMN. I WAS HOPING I'D AVOID HIM.

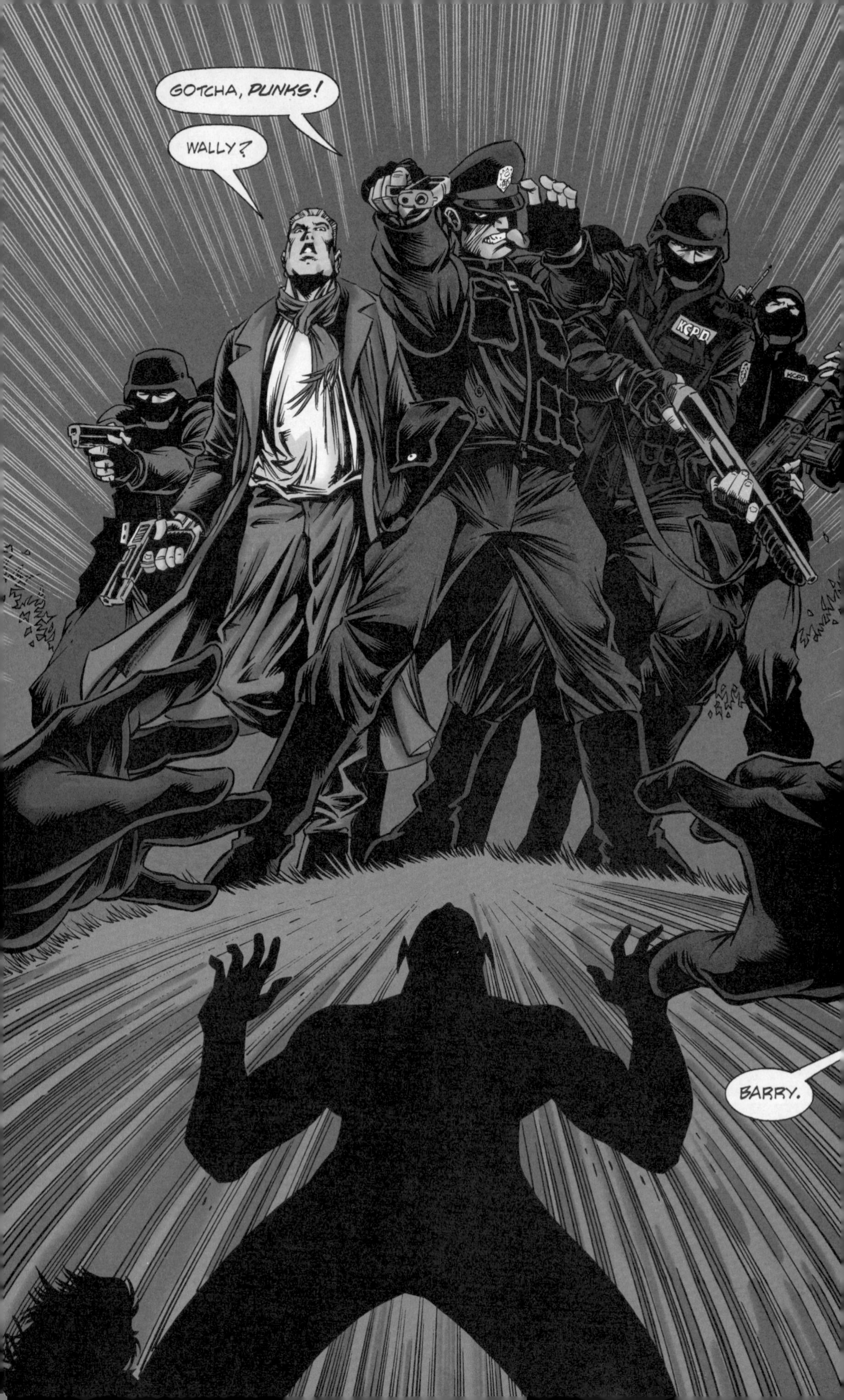
GOTCHA, PUNKS!
WALLY?
BARRY.

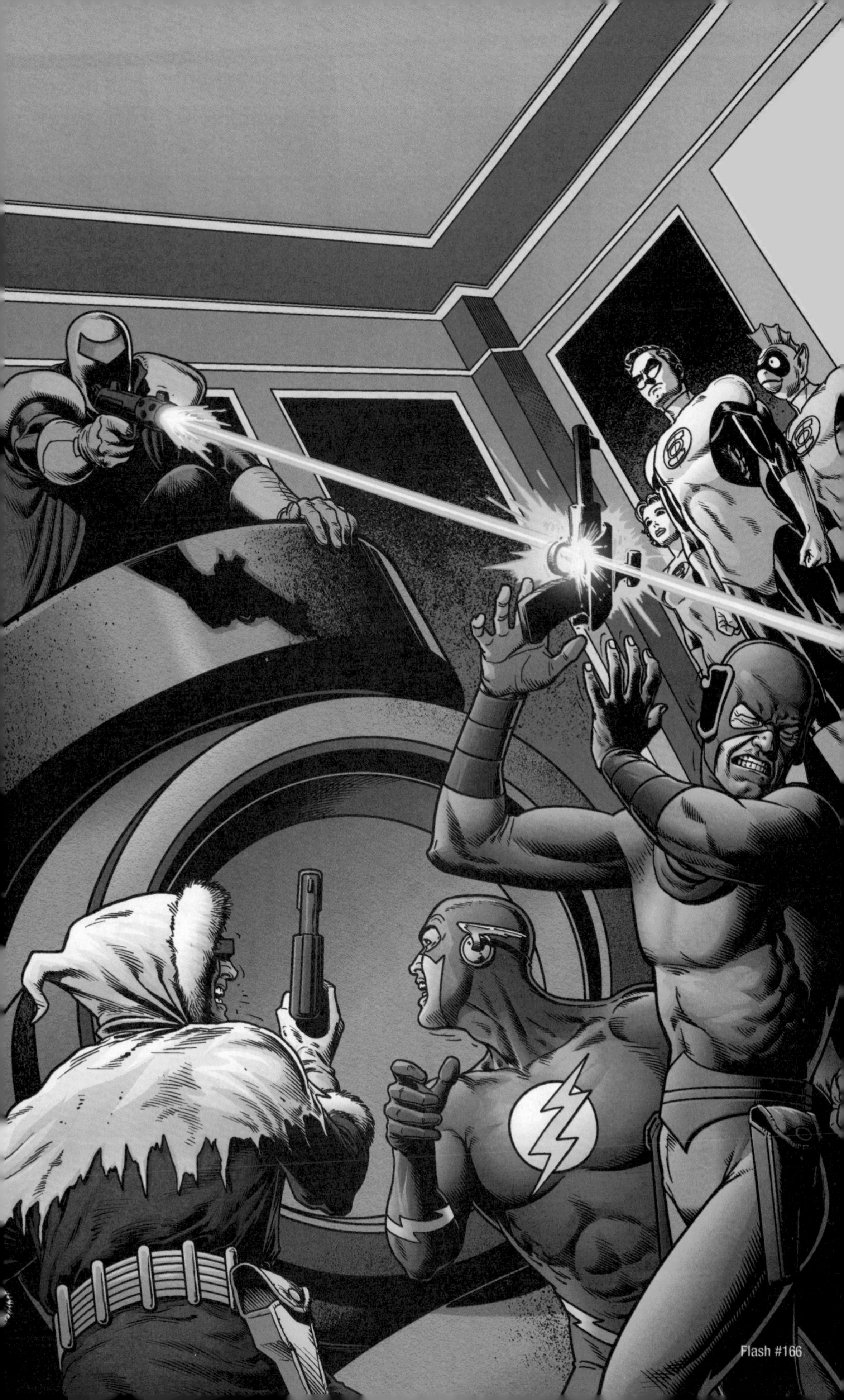

Flash #166

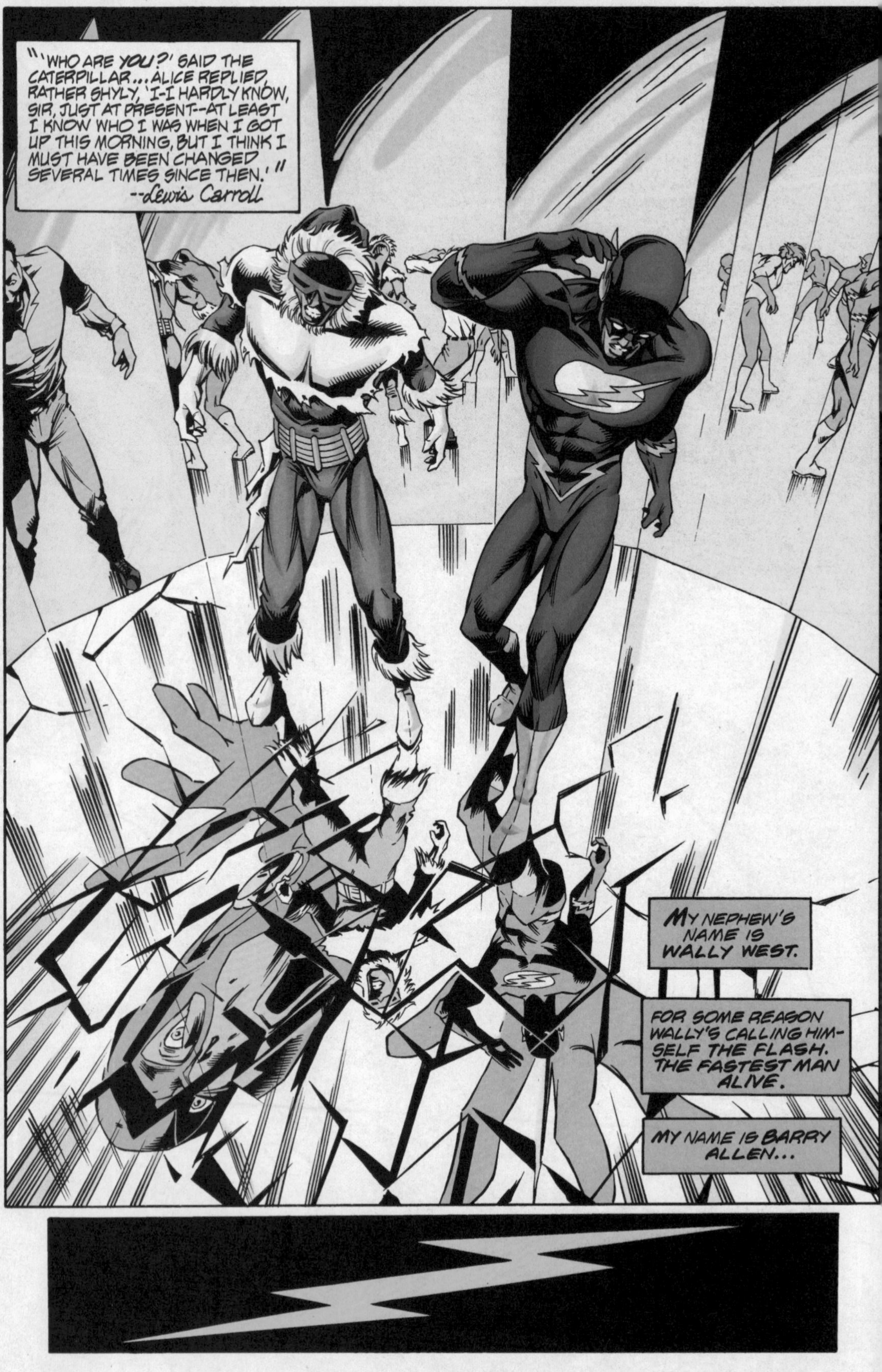
"'WHO ARE YOU?' SAID THE CATERPILLAR... ALICE REPLIED, RATHER SHYLY, 'I-I HARDLY KNOW, SIR, JUST AT PRESENT--AT LEAST I KNOW WHO I WAS WHEN I GOT UP THIS MORNING, BUT I THINK I MUST HAVE BEEN CHANGED SEVERAL TIMES SINCE THEN.'"
--Lewis Carroll
MY NEPHEW'S NAME IS WALLY WEST.
FOR SOME REASON WALLY'S CALLING HIMSELF THE FLASH. THE FASTEST MAN ALIVE.
MY NAME IS BARRY ALLEN...

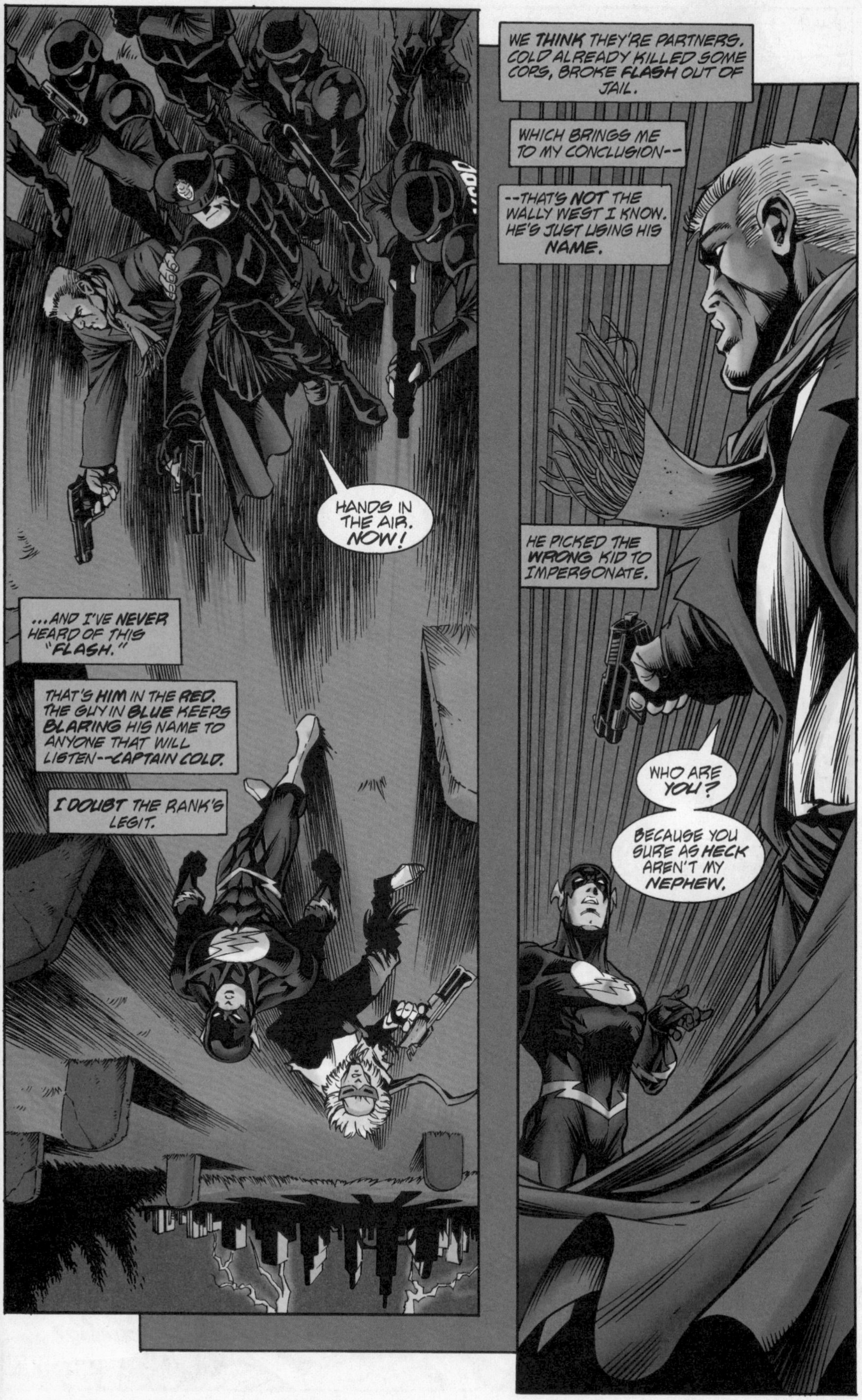
...AND I'VE NEVER HEARD OF THIS "FLASH."
THAT'S HIM IN THE RED. THE GUY IN BLUE KEEPS BLARING HIS NAME TO ANYONE THAT WILL LISTEN--CAPTAIN COLD.
I DOUBT THE RANK'S LEGIT.
HANDS IN THE AIR. NOW!
WE THINK THEY'RE PARTNERS. COLD ALREADY KILLED SOME COPS, BROKE FLASH OUT OF JAIL.
WHICH BRINGS ME TO MY CONCLUSION--
--THAT'S NOT THE WALLY WEST I KNOW. HE'S JUST USING HIS NAME.
HE PICKED THE WRONG KID TO IMPERSONATE.
WHO ARE YOU?
BECAUSE YOU SURE AS HECK AREN'T MY NEPHEW.

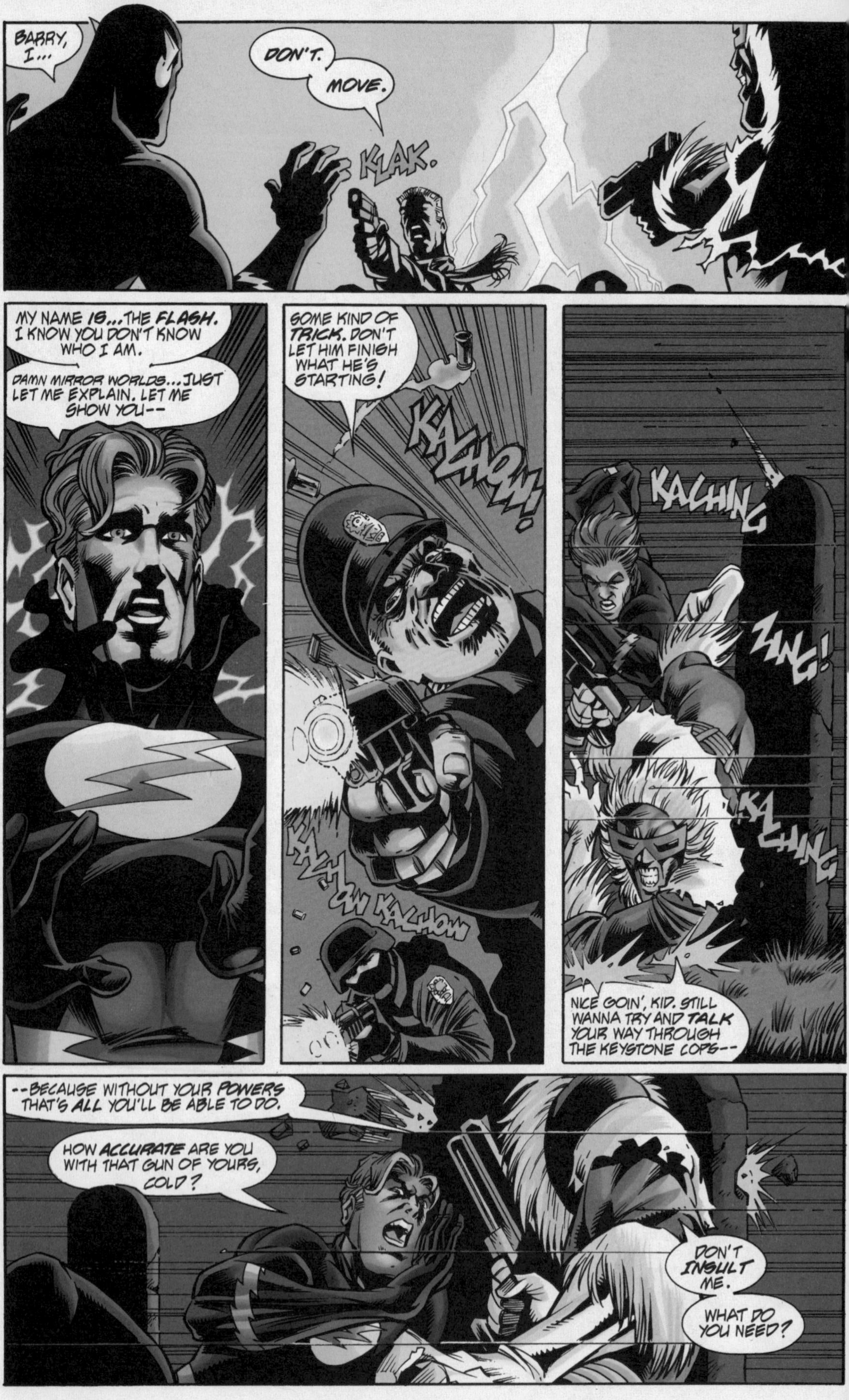
BARRY, I...
DON'T.
MOVE.
KLAK.
MY NAME IS...THE FLASH. I KNOW YOU DON'T KNOW WHO I AM.
DAMN MIRROR WORLDS...JUST LET ME EXPLAIN. LET ME SHOW YOU--
SOME KIND OF TRICK. DON'T LET HIM FINISH WHAT HE'S STARTING!
KACHOW!
KACHOW KACHOW
KACHING
ZING!
KACHING
NICE GOIN', KID. STILL WANNA TRY AND TALK YOUR WAY THROUGH THE KEYSTONE COPS--
--BECAUSE WITHOUT YOUR POWERS THAT'S ALL YOU'LL BE ABLE TO DO.
HOW ACCURATE ARE YOU WITH THAT GUN OF YOURS, COLD?
DON'T INSULT ME.
WHAT DO YOU NEED?

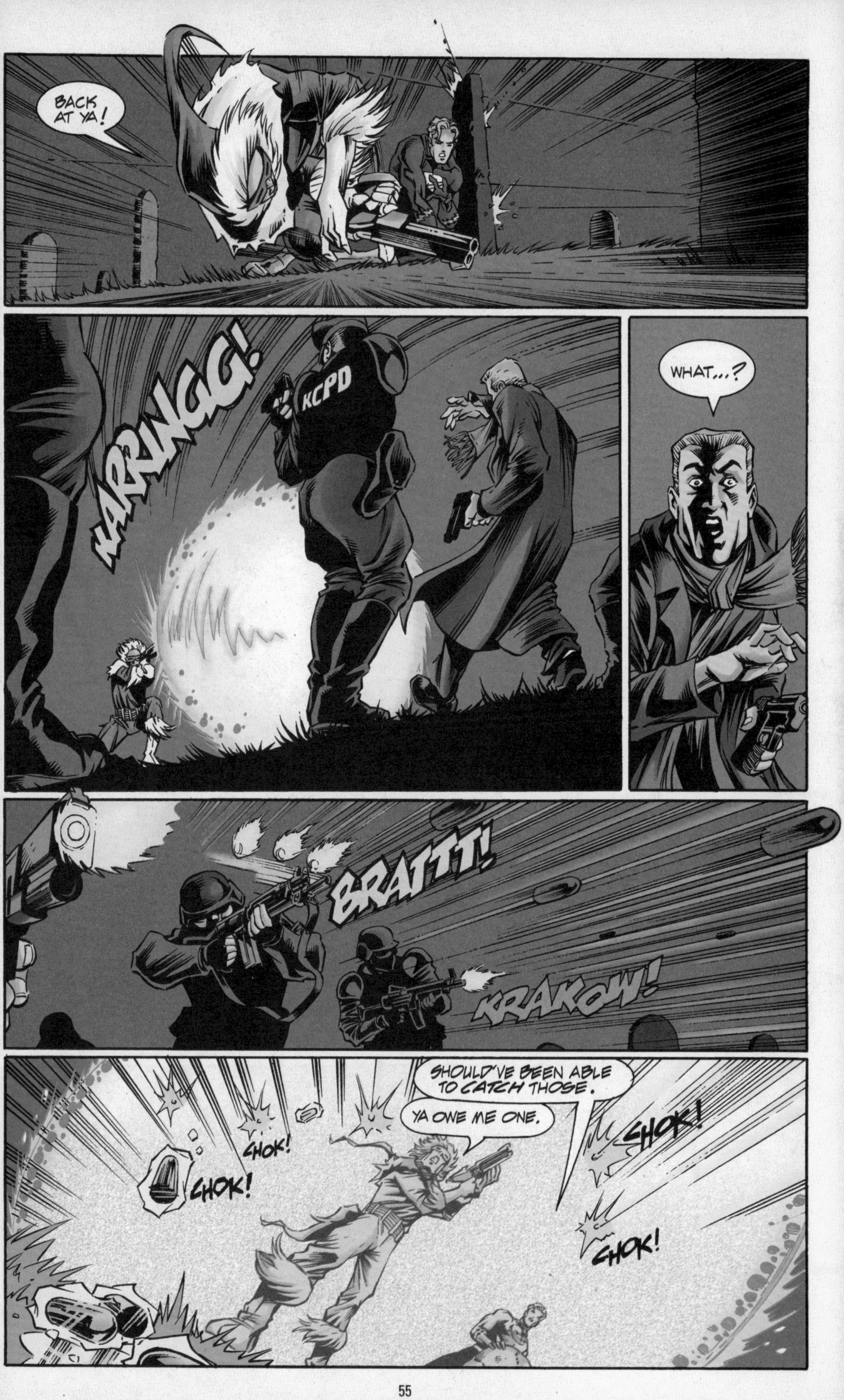

BACK AT YA!
KARRANGG!
KCPD
WHAT...?
BRATTT!
KRAKOW!
SHOULD'VE BEEN ABLE TO CATCH THOSE.
YA OWE ME ONE.
CHOK!
CHOK!
CHOK!
CHOK!

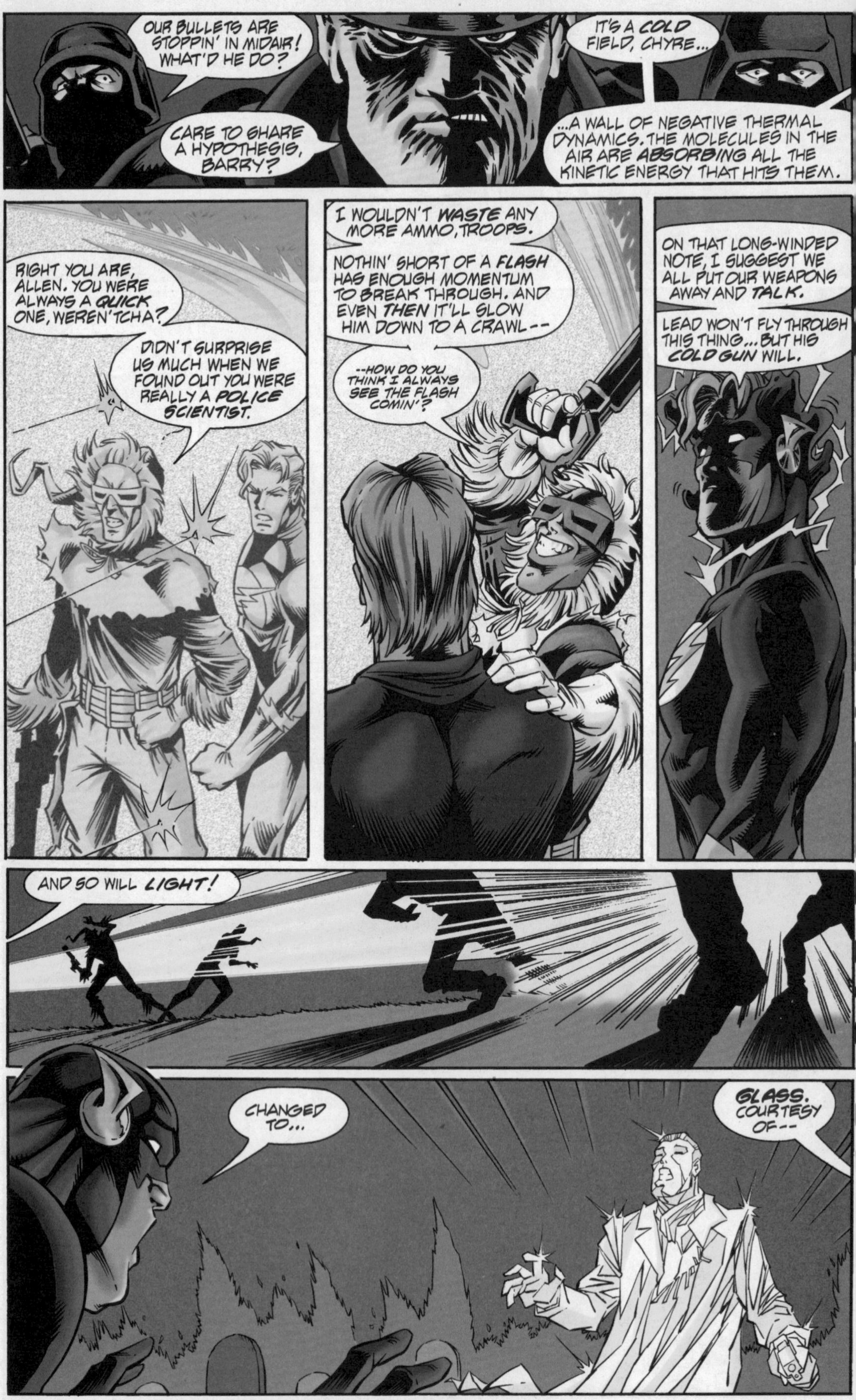
OUR BULLETS ARE STOPPIN' IN MIDAIR! WHAT'D HE DO?
CARE TO SHARE A HYPOTHESIS, BARRY?
IT'S A COLD FIELD, CHYRE...
...A WALL OF NEGATIVE THERMAL DYNAMICS. THE MOLECULES IN THE AIR ARE ABSORBING ALL THE KINETIC ENERGY THAT HITS THEM.
RIGHT YOU ARE, ALLEN. YOU WERE ALWAYS A QUICK ONE, WEREN'TCHA?
DIDN'T SURPRISE US MUCH WHEN WE FOUND OUT YOU WERE REALLY A POLICE SCIENTIST.
I WOULDN'T WASTE ANY MORE AMMO, TROOPS.
NOTHIN' SHORT OF A FLASH HAS ENOUGH MOMENTUM TO BREAK THROUGH. AND EVEN THEN IT'LL SLOW HIM DOWN TO A CRAWL--
--HOW DO YOU THINK I ALWAYS SEE THE FLASH COMIN'?
ON THAT LONG-WINDED NOTE, I SUGGEST WE ALL PUT OUR WEAPONS AWAY AND TALK.
LEAD WON'T FLY THROUGH THIS THING... BUT HIS COLD GUN WILL.
AND SO WILL LIGHT!
CHANGED TO...
GLASS. COURTESY OF--

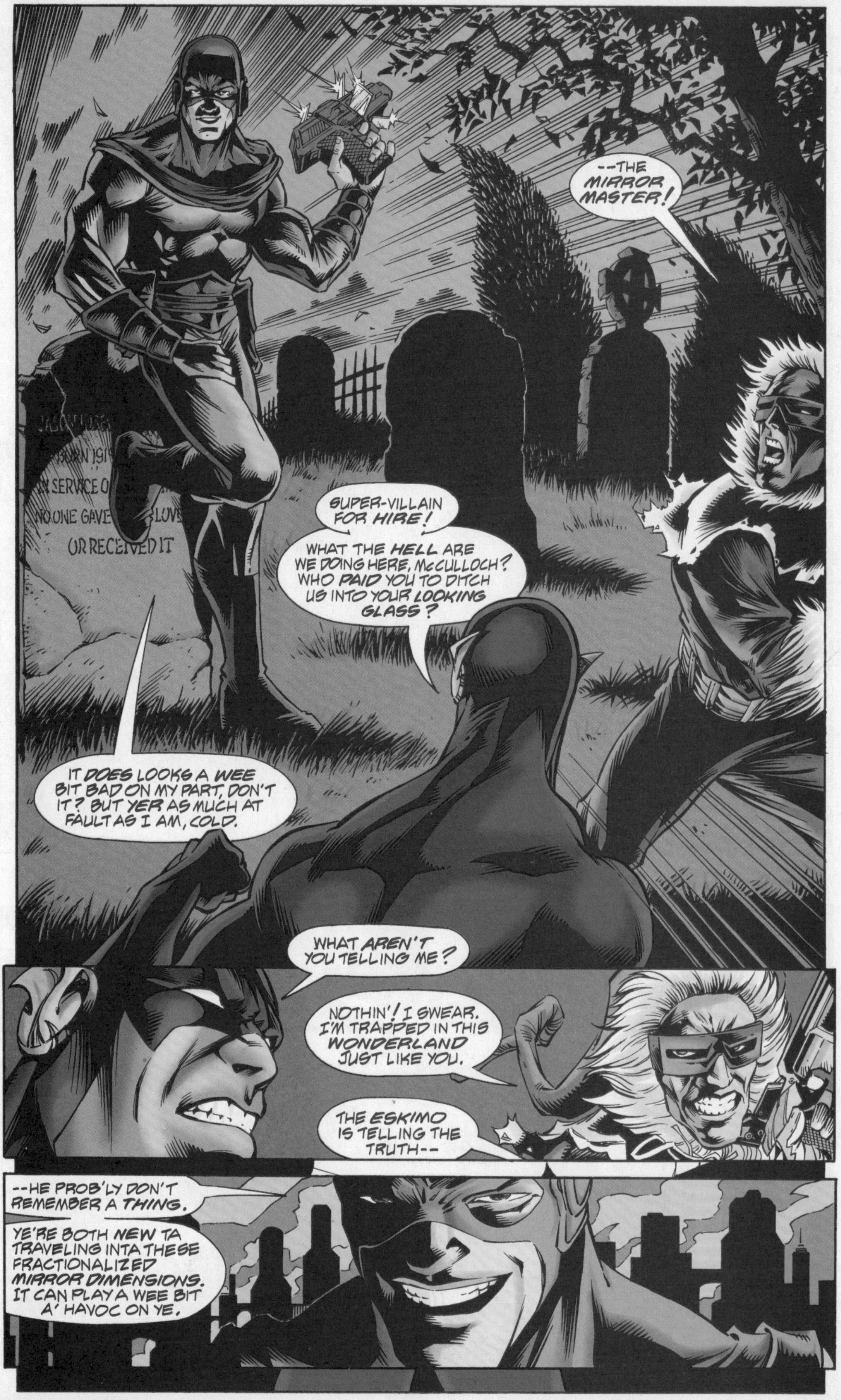
--THE MIRROR MASTER!
SUPER-VILLAIN FOR HIRE!
WHAT THE HELL ARE WE DOING HERE, McCULLOCH? WHO PAID YOU TO DITCH US INTO YOUR LOOKING GLASS?
OR RECEIVED IT
IT DOES LOOKS A WEE BIT BAD ON MY PART, DON'T IT? BUT YER AS MUCH AT FAULT AS I AM, COLD.
WHAT AREN'T YOU TELLING ME?
NOTHIN'! I SWEAR. I'M TRAPPED IN THIS WONDERLAND JUST LIKE YOU.
THE ESKIMO IS TELLING THE TRUTH--
--HE PROB'LY DON'T REMEMBER A THING.
YE'RE BOTH NEW TA TRAVELING INTA THESE FRACTIONALIZED MIRROR DIMENSIONS. IT CAN PLAY A WEE BIT A' HAVOC ON YE.

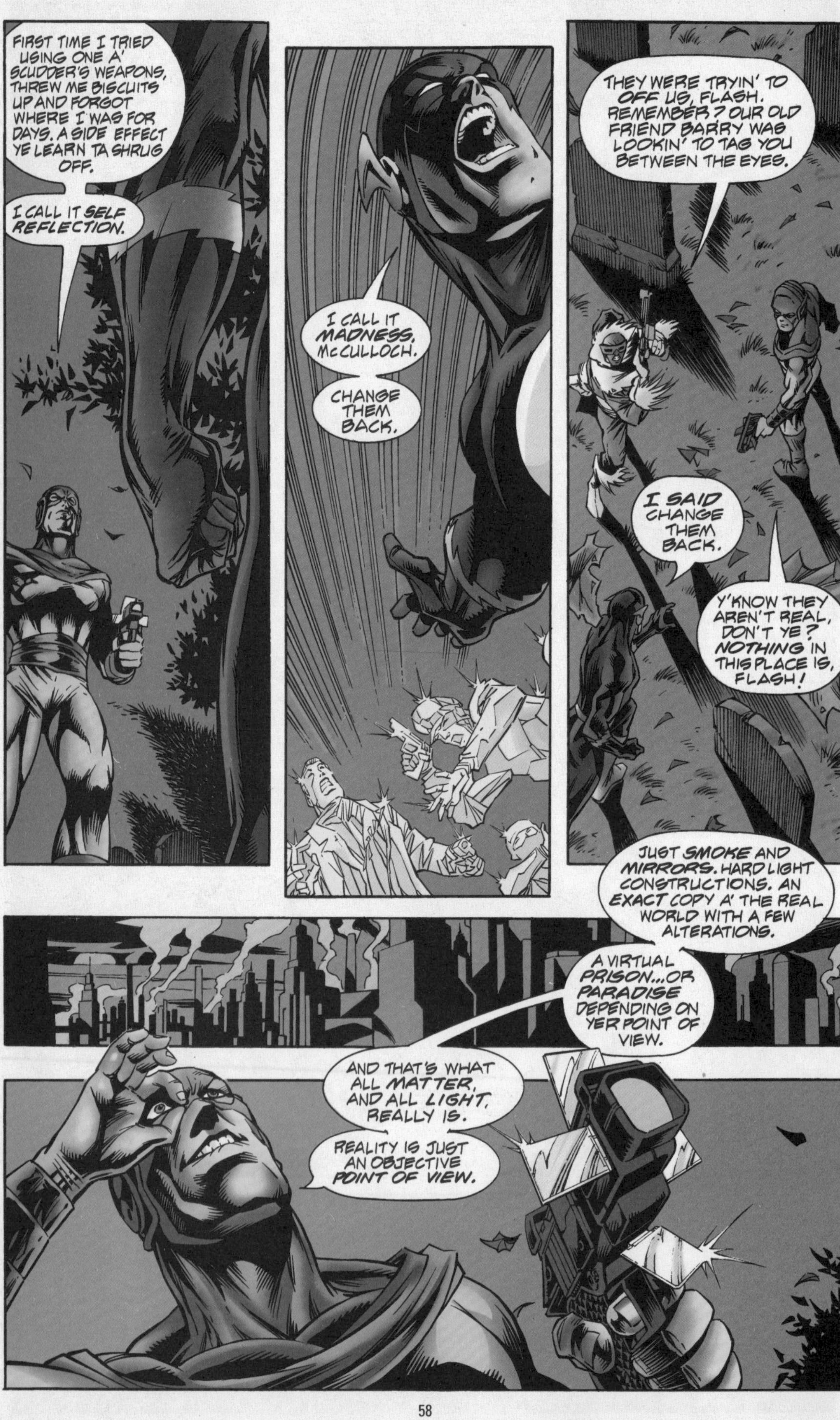
FIRST TIME I TRIED USING ONE A' SCUDDER'S WEAPONS, THREW ME BISCUITS UP AND FORGOT WHERE I WAS FOR DAYS. A SIDE EFFECT YE LEARN TA SHRUG OFF.
I CALL IT SELF REFLECTION.
I CALL IT MADNESS, McCULLOCH.
CHANGE THEM BACK.
THEY WERE TRYIN' TO OFF US, FLASH. REMEMBER? OUR OLD FRIEND BARRY WAS LOOKIN' TO TAG YOU BETWEEN THE EYES.
I SAID CHANGE THEM BACK.
Y'KNOW THEY AREN'T REAL, DON'T YE? NOTHING IN THIS PLACE IS, FLASH!
JUST SMOKE AND MIRRORS. HARD LIGHT CONSTRUCTIONS. AN EXACT COPY A' THE REAL WORLD WITH A FEW ALTERATIONS.
A VIRTUAL PRISON...OR PARADISE DEPENDING ON YER POINT OF VIEW.
AND THAT'S WHAT ALL MATTER, AND ALL LIGHT, REALLY IS.
REALITY IS JUST AN OBJECTIVE POINT OF VIEW.

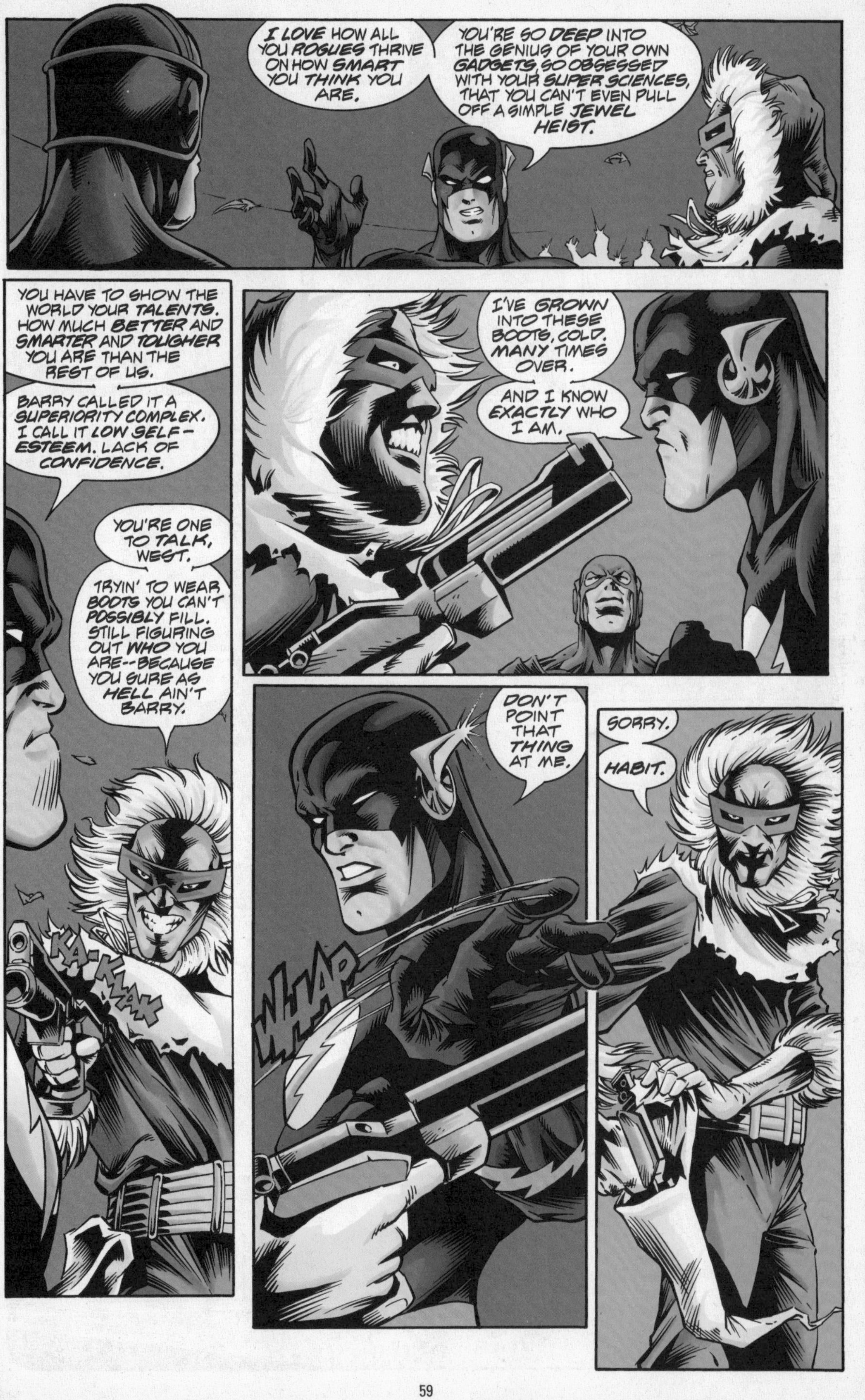
I LOVE HOW ALL YOU ROGUES THRIVE ON HOW SMART YOU THINK YOU ARE.
YOU'RE SO DEEP INTO THE GENIUS OF YOUR OWN GADGETS, SO OBSESSED WITH YOUR SUPER SCIENCES, THAT YOU CAN'T EVEN PULL OFF A SIMPLE JEWEL HEIST.
YOU HAVE TO SHOW THE WORLD YOUR TALENTS. HOW MUCH BETTER AND SMARTER AND TOUGHER YOU ARE THAN THE REST OF US.
BARRY CALLED IT A SUPERIORITY COMPLEX. I CALL IT LOW SELF-ESTEEM. LACK OF CONFIDENCE.
YOU'RE ONE TO TALK, WEST.
TRYIN' TO WEAR BOOTS YOU CAN'T POSSIBLY FILL. STILL FIGURING OUT WHO YOU ARE--BECAUSE YOU SURE AS HELL AIN'T BARRY.
KA-KLAK
I'VE GROWN INTO THESE BOOTS, COLD. MANY TIMES OVER.
AND I KNOW EXACTLY WHO I AM.
DON'T POINT THAT THING AT ME.
WHAP
SORRY.
HABIT.

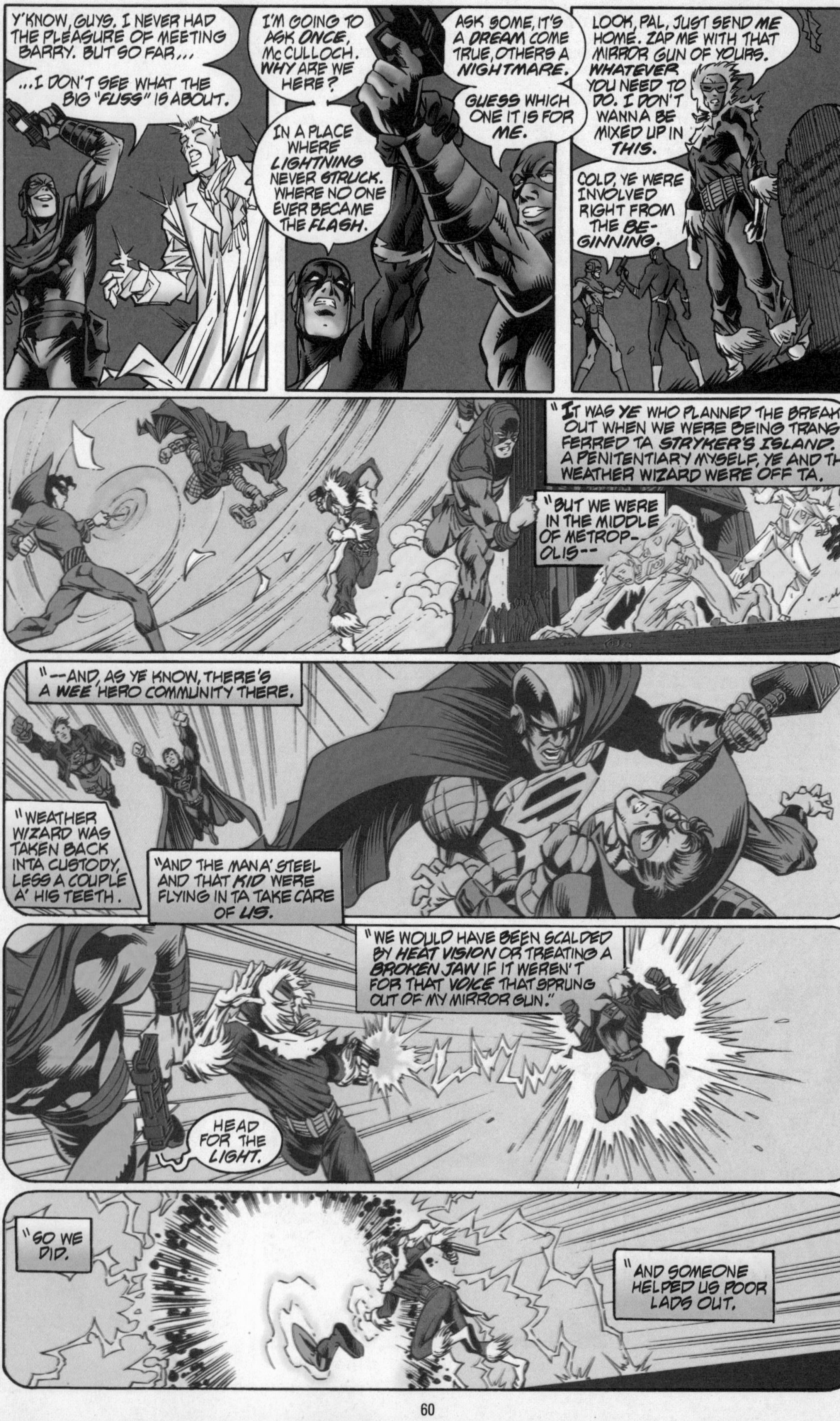

Y'KNOW, GUYS. I NEVER HAD THE PLEASURE OF MEETING BARRY. BUT SO FAR,...
...I DON'T SEE WHAT THE BIG "FUSS" IS ABOUT.
I'M GOING TO ASK ONCE, McCULLOCH. WHY ARE WE HERE?
IN A PLACE WHERE LIGHTNING NEVER STRUCK. WHERE NO ONE EVER BECAME THE FLASH.
ASK SOME, IT'S A DREAM COME TRUE, OTHERS A NIGHTMARE.
GUESS WHICH ONE IT IS FOR ME.
LOOK, PAL, JUST SEND ME HOME. ZAP ME WITH THAT MIRROR GUN OF YOURS. WHATEVER YOU NEED TO DO. I DON'T WANNA BE MIXED UP IN THIS.
COLD, YE WERE INVOLVED RIGHT FROM THE BE-GINNING.
"IT WAS YE WHO PLANNED THE BREAK-OUT WHEN WE WERE BEING TRANS-FERRED TA STRYKER'S ISLAND. A PENITENTIARY MYSELF, YE AND THE WEATHER WIZARD WERE OFF TA.
"BUT WE WERE IN THE MIDDLE OF METROP-OLIS--
"--AND, AS YE KNOW, THERE'S A WEE HERO COMMUNITY THERE.
"WEATHER WIZARD WAS TAKEN BACK INTA CUSTODY, LESS A COUPLE A' HIS TEETH.
"AND THE MAN A' STEEL AND THAT KID WERE FLYING IN TA TAKE CARE OF US.
"WE WOULD HAVE BEEN SCALDED BY HEAT VISION OR TREATING A BROKEN JAW IF IT WEREN'T FOR THAT VOICE THAT SPRUNG OUT OF MY MIRROR GUN."
HEAD FOR THE LIGHT.
"SO WE DID.
"AND SOMEONE HELPED US POOR LADS OUT.

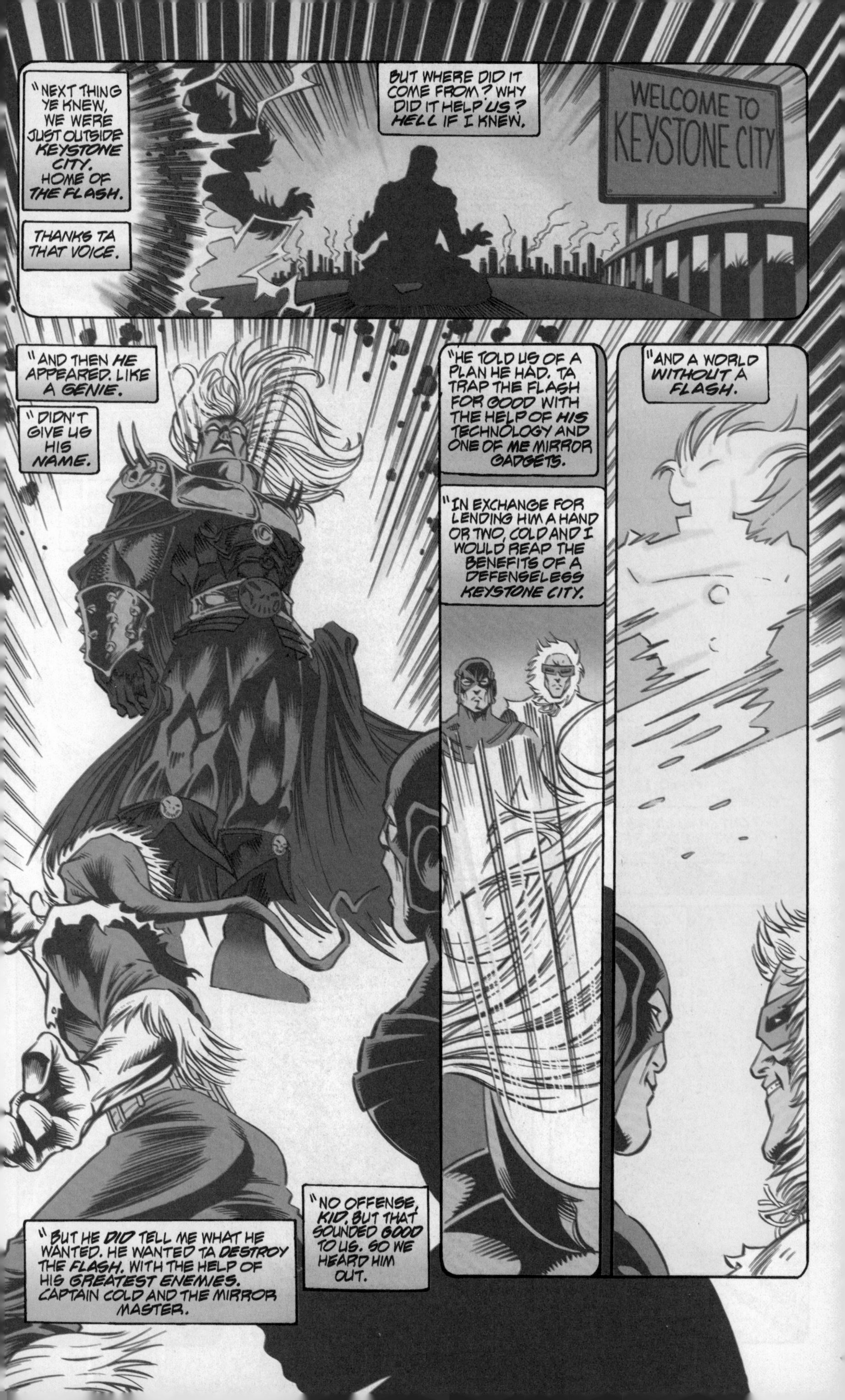
"NEXT THING YE KNEW, WE WERE JUST OUTSIDE KEYSTONE CITY. HOME OF THE FLASH.
THANKS TA THAT VOICE.
BUT WHERE DID IT COME FROM? WHY DID IT HELP US? HELL IF I KNEW.
WELCOME TO KEYSTONE CITY
"AND THEN HE APPEARED. LIKE A GENIE.
"DIDN'T GIVE US HIS NAME.
"BUT HE DID TELL ME WHAT HE WANTED. HE WANTED TA DESTROY THE FLASH. WITH THE HELP OF HIS GREATEST ENEMIES. CAPTAIN COLD AND THE MIRROR MASTER.
"NO OFFENSE, KID. BUT THAT SOUNDED GOOD TO US. SO WE HEARD HIM OUT.
"HE TOLD US OF A PLAN HE HAD. TA TRAP THE FLASH FOR GOOD WITH THE HELP OF HIS TECHNOLOGY AND ONE OF ME MIRROR GADGETS.
"IN EXCHANGE FOR LENDING HIM A HAND OR TWO, COLD AND I WOULD REAP THE BENEFITS OF A DEFENSELESS KEYSTONE CITY.
"AND A WORLD WITHOUT A FLASH.

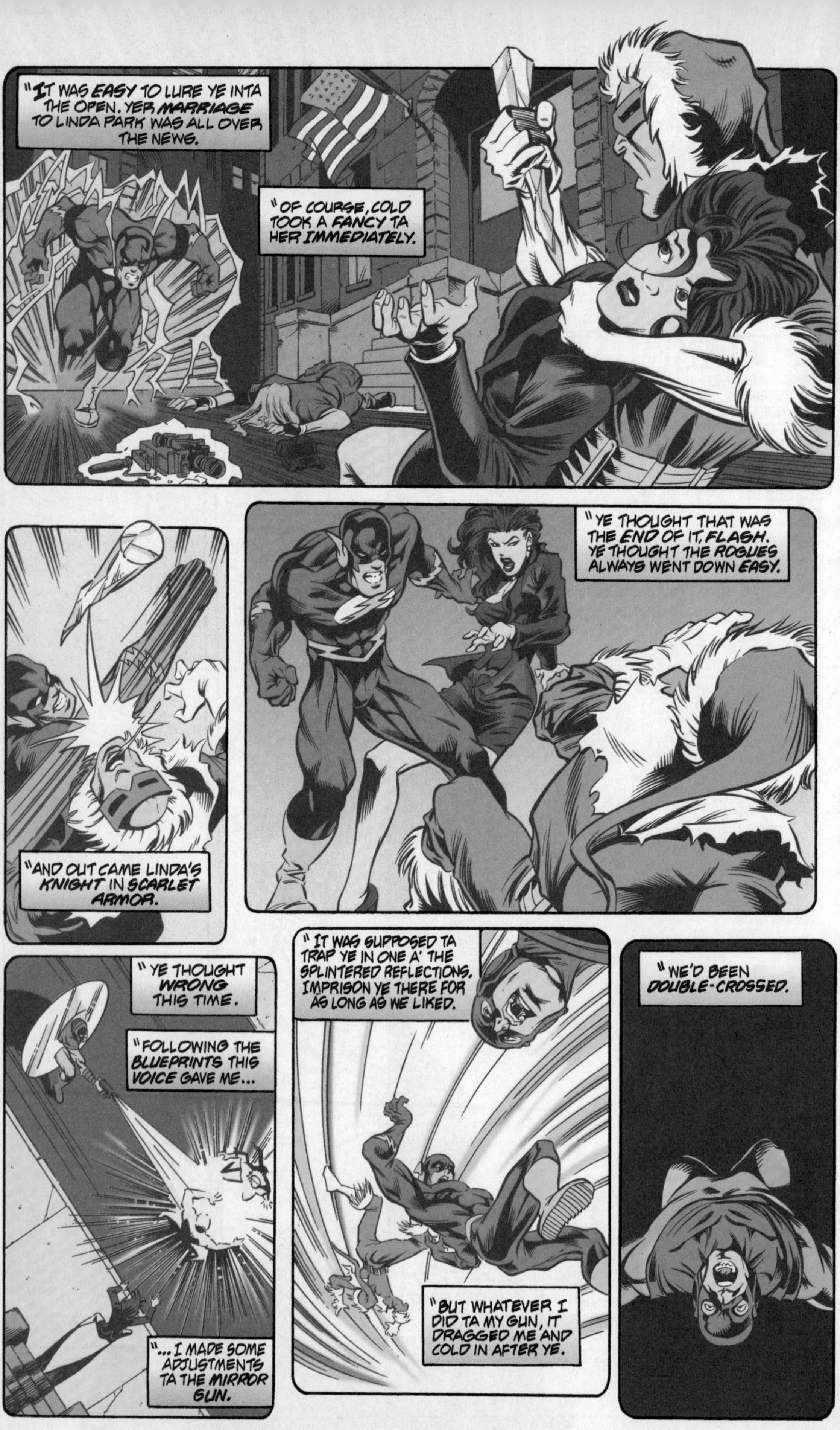
"IT WAS EASY TO LURE YE INTA THE OPEN. YER MARRIAGE TO LINDA PARK WAS ALL OVER THE NEWS.
"OF COURSE, COLD TOOK A FANCY TA HER IMMEDIATELY.
"AND OUT CAME LINDA'S KNIGHT IN SCARLET ARMOR.
"YE THOUGHT THAT WAS THE END OF IT, FLASH. YE THOUGHT THE ROGUES ALWAYS WENT DOWN EASY.
"YE THOUGHT WRONG THIS TIME.
"FOLLOWING THE BLUEPRINTS THIS VOICE GAVE ME...
"...I MADE SOME ADJUSTMENTS TA THE MIRROR GUN.
"IT WAS SUPPOSED TA TRAP YE IN ONE A' THE SPLINTERED REFLECTIONS. IMPRISON YE THERE FOR AS LONG AS WE LIKED.
"BUT WHATEVER I DID TA MY GUN, IT DRAGGED ME AND COLD IN AFTER YE.
"WE'D BEEN DOUBLE-CROSSED.

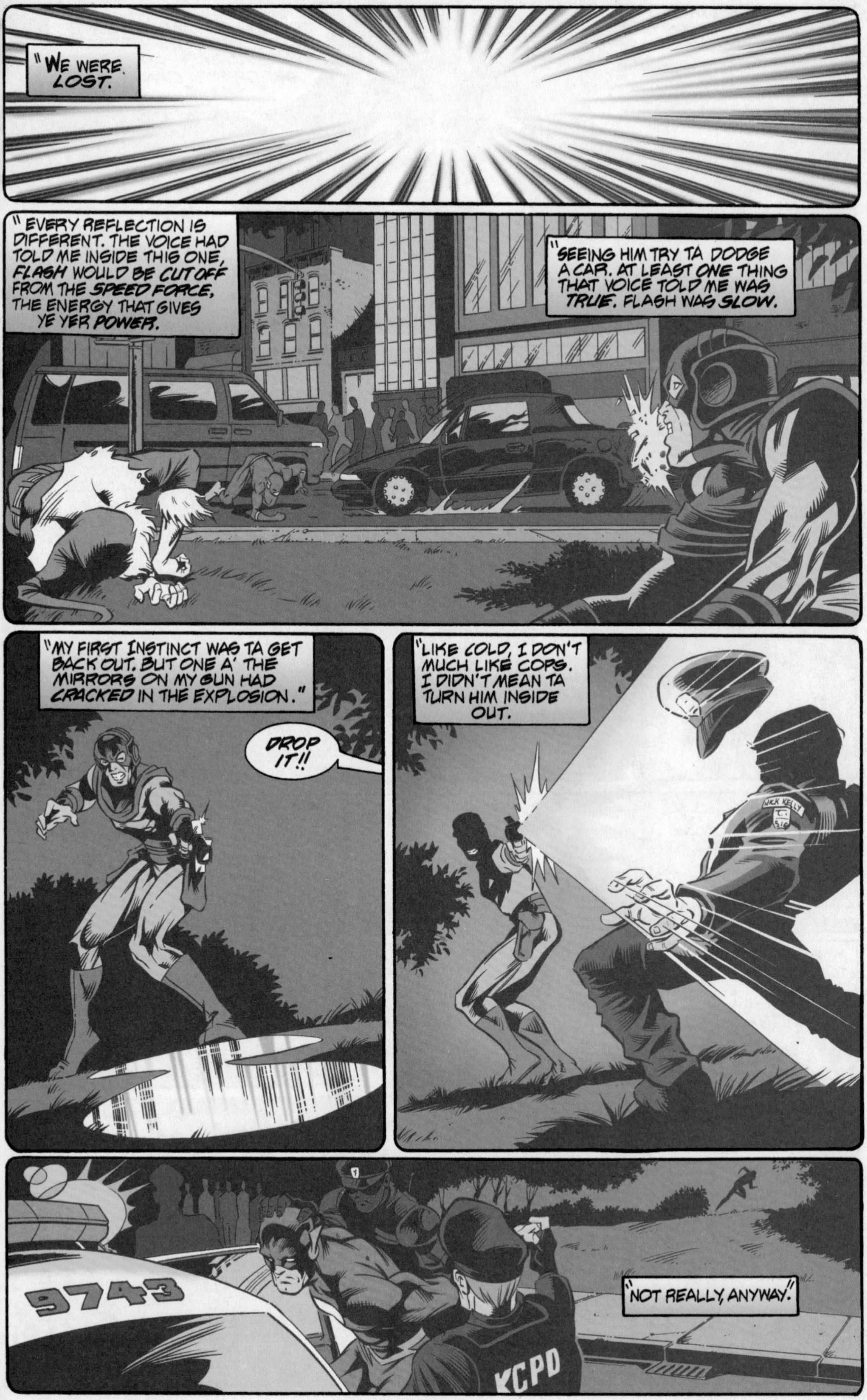
"WE WERE LOST.
"EVERY REFLECTION IS DIFFERENT. THE VOICE HAD TOLD ME INSIDE THIS ONE, FLASH WOULD BE CUT OFF FROM THE SPEED FORCE, THE ENERGY THAT GIVES YE YER POWER.
"SEEING HIM TRY TA DODGE A CAR. AT LEAST ONE THING THAT VOICE TOLD ME WAS TRUE. FLASH WAS SLOW.
"MY FIRST INSTINCT WAS TA GET BACK OUT. BUT ONE A' THE MIRRORS ON MY GUN HAD CRACKED IN THE EXPLOSION."
DROP IT!!
"LIKE COLD, I DON'T MUCH LIKE COPS. I DIDN'T MEAN TA TURN HIM INSIDE OUT.
9743
"NOT REALLY, ANYWAY."
KCPD

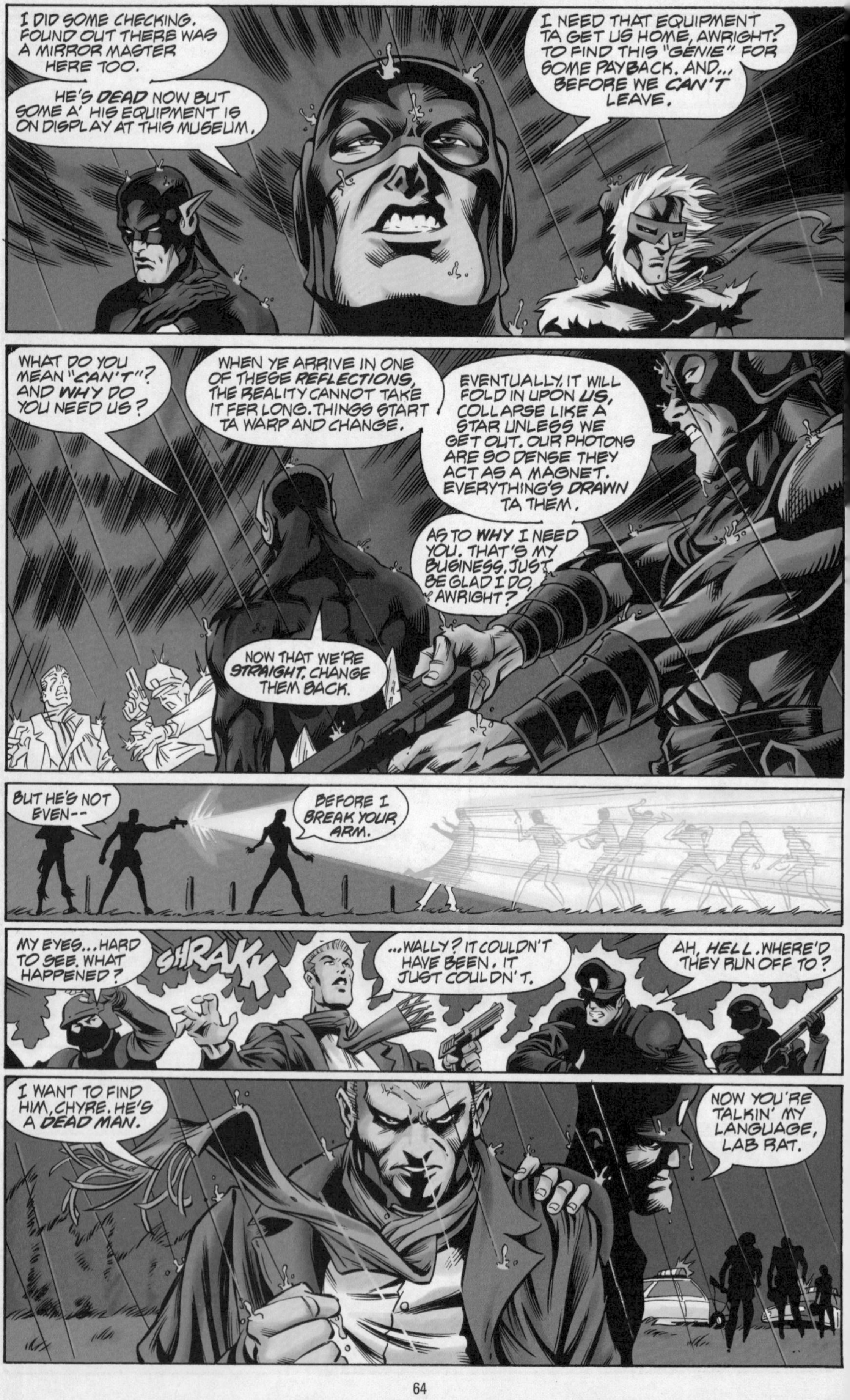
I DID SOME CHECKING. FOUND OUT THERE WAS A MIRROR MASTER HERE TOO.
HE'S DEAD NOW BUT SOME A' HIS EQUIPMENT IS ON DISPLAY AT THIS MUSEUM.
I NEED THAT EQUIPMENT TA GET US HOME, AWRIGHT? TO FIND THIS "GENIE" FOR SOME PAYBACK. AND... BEFORE WE CAN'T LEAVE.
WHAT DO YOU MEAN "CAN'T"? AND WHY DO YOU NEED US?
WHEN YE ARRIVE IN ONE OF THESE REFLECTIONS, THE REALITY CANNOT TAKE IT FER LONG. THINGS START TA WARP AND CHANGE.
EVENTUALLY, IT WILL FOLD IN UPON US, COLLAPSE LIKE A STAR UNLESS WE GET OUT. OUR PHOTONS ARE SO DENSE THEY ACT AS A MAGNET. EVERYTHING'S DRAWN TA THEM.
AS TO WHY I NEED YOU. THAT'S MY BUSINESS. JUST BE GLAD I DO, AWRIGHT?
NOW THAT WE'RE STRAIGHT, CHANGE THEM BACK.
BUT HE'S NOT EVEN--
BEFORE I BREAK YOUR ARM.
MY EYES... HARD TO SEE. WHAT HAPPENED?
SHRAKK
...WALLY? IT COULDN'T HAVE BEEN. IT JUST COULDN'T.
AH, HELL. WHERE'D THEY RUN OFF TO?
I WANT TO FIND HIM, CHYRE. HE'S A DEAD MAN.
NOW YOU'RE TALKIN' MY LANGUAGE, LAB RAT.

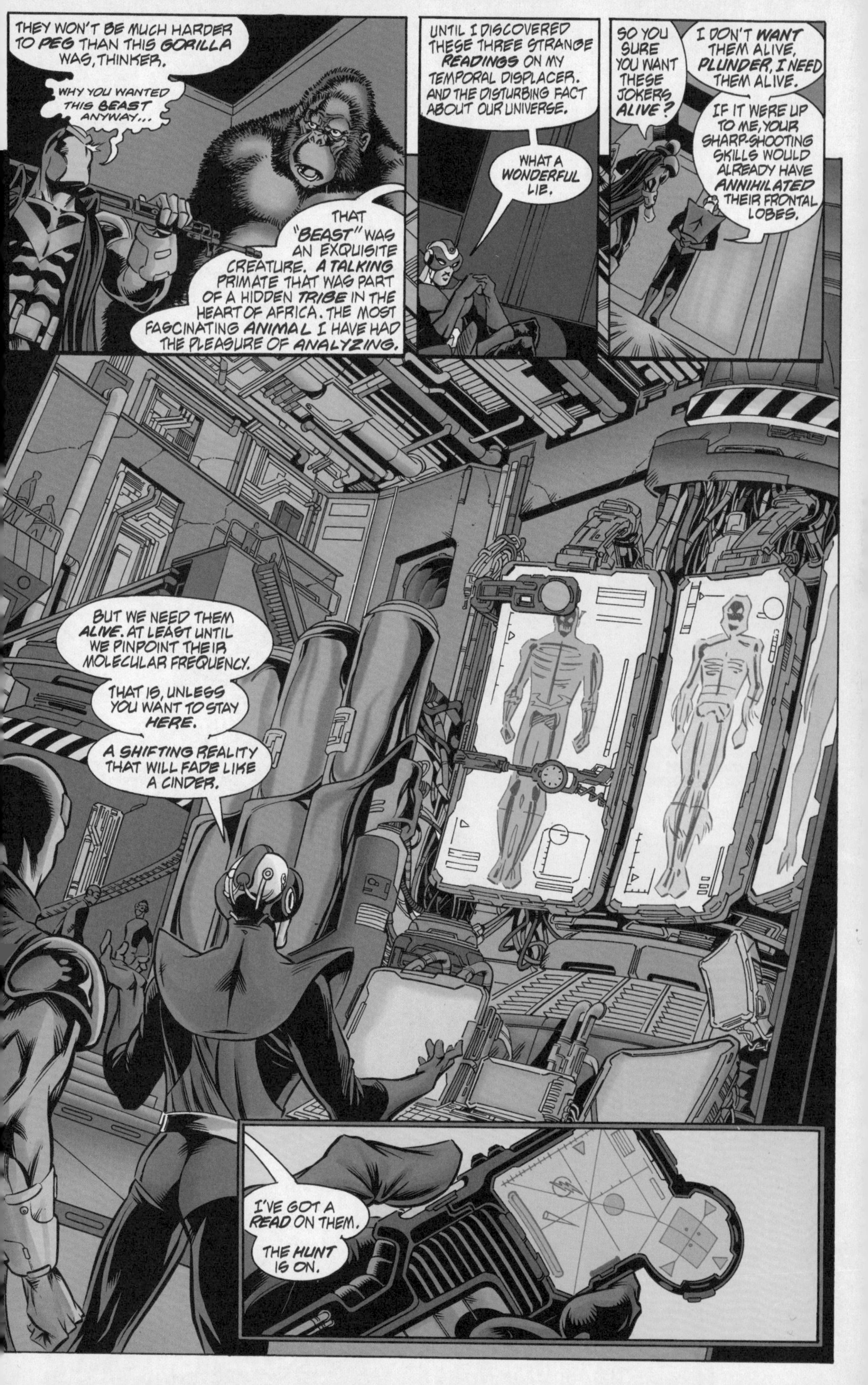
THEY WON'T BE MUCH HARDER TO PEG THAN THIS GORILLA WAS, THINKER.
WHY YOU WANTED THIS BEAST ANYWAY...
THAT "BEAST" WAS AN EXQUISITE CREATURE. A TALKING PRIMATE THAT WAS PART OF A HIDDEN TRIBE IN THE HEART OF AFRICA. THE MOST FASCINATING ANIMAL I HAVE HAD THE PLEASURE OF ANALYZING.
UNTIL I DISCOVERED THESE THREE STRANGE READINGS ON MY TEMPORAL DISPLACER. AND THE DISTURBING FACT ABOUT OUR UNIVERSE.
WHAT A WONDERFUL LIE.
SO YOU SURE YOU WANT THESE JOKERS ALIVE?
I DON'T WANT THEM ALIVE, PLUNDER, I NEED THEM ALIVE.
IF IT WERE UP TO ME, YOUR SHARP-SHOOTING SKILLS WOULD ALREADY HAVE ANNIHILATED THEIR FRONTAL LOBES.
BUT WE NEED THEM ALIVE. AT LEAST UNTIL WE PINPOINT THEIR MOLECULAR FREQUENCY.
THAT IS, UNLESS YOU WANT TO STAY HERE.
A SHIFTING REALITY THAT WILL FADE LIKE A CINDER.
I'VE GOT A READ ON THEM.
THE HUNT IS ON.

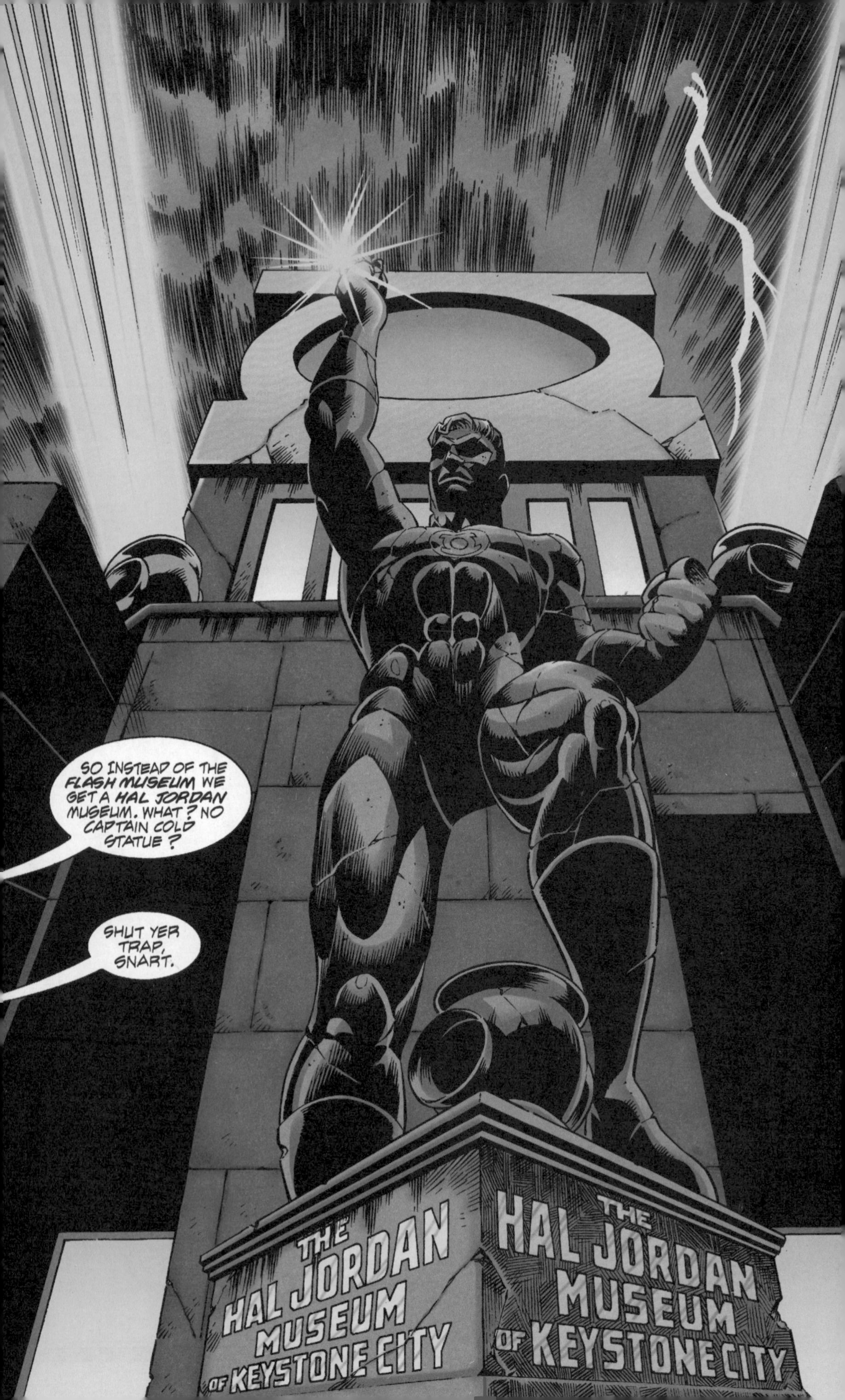

SO INSTEAD OF THE FLASH MUSEUM WE GET A HAL JORDAN MUSEUM. WHAT? NO CAPTAIN COLD STATUE?
SHUT YER TRAP, SNART.
THE HAL JORDAN MUSEUM OF KEYSTONE CITY
THE HAL JORDAN MUSEUM OF KEYSTONE CITY

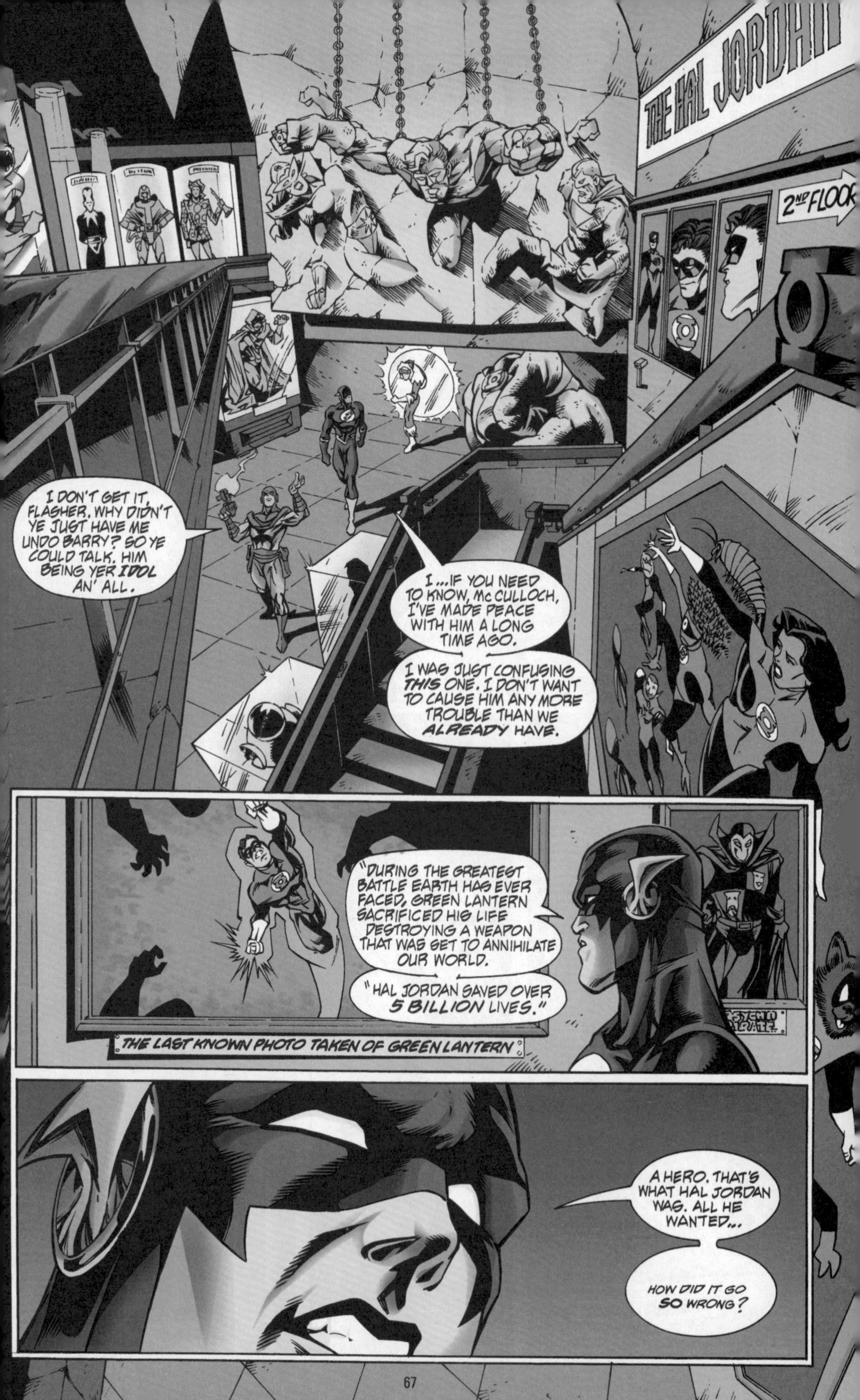
THE HAL JORDAN
2ND FLOOR
I DON'T GET IT, FLASHER. WHY DIDN'T YE JUST HAVE ME UNDO BARRY? SO YE COULD TALK. HIM BEING YER IDOL AN' ALL.
I...IF YOU NEED TO KNOW, McCULLOCH, I'VE MADE PEACE WITH HIM A LONG TIME AGO.
I WAS JUST CONFUSING THIS ONE. I DON'T WANT TO CAUSE HIM ANY MORE TROUBLE THAN WE ALREADY HAVE.
"DURING THE GREATEST BATTLE EARTH HAS EVER FACED, GREEN LANTERN SACRIFICED HIS LIFE DESTROYING A WEAPON THAT WAS SET TO ANNIHILATE OUR WORLD.
"HAL JORDAN SAVED OVER 5 BILLION LIVES."
THE LAST KNOWN PHOTO TAKEN OF GREEN LANTERN
A HERO. THAT'S WHAT HAL JORDAN WAS. ALL HE WANTED...
HOW DID IT GO SO WRONG?

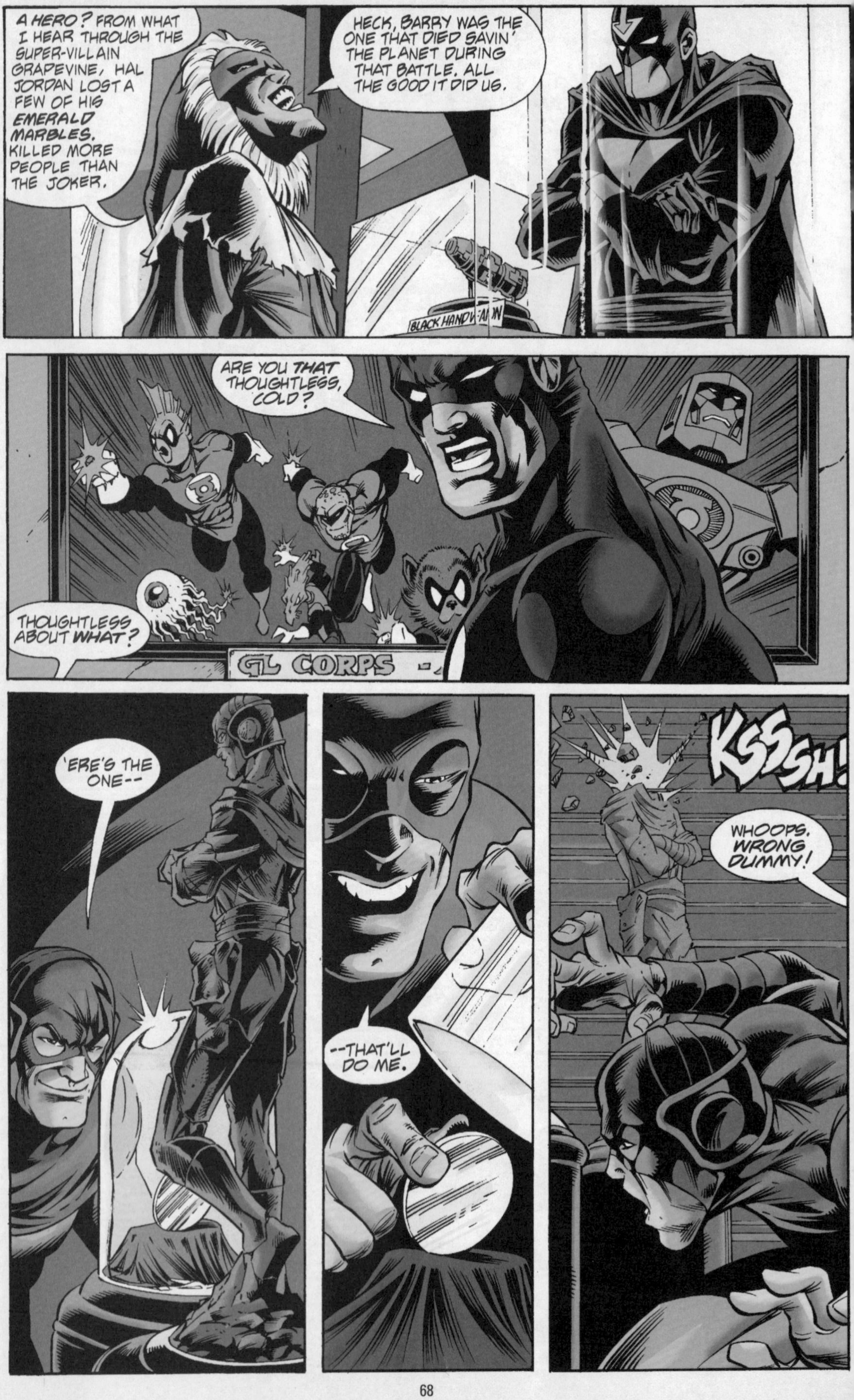
A HERO? FROM WHAT I HEAR THROUGH THE SUPER-VILLAIN GRAPEVINE, HAL JORDAN LOST A FEW OF HIS EMERALD MARBLES. KILLED MORE PEOPLE THAN THE JOKER.
HECK, BARRY WAS THE ONE THAT DIED SAVIN' THE PLANET DURING THAT BATTLE. ALL THE GOOD IT DID US.
ARE YOU THAT THOUGHTLESS, COLD?
THOUGHTLESS ABOUT WHAT?
GL CORPS
'ERE'S THE ONE--
--THAT'LL DO ME.
KSSSH!
WHOOPS. WRONG DUMMY!

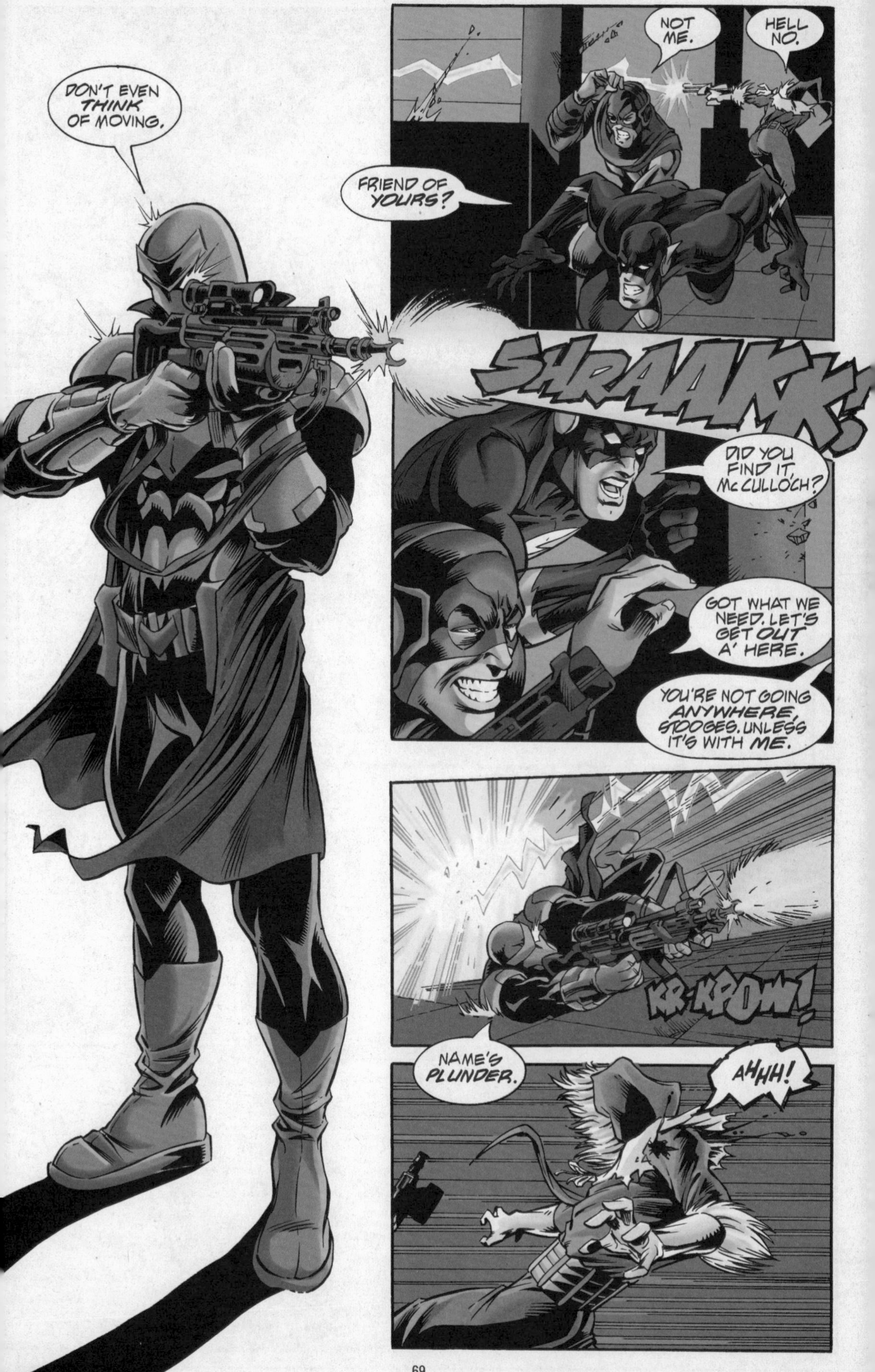
DON'T EVEN THINK OF MOVING.
FRIEND OF YOURS?
NOT ME.
HELL NO.
SHRAAAKK!
DID YOU FIND IT, McCULLOCH?
GOT WHAT WE NEED. LET'S GET OUT A' HERE.
YOU'RE NOT GOING ANYWHERE, STOOGES. UNLESS IT'S WITH ME.
KR-KPOW!
NAME'S PLUNDER.
AHHH!

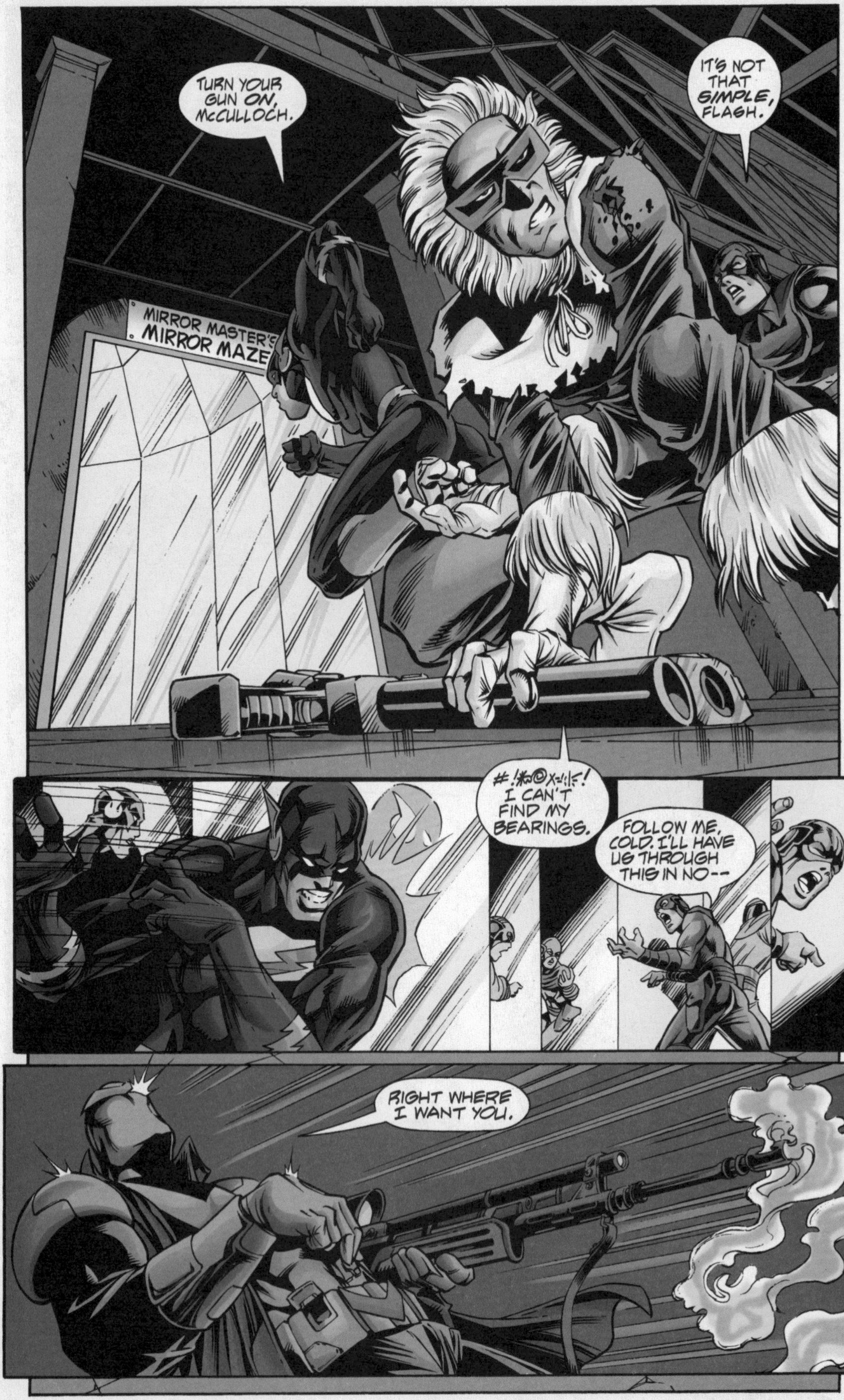
TURN YOUR GUN ON, McCULLOCH.
IT'S NOT THAT SIMPLE, FLASH.
MIRROR MASTER'S MIRROR MAZE
#!%©X=!&! I CAN'T FIND MY BEARINGS.
FOLLOW ME, COLD. I'LL HAVE US THROUGH THIS IN NO--
RIGHT WHERE I WANT YOU.

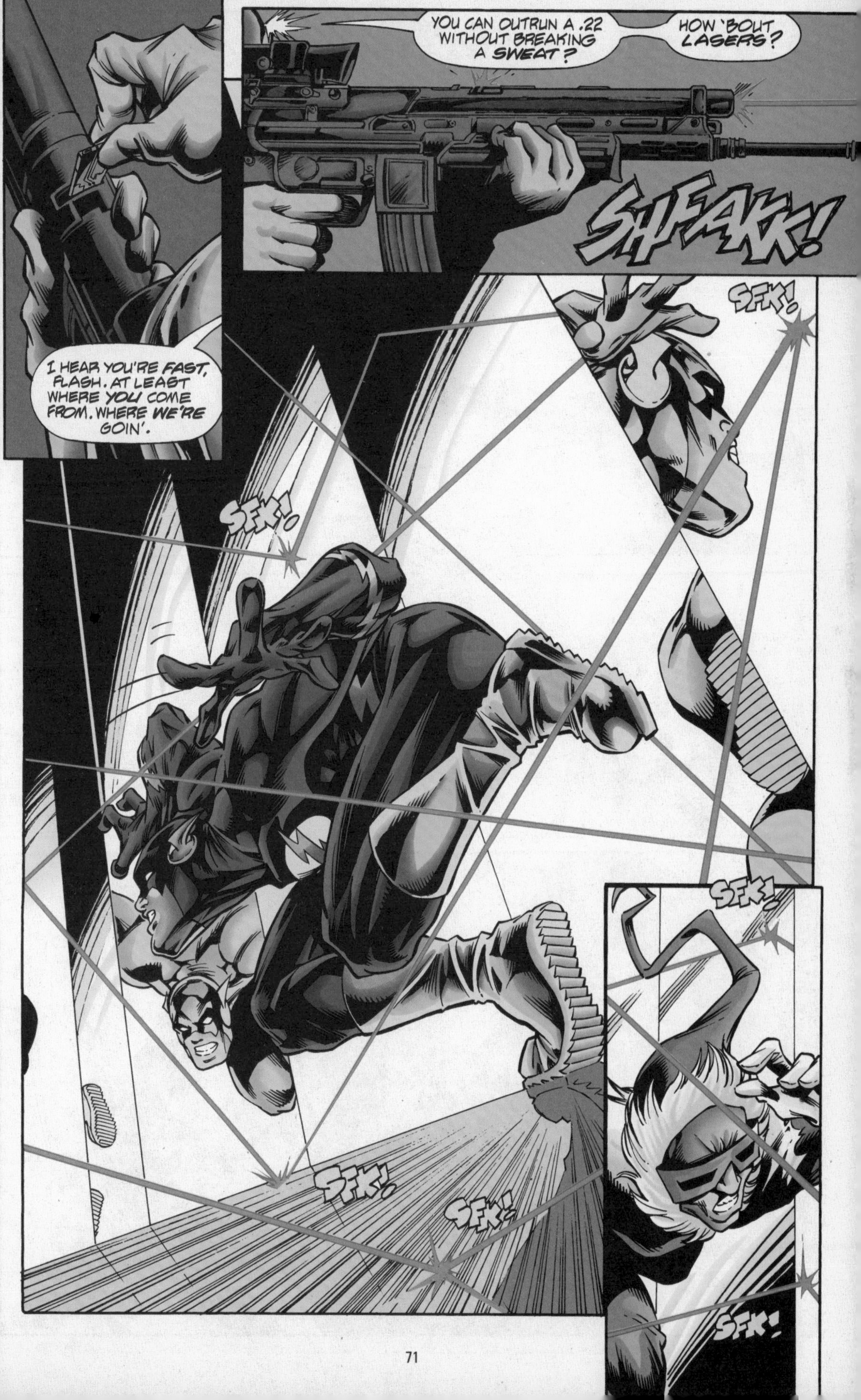
I HEAR YOU'RE FAST, FLASH. AT LEAST WHERE YOU COME FROM. WHERE WE'RE GOIN'.
YOU CAN OUTRUN A .22 WITHOUT BREAKING A SWEAT?
HOW 'BOUT LASERS?
SHFAKK!
SFK!
SFK!
SFK!
SFK!
SFK!
SFK!

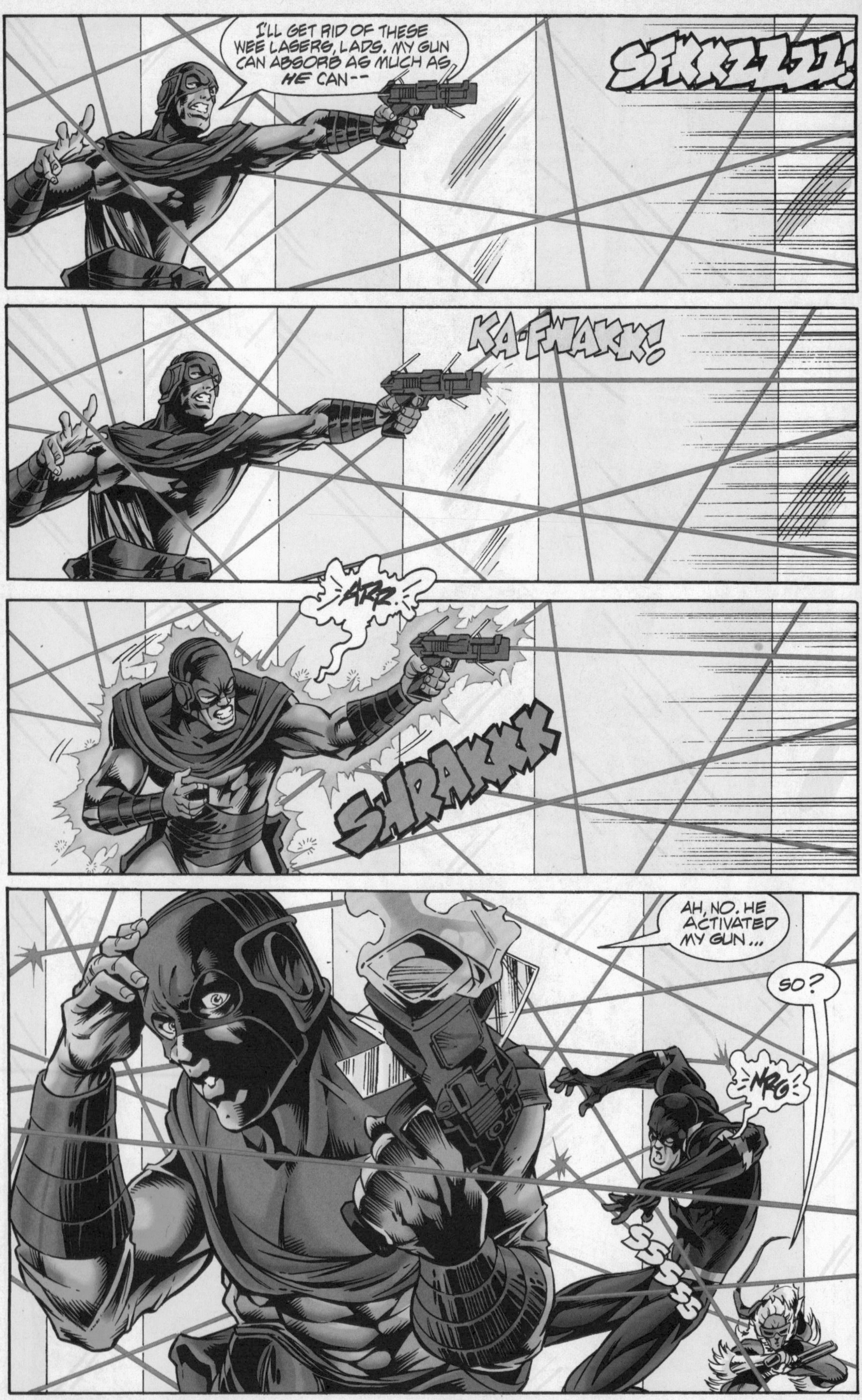
I'LL GET RID OF THESE WEE LASERS, LADS. MY GUN CAN ABSORB AS MUCH AS HE CAN--
SFKKZZZZ!
KA-FWAKK!
ARR
SHRAKKK
AH, NO. HE ACTIVATED MY GUN...
SO?
NRG
SSSSS

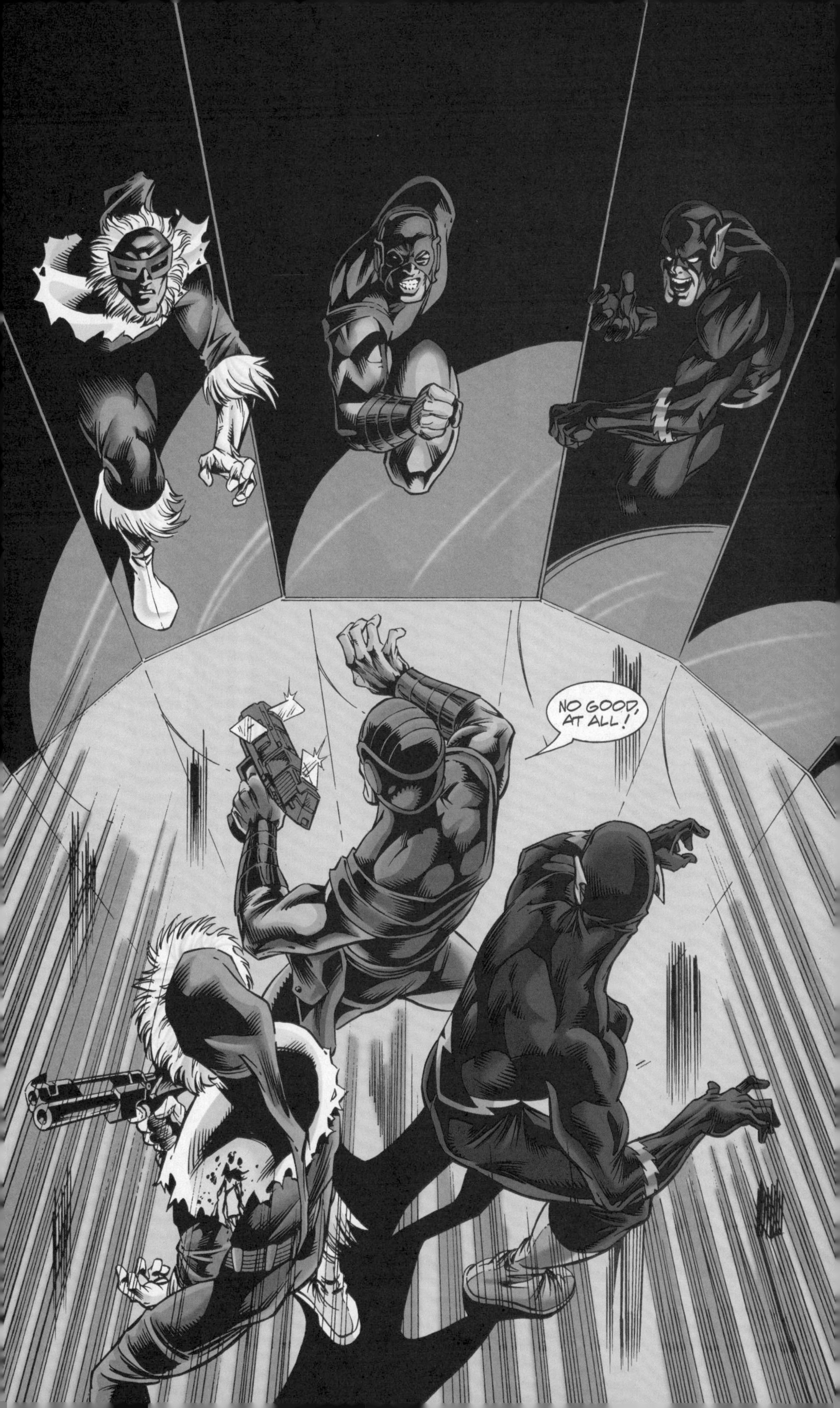
NO GOOD, AT ALL!

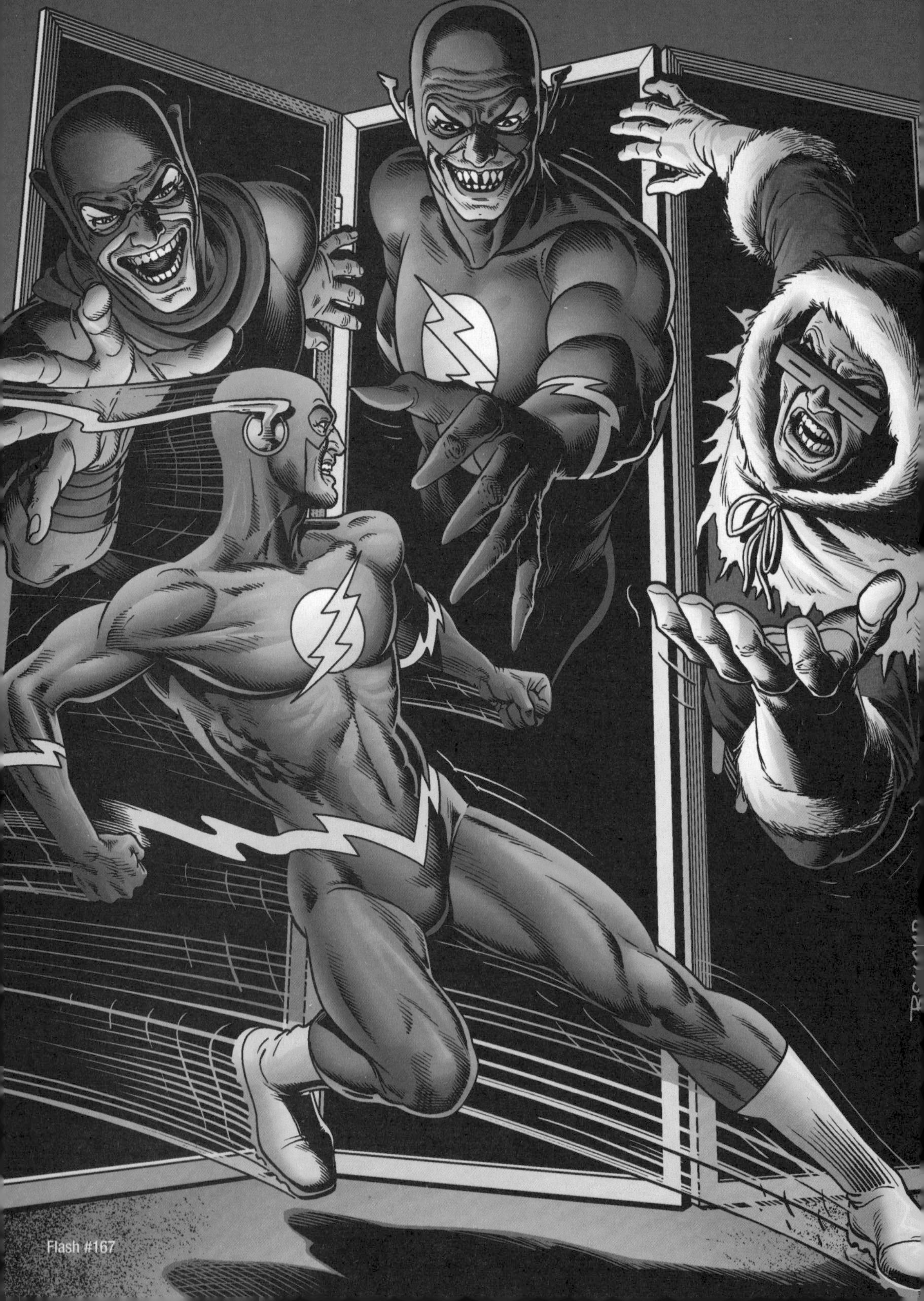

Flash #167

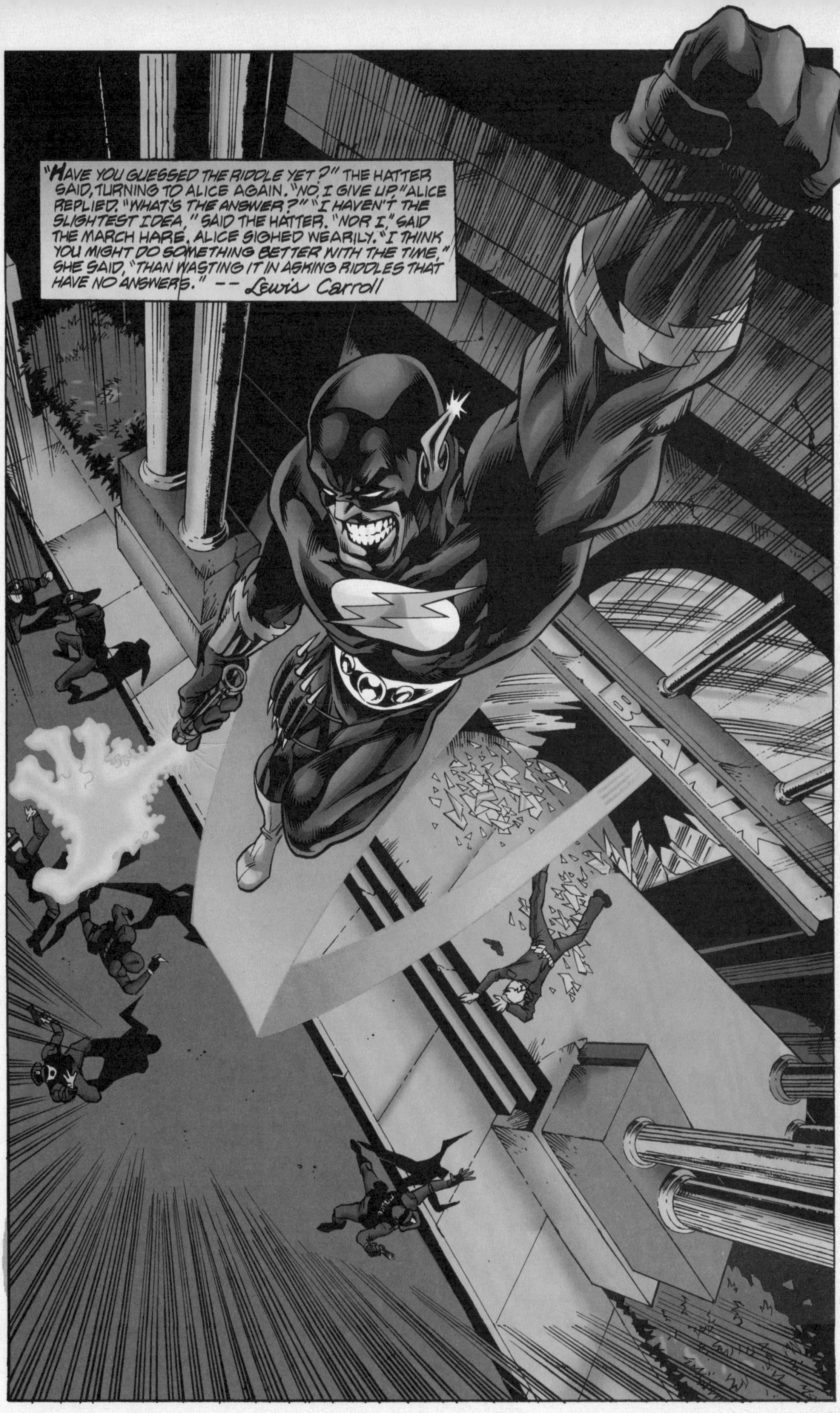
"HAVE YOU GUESSED THE RIDDLE YET?" THE HATTER SAID, TURNING TO ALICE AGAIN. "NO, I GIVE UP," ALICE REPLIED. "WHAT'S THE ANSWER?" "I HAVEN'T THE SLIGHTEST IDEA," SAID THE HATTER. "NOR I," SAID THE MARCH HARE. ALICE SIGHED WEARILY. "I THINK YOU MIGHT DO SOMETHING BETTER WITH THE TIME," SHE SAID, "THAN WASTING IT IN ASKING RIDDLES THAT HAVE NO ANSWERS." -- Lewis Carroll
BANK

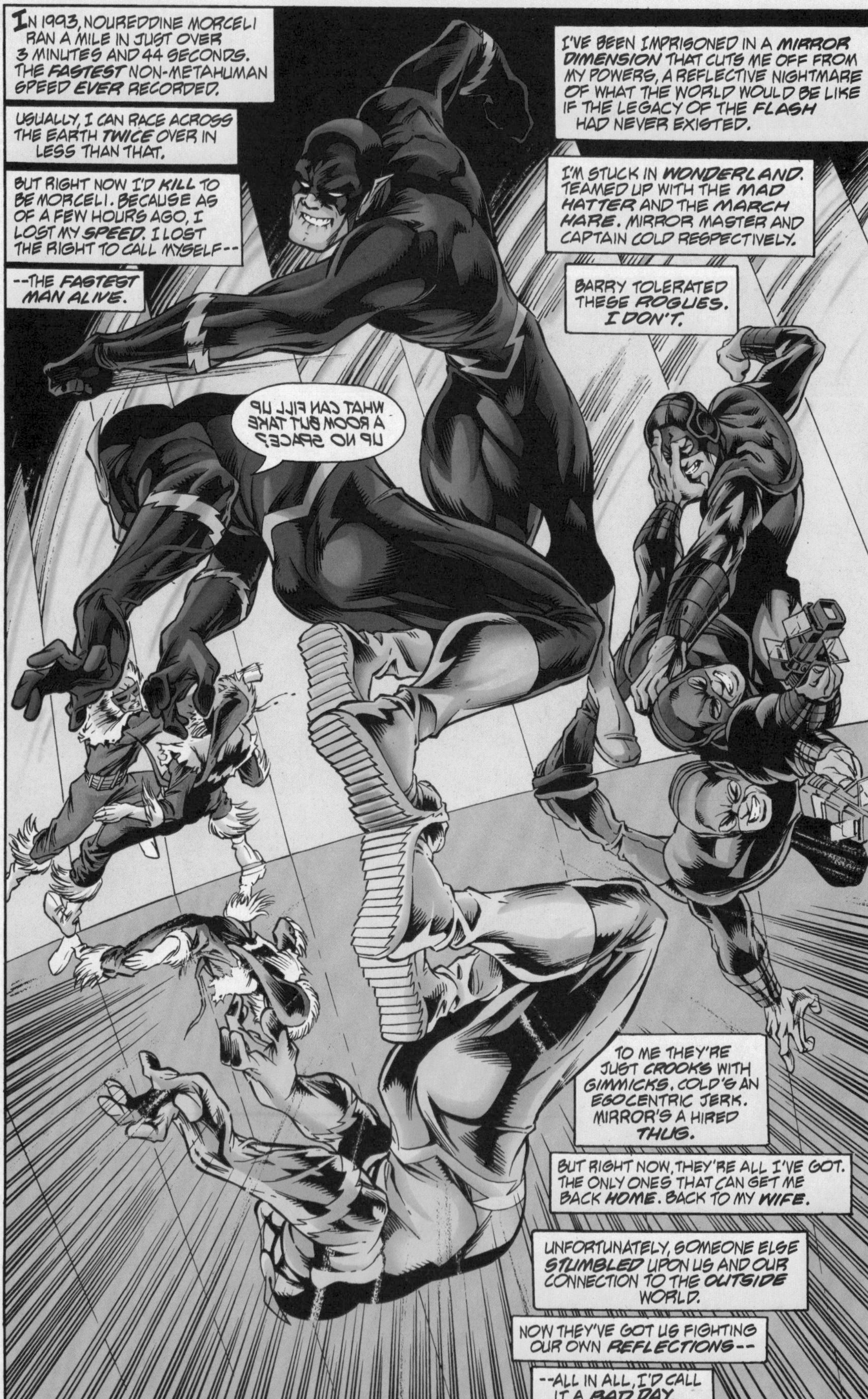
IN 1993, NOUREDDINE MORCELI RAN A MILE IN JUST OVER 3 MINUTES AND 44 SECONDS. THE FASTEST NON-METAHUMAN SPEED EVER RECORDED.
USUALLY, I CAN RACE ACROSS THE EARTH TWICE OVER IN LESS THAN THAT.
BUT RIGHT NOW I'D KILL TO BE MORCELI. BECAUSE AS OF A FEW HOURS AGO, I LOST MY SPEED. I LOST THE RIGHT TO CALL MYSELF--
--THE FASTEST MAN ALIVE.
I'VE BEEN IMPRISONED IN A MIRROR DIMENSION THAT CUTS ME OFF FROM MY POWERS, A REFLECTIVE NIGHTMARE OF WHAT THE WORLD WOULD BE LIKE IF THE LEGACY OF THE FLASH HAD NEVER EXISTED.
I'M STUCK IN WONDERLAND. TEAMED UP WITH THE MAD HATTER AND THE MARCH HARE. MIRROR MASTER AND CAPTAIN COLD RESPECTIVELY.
BARRY TOLERATED THESE ROGUES. I DON'T.
WHAT CAN FILL UP A ROOM BUT TAKE UP NO SPACE?
TO ME THEY'RE JUST CROOKS WITH GIMMICKS. COLD'S AN EGOCENTRIC JERK. MIRROR'S A HIRED THUG.
BUT RIGHT NOW, THEY'RE ALL I'VE GOT. THE ONLY ONES THAT CAN GET ME BACK HOME. BACK TO MY WIFE.
UNFORTUNATELY, SOMEONE ELSE STUMBLED UPON US AND OUR CONNECTION TO THE OUTSIDE WORLD.
NOW THEY'VE GOT US FIGHTING OUR OWN REFLECTIONS--
--ALL IN ALL, I'D CALL IT A BAD DAY.

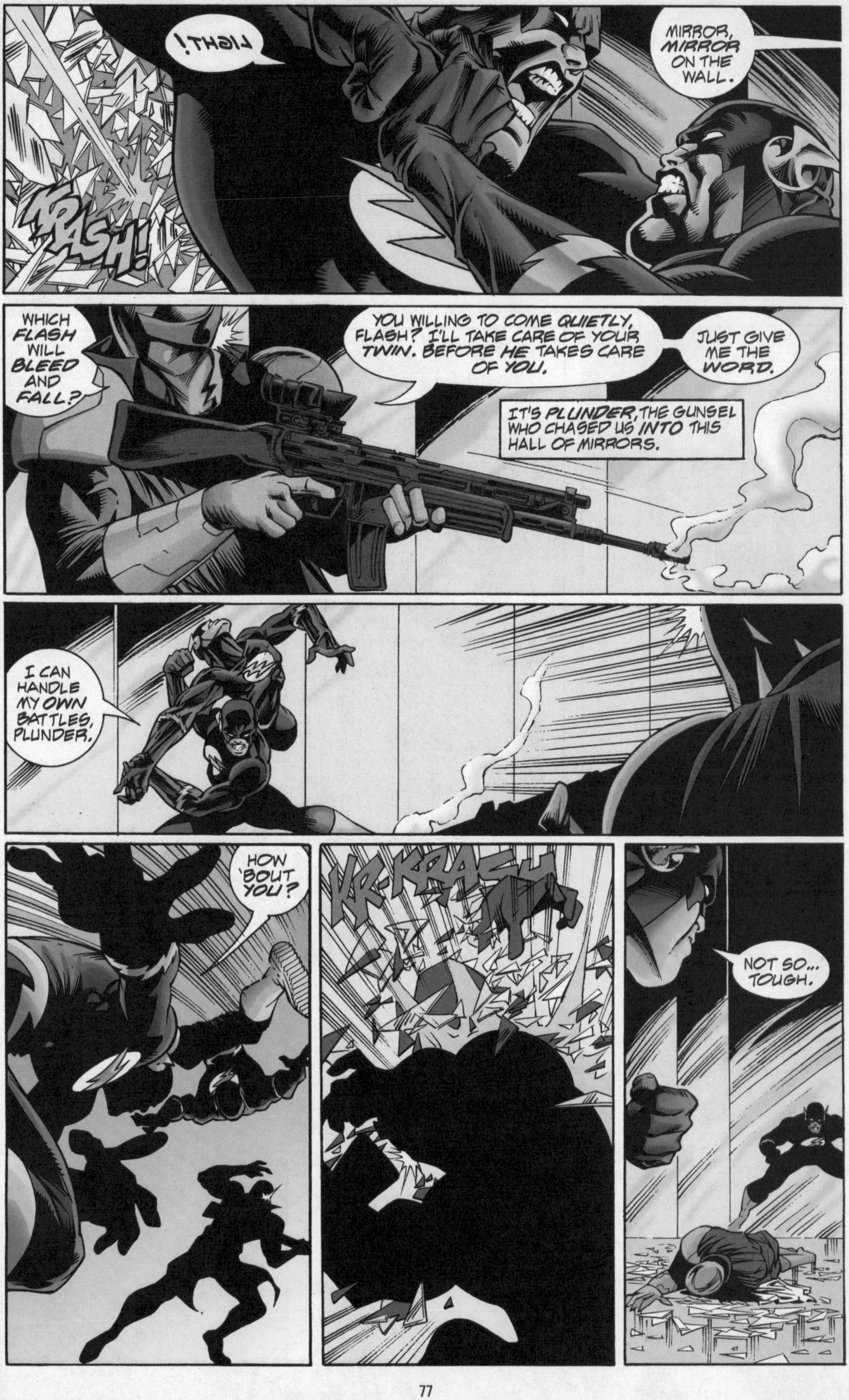
MIRROR, MIRROR ON THE WALL.
KRASH!
WHICH FLASH WILL BLEED AND FALL?
YOU WILLING TO COME QUIETLY, FLASH? I'LL TAKE CARE OF YOUR TWIN. BEFORE HE TAKES CARE OF YOU.
JUST GIVE ME THE WORD.
IT'S PLUNDER, THE GUNSEL WHO CHASED US INTO THIS HALL OF MIRRORS.
I CAN HANDLE MY OWN BATTLES, PLUNDER.
HOW 'BOUT YOU?
NOT SO... TOUGH.

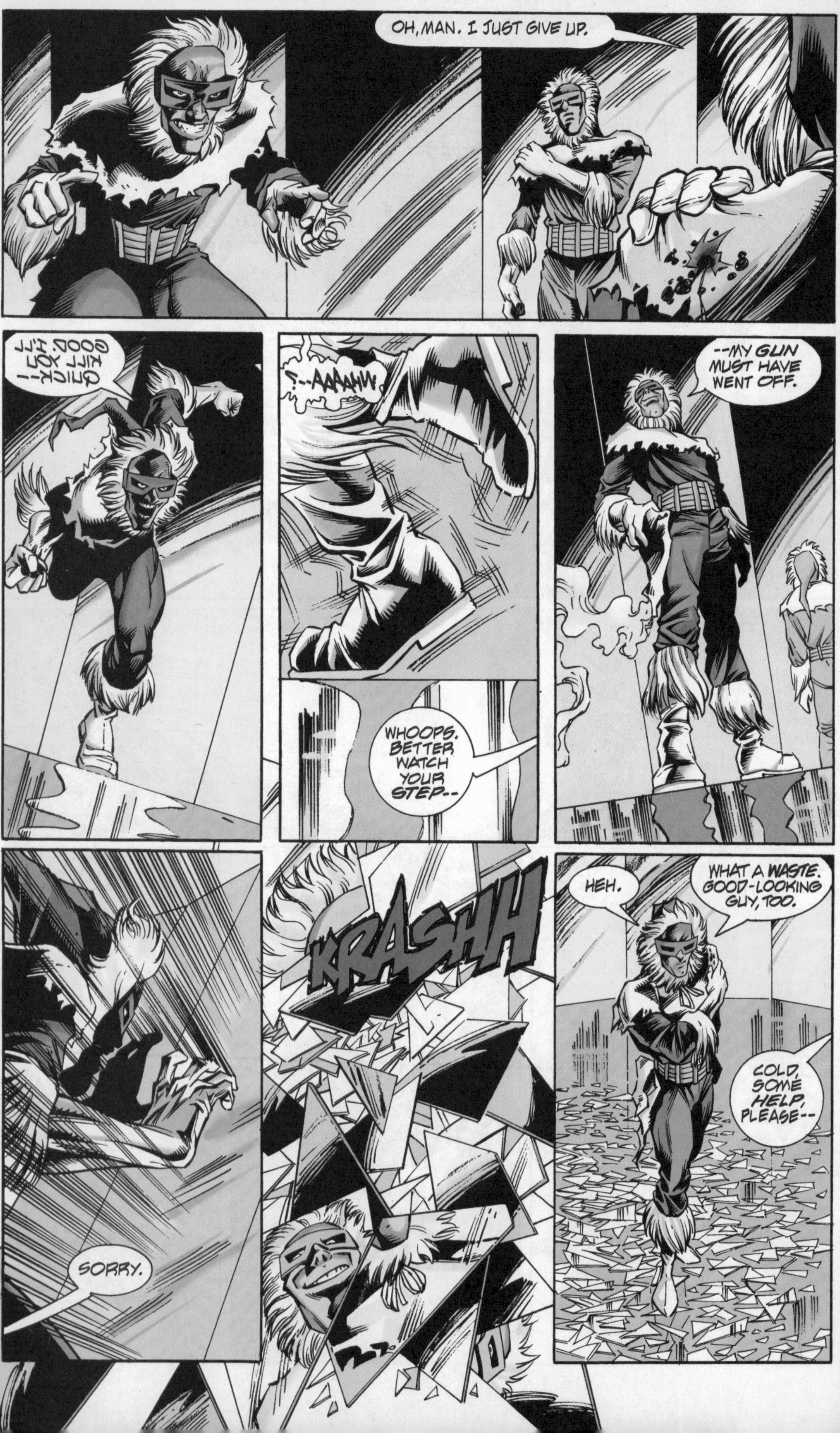
OH, MAN. I JUST GIVE UP.
GOOD. I'LL KILL YOU QUICK--
WHAAAA--?!
WHOOPS. BETTER WATCH YOUR STEP--
--MY GUN MUST HAVE WENT OFF.
SORRY.
KRASHH
HEH.
WHAT A WASTE. GOOD-LOOKING GUY, TOO.
COLD, SOME HELP, PLEASE--

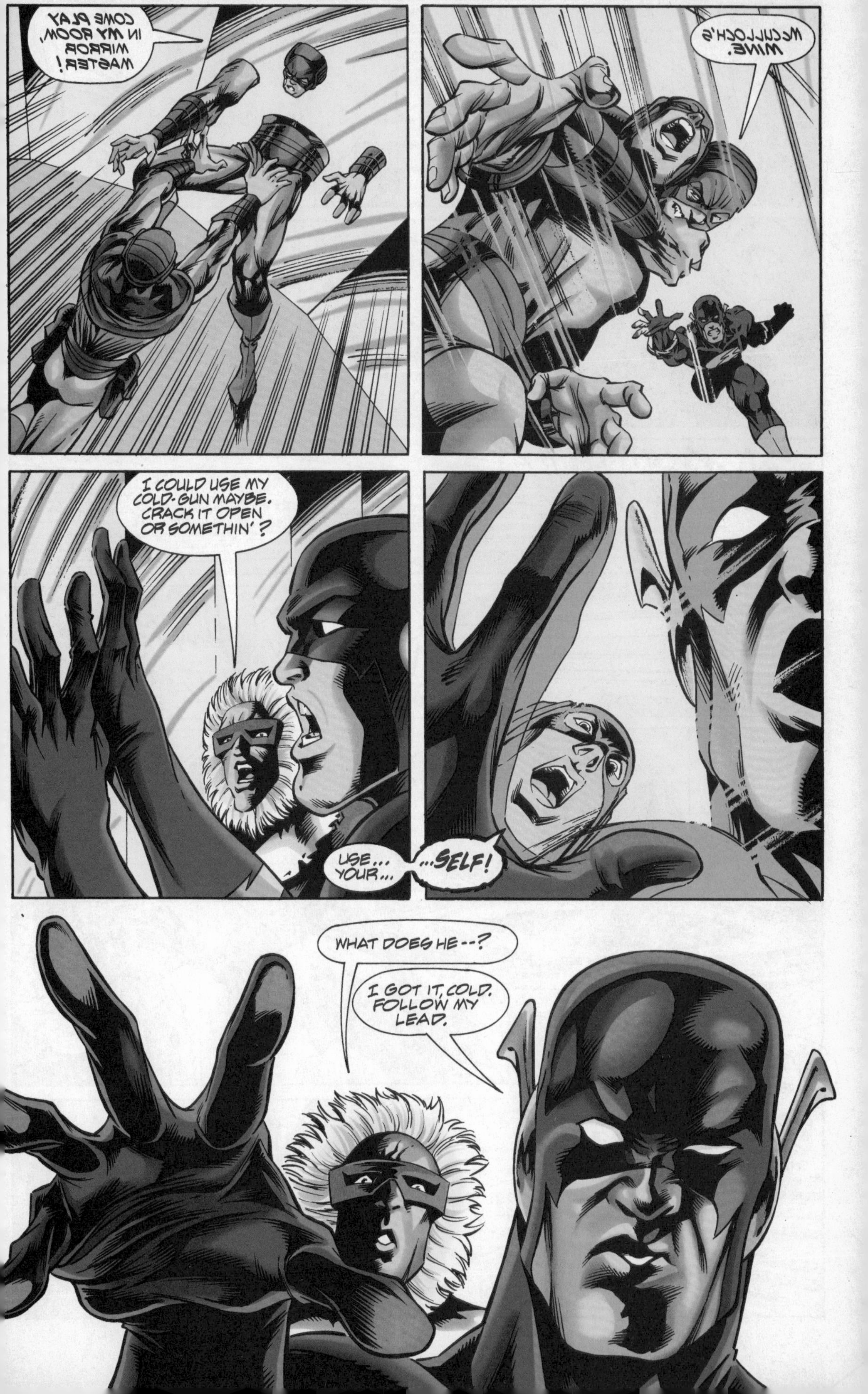
COME PLAY IN MY ROOM, MIRROR MASTER!
McCULLOCH'S MINE.
I COULD USE MY COLD-GUN MAYBE. CRACK IT OPEN OR SOMETHIN'?
USE... YOUR...
...SELF!
WHAT DOES HE--?
I GOT IT, COLD. FOLLOW MY LEAD.

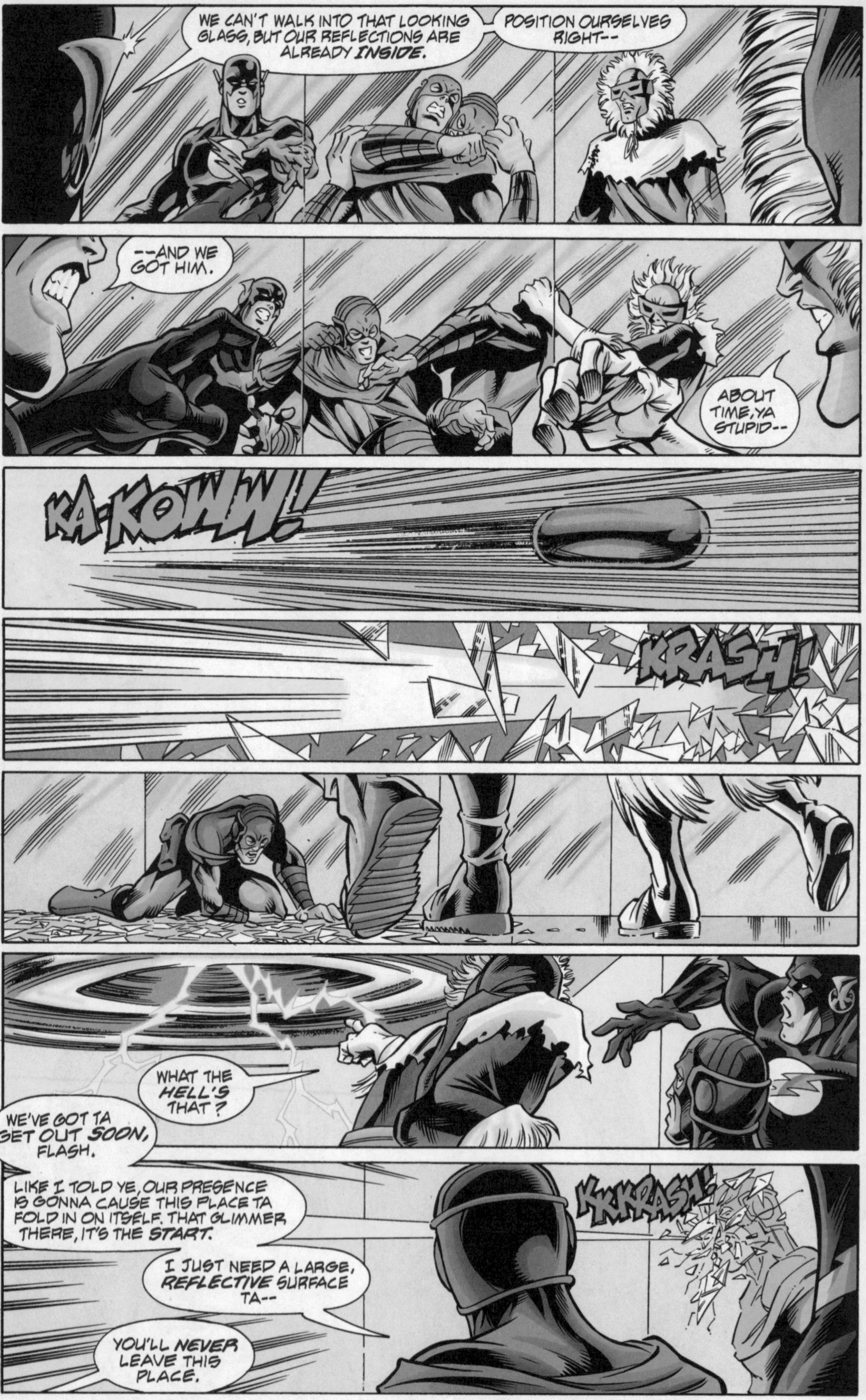
WE CAN'T WALK INTO THAT LOOKING GLASS, BUT OUR REFLECTIONS ARE ALREADY INSIDE.
POSITION OURSELVES RIGHT--
--AND WE GOT HIM.
ABOUT TIME, YA STUPID--
KA-KOWW!
KRASH!
WHAT THE HELL'S THAT?
WE'VE GOT TA GET OUT SOON, FLASH.
LIKE I TOLD YE, OUR PRESENCE IS GONNA CAUSE THIS PLACE TA FOLD IN ON ITSELF. THAT GLIMMER THERE, IT'S THE START.
KKKRASH!
I JUST NEED A LARGE, REFLECTIVE SURFACE TA--
YOU'LL NEVER LEAVE THIS PLACE.

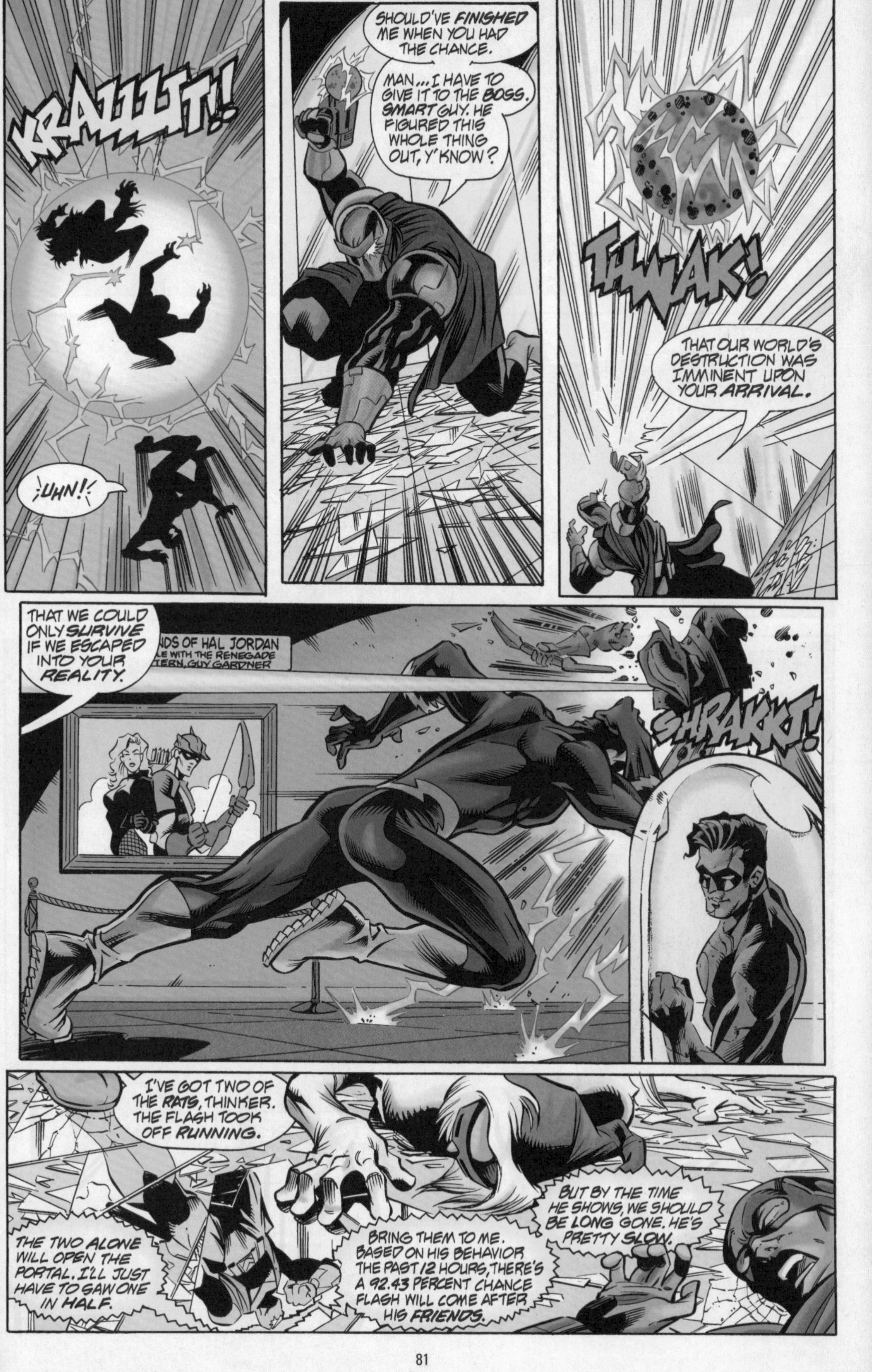
KRALLLT!
¡UHN!¡
SHOULD'VE FINISHED ME WHEN YOU HAD THE CHANCE.
MAN... I HAVE TO GIVE IT TO THE BOSS. SMART GUY. HE FIGURED THIS WHOLE THING OUT, Y'KNOW?
THWAK!
THAT OUR WORLD'S DESTRUCTION WAS IMMINENT UPON YOUR ARRIVAL.
THAT WE COULD ONLY SURVIVE IF WE ESCAPED INTO YOUR REALITY.
NDS OF HAL JORDAN
LE WITH THE RENEGADE
TERN, GUY GARDNER
SHRAKKT!
I'VE GOT TWO OF THE RATS, THINKER. THE FLASH TOOK OFF RUNNING.
THE TWO ALONE WILL OPEN THE PORTAL. I'LL JUST HAVE TO SAW ONE IN HALF.
BRING THEM TO ME. BASED ON HIS BEHAVIOR THE PAST 12 HOURS, THERE'S A 92.43 PERCENT CHANCE FLASH WILL COME AFTER HIS FRIENDS.
BUT BY THE TIME HE SHOWS, WE SHOULD BE LONG GONE. HE'S PRETTY SLOW.

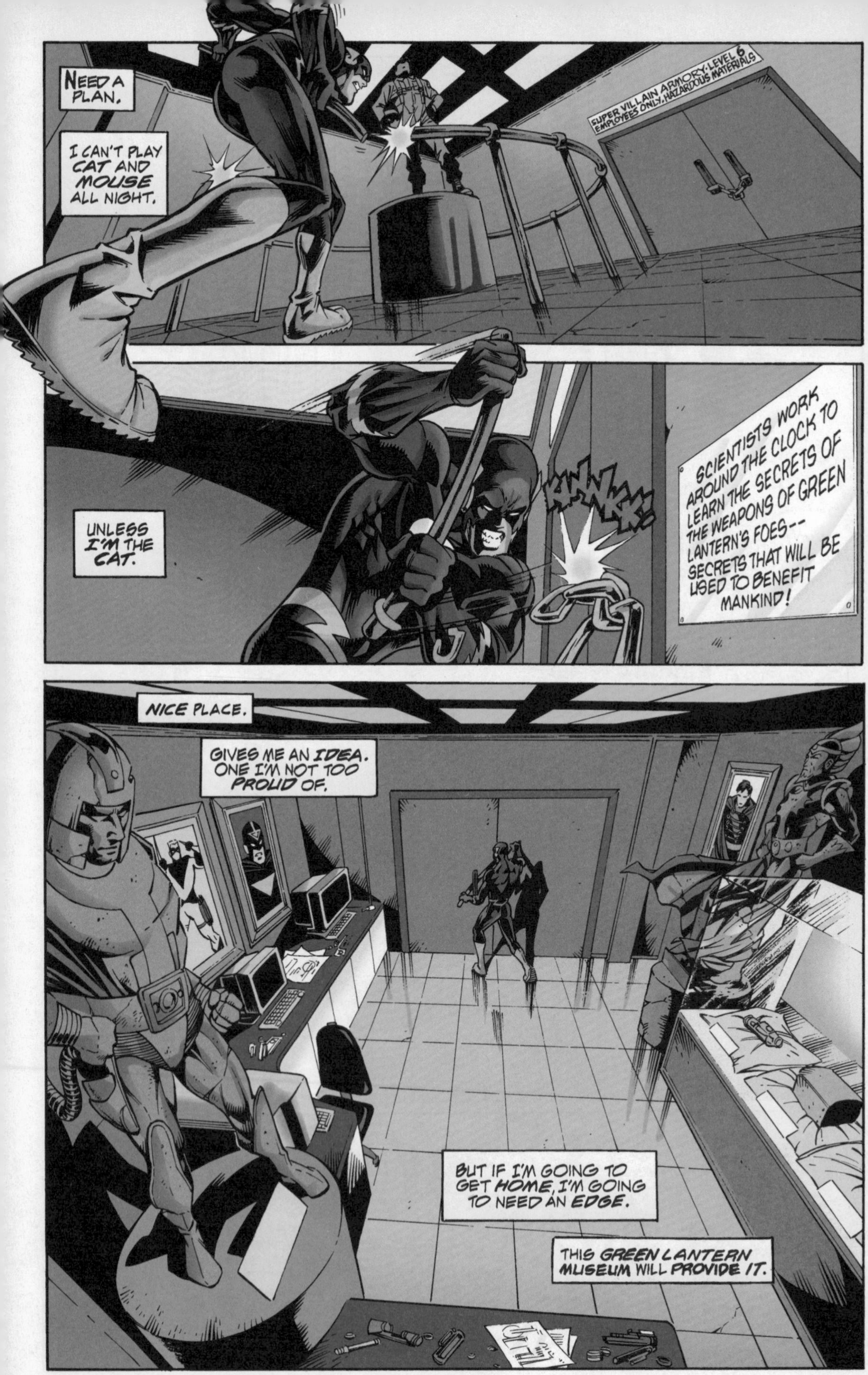
NEED A PLAN.
I CAN'T PLAY CAT AND MOUSE ALL NIGHT.
SUPER VILLAIN ARMORY: LEVEL 6
EMPLOYEES ONLY, HAZARDOUS MATERIALS
UNLESS I'M THE CAT.
KLNNKK!
SCIENTISTS WORK AROUND THE CLOCK TO LEARN THE SECRETS OF THE WEAPONS OF GREEN LANTERN'S FOES-- SECRETS THAT WILL BE USED TO BENEFIT MANKIND!
NICE PLACE.
GIVES ME AN IDEA. ONE I'M NOT TOO PROUD OF.
BUT IF I'M GOING TO GET HOME, I'M GOING TO NEED AN EDGE.
THIS GREEN LANTERN MUSEUM WILL PROVIDE IT.

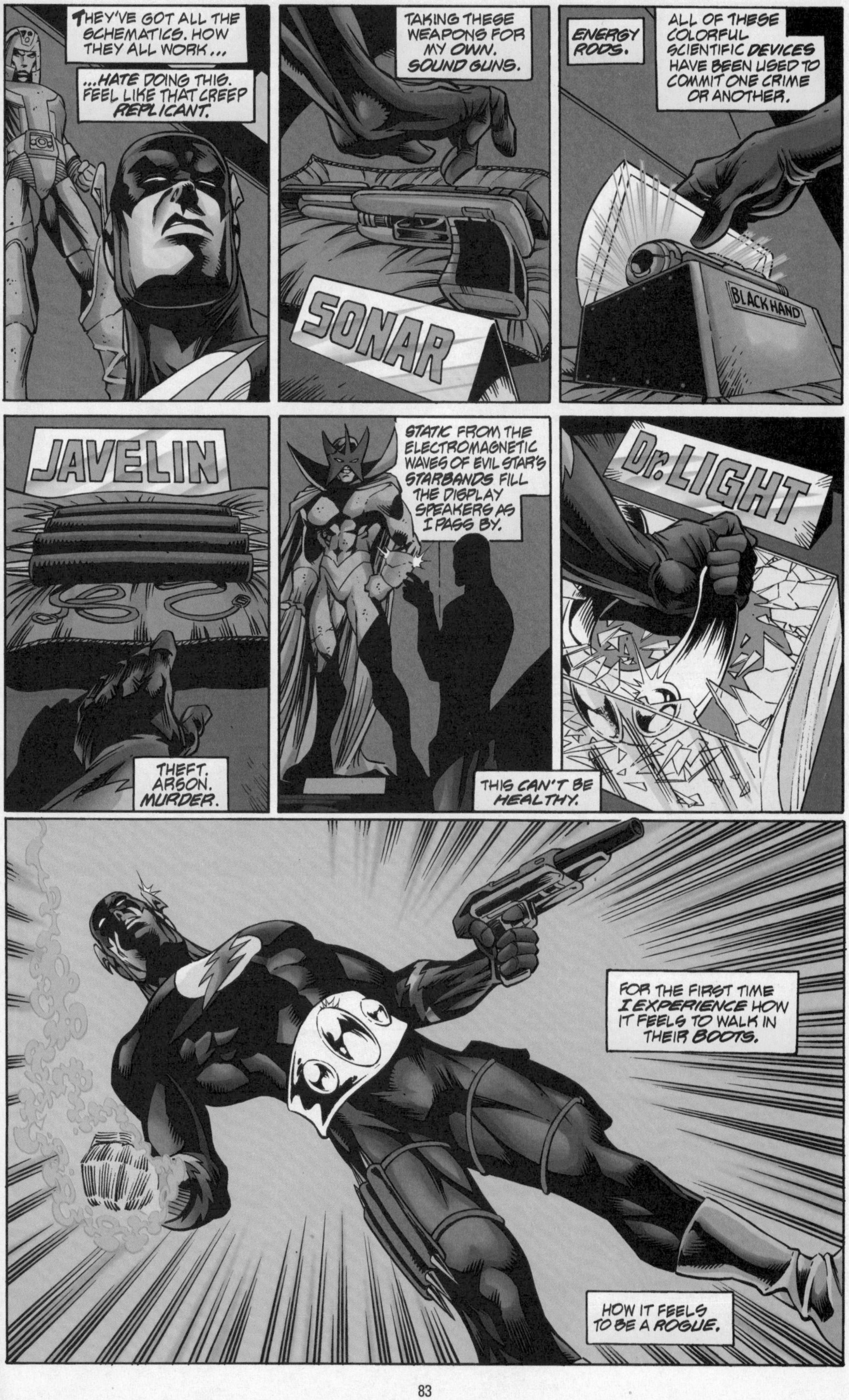
THEY'VE GOT ALL THE SCHEMATICS. HOW THEY ALL WORK...
...HATE DOING THIS. FEEL LIKE THAT CREEP REPLICANT.
TAKING THESE WEAPONS FOR MY OWN. SOUND GUNS.
SONAR
ENERGY RODS.
ALL OF THESE COLORFUL SCIENTIFIC DEVICES HAVE BEEN USED TO COMMIT ONE CRIME OR ANOTHER.
BLACK HAND
JAVELIN
THEFT. ARSON. MURDER.
STATIC FROM THE ELECTROMAGNETIC WAVES OF EVIL STAR'S STARBANDS FILL THE DISPLAY SPEAKERS AS I PASS BY.
THIS CAN'T BE HEALTHY.
Dr. LIGHT
FOR THE FIRST TIME I EXPERIENCE HOW IT FEELS TO WALK IN THEIR BOOTS.
HOW IT FEELS TO BE A ROGUE.

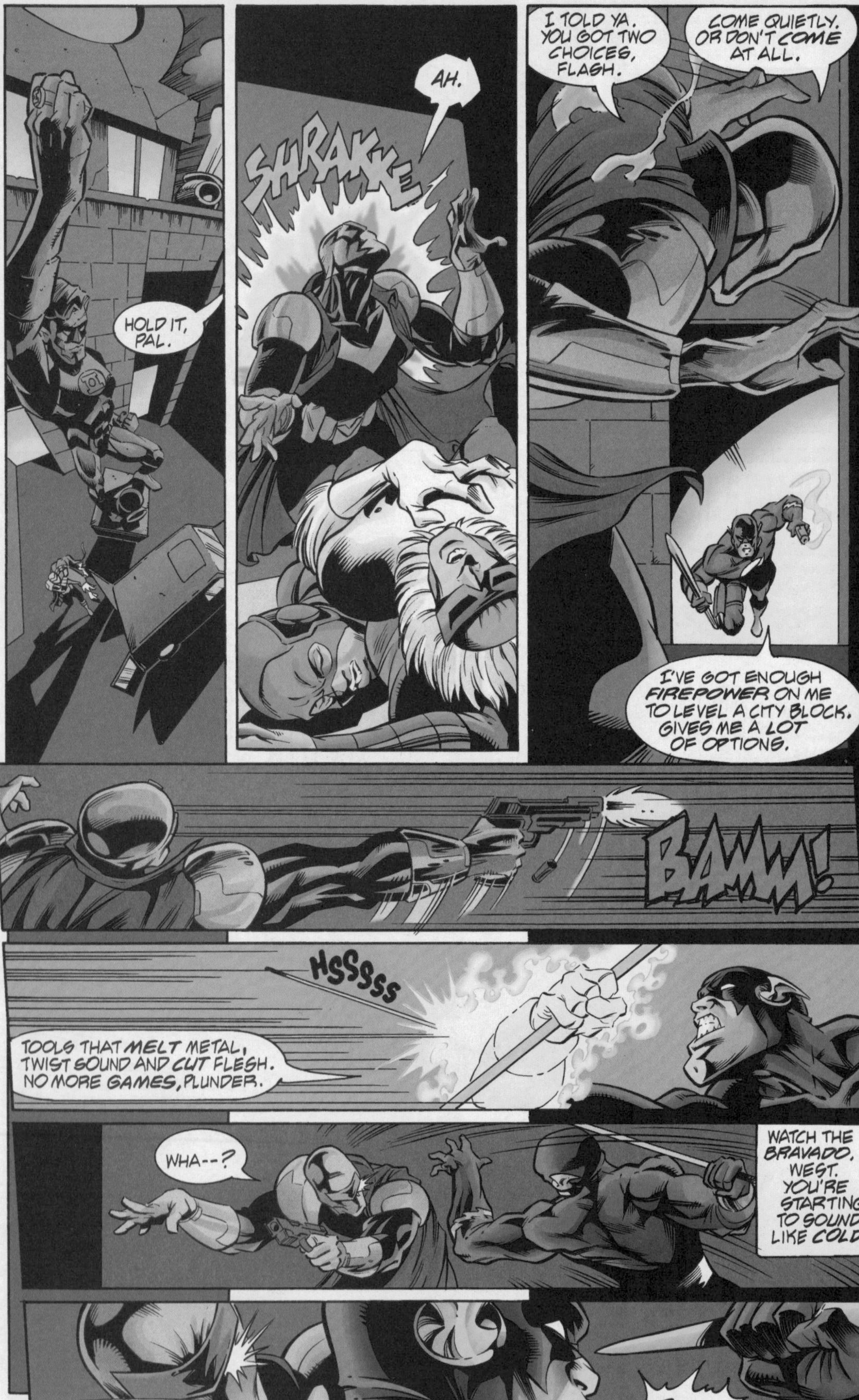

HOLD IT, PAL.
SHRAKKE
AH.
I TOLD YA. YOU GOT TWO CHOICES, FLASH.
COME QUIETLY. OR DON'T COME AT ALL.
I'VE GOT ENOUGH FIREPOWER ON ME TO LEVEL A CITY BLOCK. GIVES ME A LOT OF OPTIONS.
BAMM!
HSSSSS
TOOLS THAT MELT METAL, TWIST SOUND AND CUT FLESH. NO MORE GAMES, PLUNDER.
WHA--?
WATCH THE BRAVADO, WEST. YOU'RE STARTING TO SOUND LIKE COLD.
STAND ASIDE AND LET US GO. ONCE WE'RE GONE, YOUR WORLD WILL BE SAFE...
FIRE!!

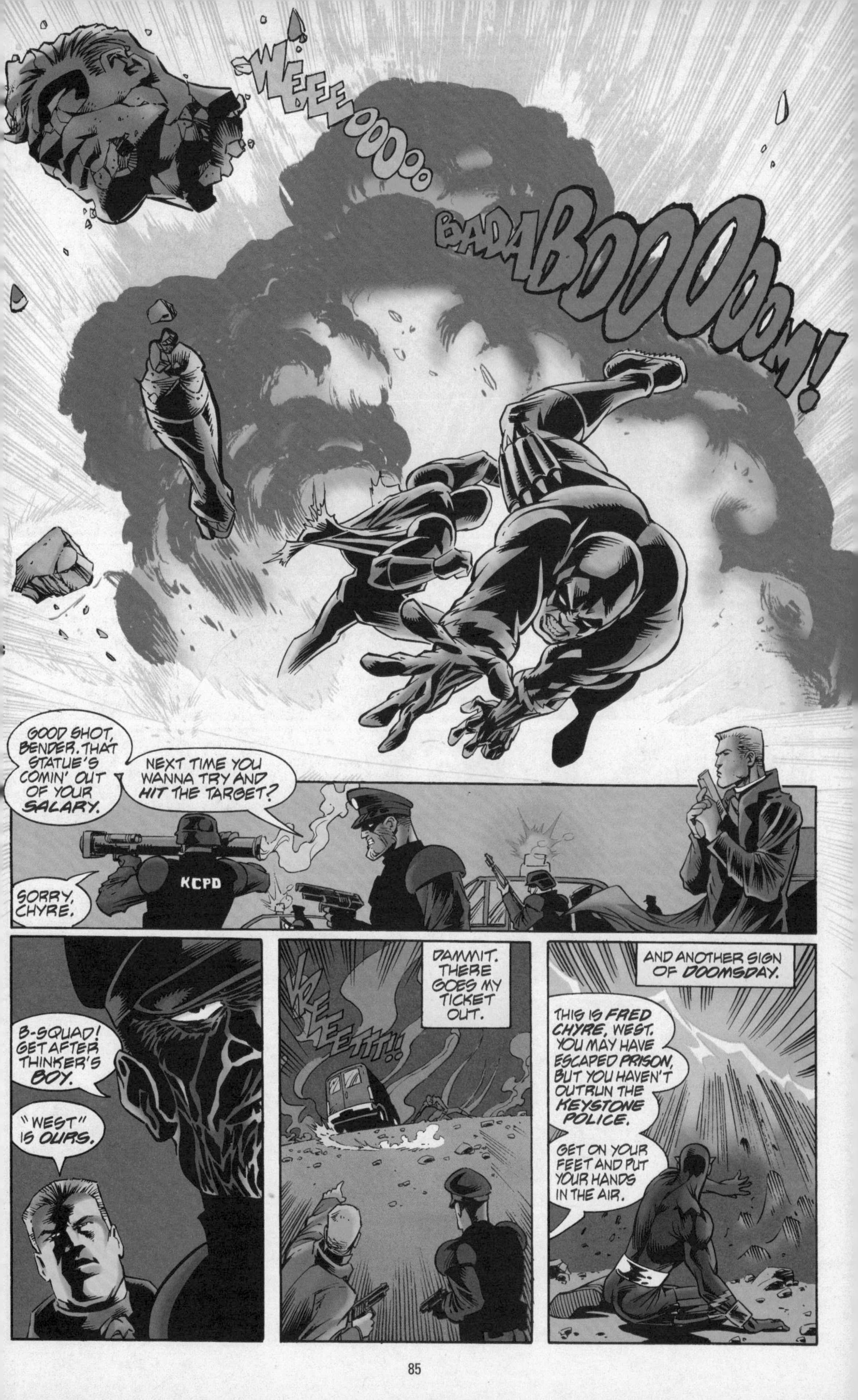
WEEEOOOOoo
BADABOOOOoom!
GOOD SHOT, BENDER. THAT STATUE'S COMIN' OUT OF YOUR SALARY.
NEXT TIME YOU WANNA TRY AND HIT THE TARGET?
KCPD
SORRY, CHYRE.
B-SQUAD! GET AFTER THINKER'S BOY.
"WEST" IS OURS.
DAMMIT. THERE GOES MY TICKET OUT.
AND ANOTHER SIGN OF DOOMSDAY.
THIS IS FRED CHYRE, WEST. YOU MAY HAVE ESCAPED PRISON, BUT YOU HAVEN'T OUTRUN THE KEYSTONE POLICE.
GET ON YOUR FEET AND PUT YOUR HANDS IN THE AIR.

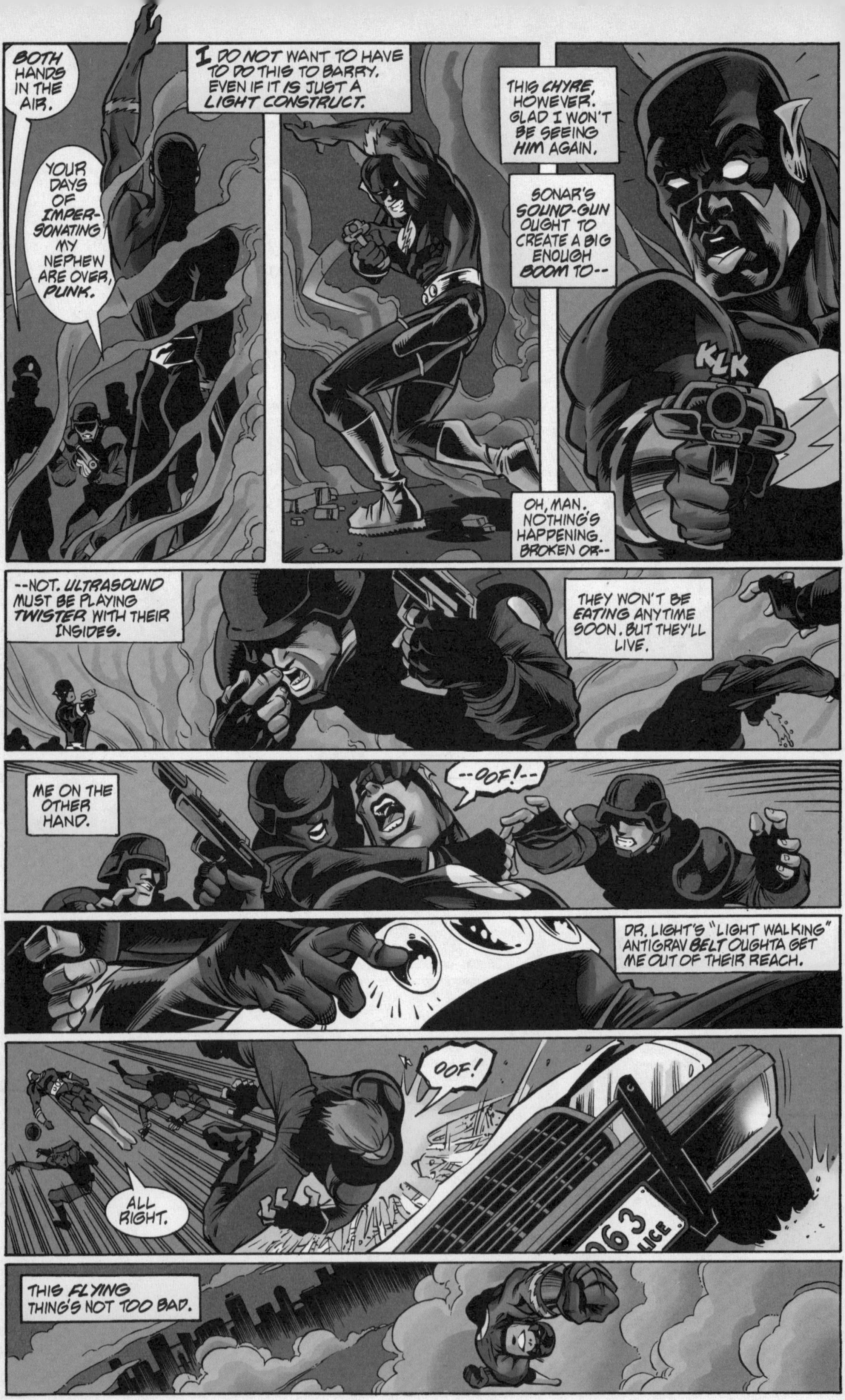
BOTH HANDS IN THE AIR.
YOUR DAYS OF IMPERSONATING MY NEPHEW ARE OVER, PUNK.
I DO NOT WANT TO HAVE TO DO THIS TO BARRY. EVEN IF IT IS JUST A LIGHT CONSTRUCT.
THIS CHYRE, HOWEVER. GLAD I WON'T BE SEEING HIM AGAIN.
SONAR'S SOUND-GUN OUGHT TO CREATE A BIG ENOUGH BOOM TO--
KLK
OH, MAN. NOTHING'S HAPPENING. BROKEN OR--
--NOT. ULTRASOUND MUST BE PLAYING TWISTER WITH THEIR INSIDES.
THEY WON'T BE EATING ANYTIME SOON. BUT THEY'LL LIVE.
ME ON THE OTHER HAND.
--OOF!--
DR. LIGHT'S "LIGHT WALKING" ANTIGRAV BELT OUGHTA GET ME OUT OF THEIR REACH.
OOF!
ALL RIGHT.
THIS FLYING THING'S NOT TOO BAD.

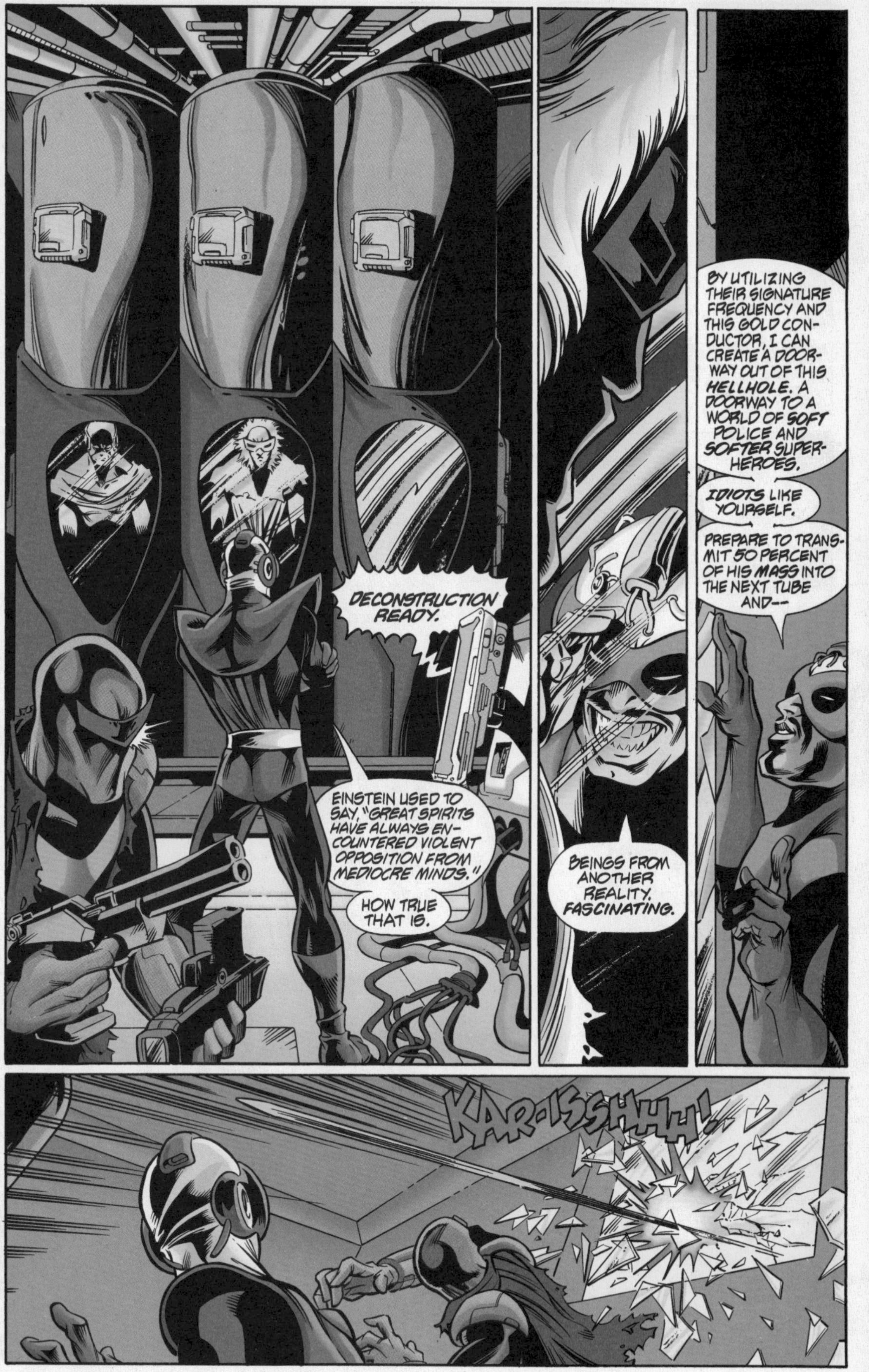
DECONSTRUCTION READY.
EINSTEIN USED TO SAY, "GREAT SPIRITS HAVE ALWAYS ENCOUNTERED VIOLENT OPPOSITION FROM MEDIOCRE MINDS."
HOW TRUE THAT IS.
BEINGS FROM ANOTHER REALITY. FASCINATING.
BY UTILIZING THEIR SIGNATURE FREQUENCY AND THIS GOLD CONDUCTOR, I CAN CREATE A DOORWAY OUT OF THIS HELLHOLE. A DOORWAY TO A WORLD OF SOFT POLICE AND SOFTER SUPERHEROES.
IDIOTS LIKE YOURSELF.
PREPARE TO TRANSMIT 50 PERCENT OF HIS MASS INTO THE NEXT TUBE AND--
KAR-ISSHHH!

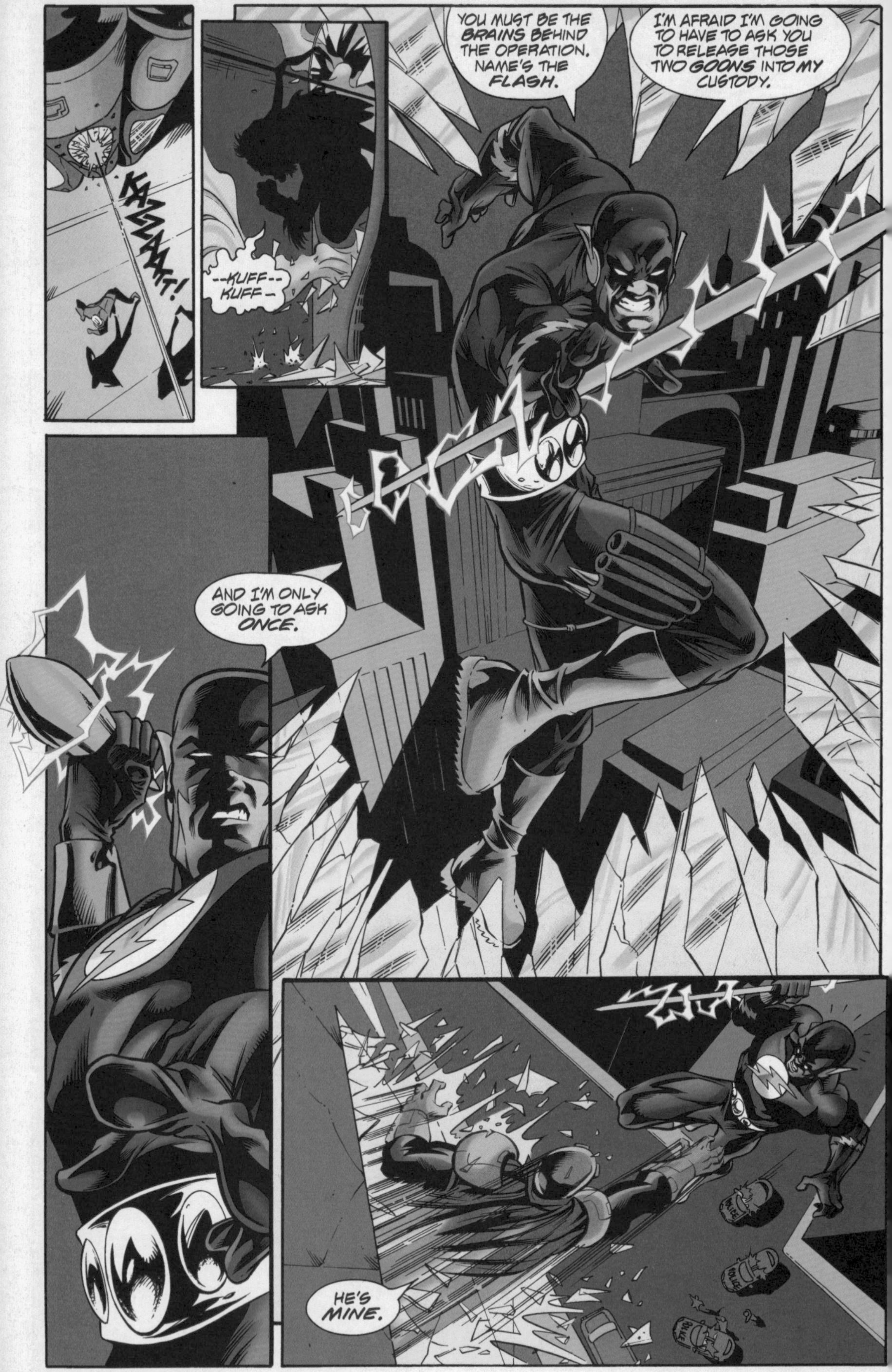
KAZAAAKT!
--KUFF--
KUFF--
YOU MUST BE THE BRAINS BEHIND THE OPERATION. NAME'S THE FLASH.
I'M AFRAID I'M GOING TO HAVE TO ASK YOU TO RELEASE THOSE TWO GOONS INTO MY CUSTODY.
AND I'M ONLY GOING TO ASK ONCE.
HE'S MINE.

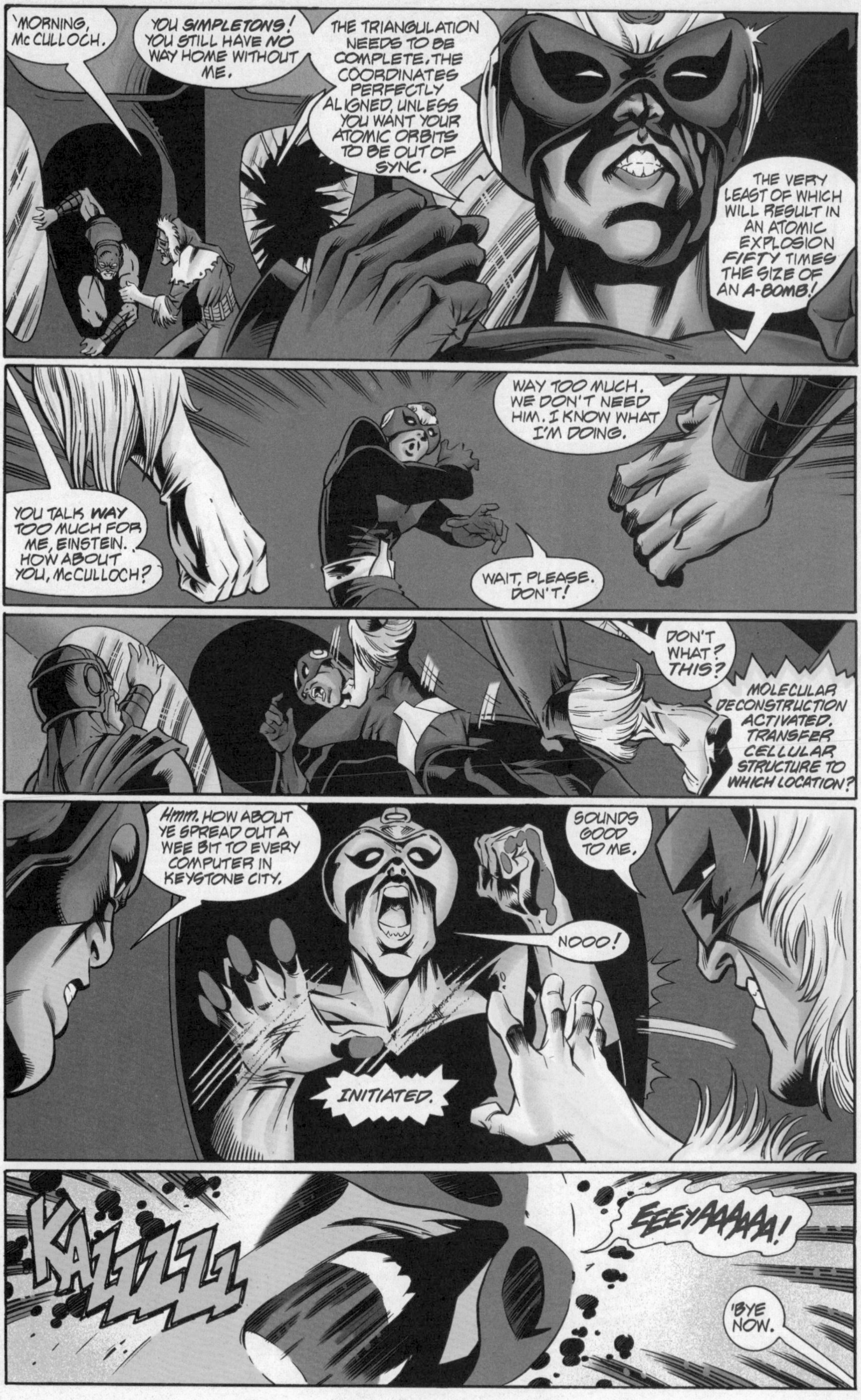

`MORNING, McCULLOCH.
YOU SIMPLETONS! YOU STILL HAVE NO WAY HOME WITHOUT ME.
THE TRIANGULATION NEEDS TO BE COMPLETE, THE COORDINATES PERFECTLY ALIGNED, UNLESS YOU WANT YOUR ATOMIC ORBITS TO BE OUT OF SYNC.
THE VERY LEAST OF WHICH WILL RESULT IN AN ATOMIC EXPLOSION FIFTY TIMES THE SIZE OF AN A-BOMB!
YOU TALK WAY TOO MUCH FOR ME, EINSTEIN. HOW ABOUT YOU, McCULLOCH?
WAY TOO MUCH. WE DON'T NEED HIM. I KNOW WHAT I'M DOING.
WAIT, PLEASE. DON'T!
DON'T WHAT? THIS?
MOLECULAR DECONSTRUCTION ACTIVATED. TRANSFER CELLULAR STRUCTURE TO WHICH LOCATION?
Hmm. HOW ABOUT YE SPREAD OUT A WEE BIT TO EVERY COMPUTER IN KEYSTONE CITY.
SOUNDS GOOD TO ME.
NOOO!
INITIATED.
KAZZZZZ
EEEYAAAAAA!
'BYE NOW.

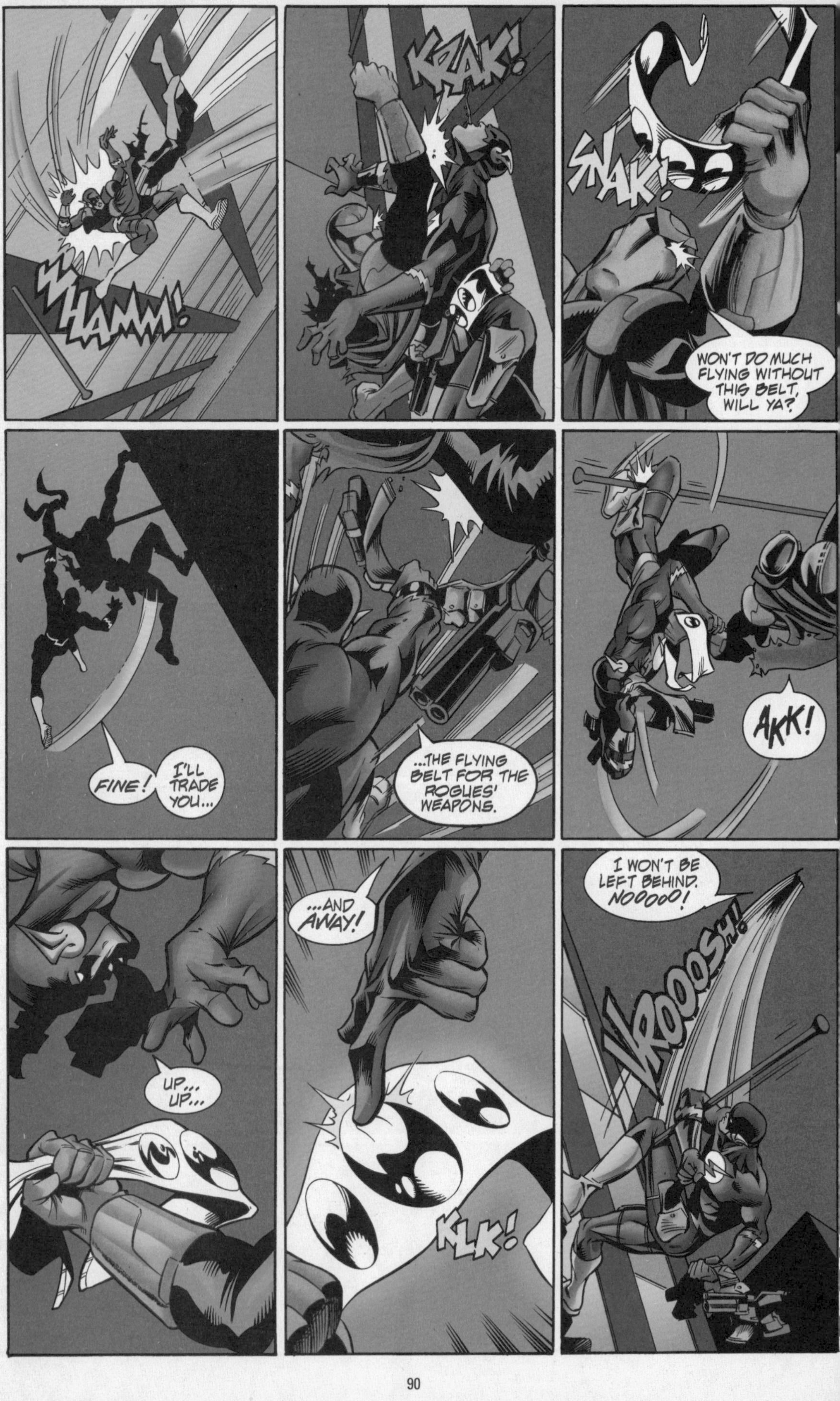
WHAMM!
KRAK!
SNAK!
WON'T DO MUCH FLYING WITHOUT THIS BELT, WILL YA?
FINE!
I'LL TRADE YOU...
...THE FLYING BELT FOR THE ROGUES' WEAPONS.
AKK!
UP... UP...
...AND AWAY!
KLK!
I WON'T BE LEFT BEHIND. NOOOOO!
VROOOSH!

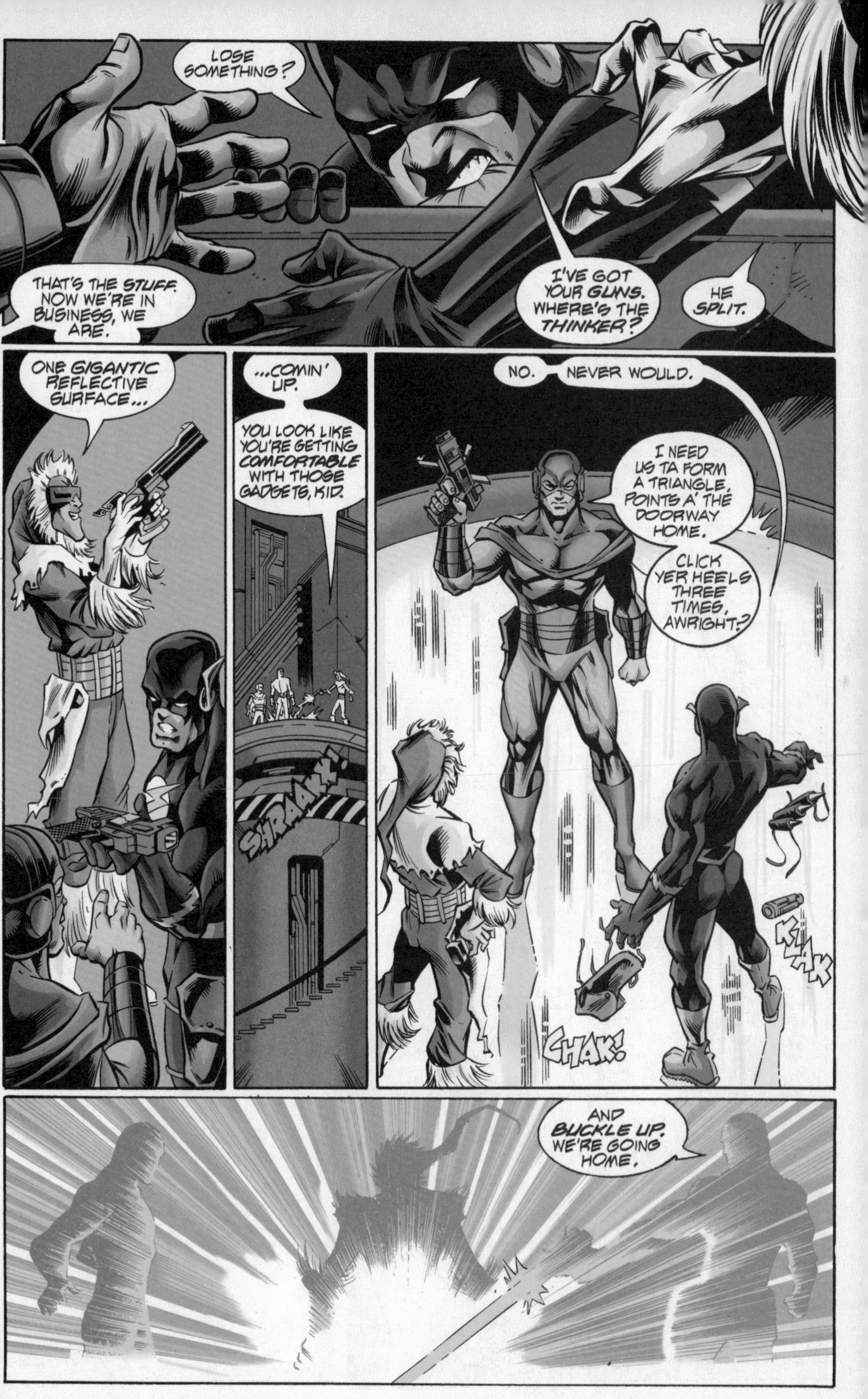
LOSE SOMETHING?
THAT'S THE STUFF. NOW WE'RE IN BUSINESS, WE ARE.
I'VE GOT YOUR GUNS. WHERE'S THE THINKER?
HE SPLIT.
ONE GIGANTIC REFLECTIVE SURFACE...
...COMIN' UP.
YOU LOOK LIKE YOU'RE GETTING COMFORTABLE WITH THOSE GADGETS, KID.
SHRAAKK!
NO.
NEVER WOULD.
I NEED US TA FORM A TRIANGLE, POINTS A' THE DOORWAY HOME.
CLICK YER HEELS THREE TIMES, AWRIGHT?
KLAK
CHAK!
AND BUCKLE UP. WE'RE GOING HOME.

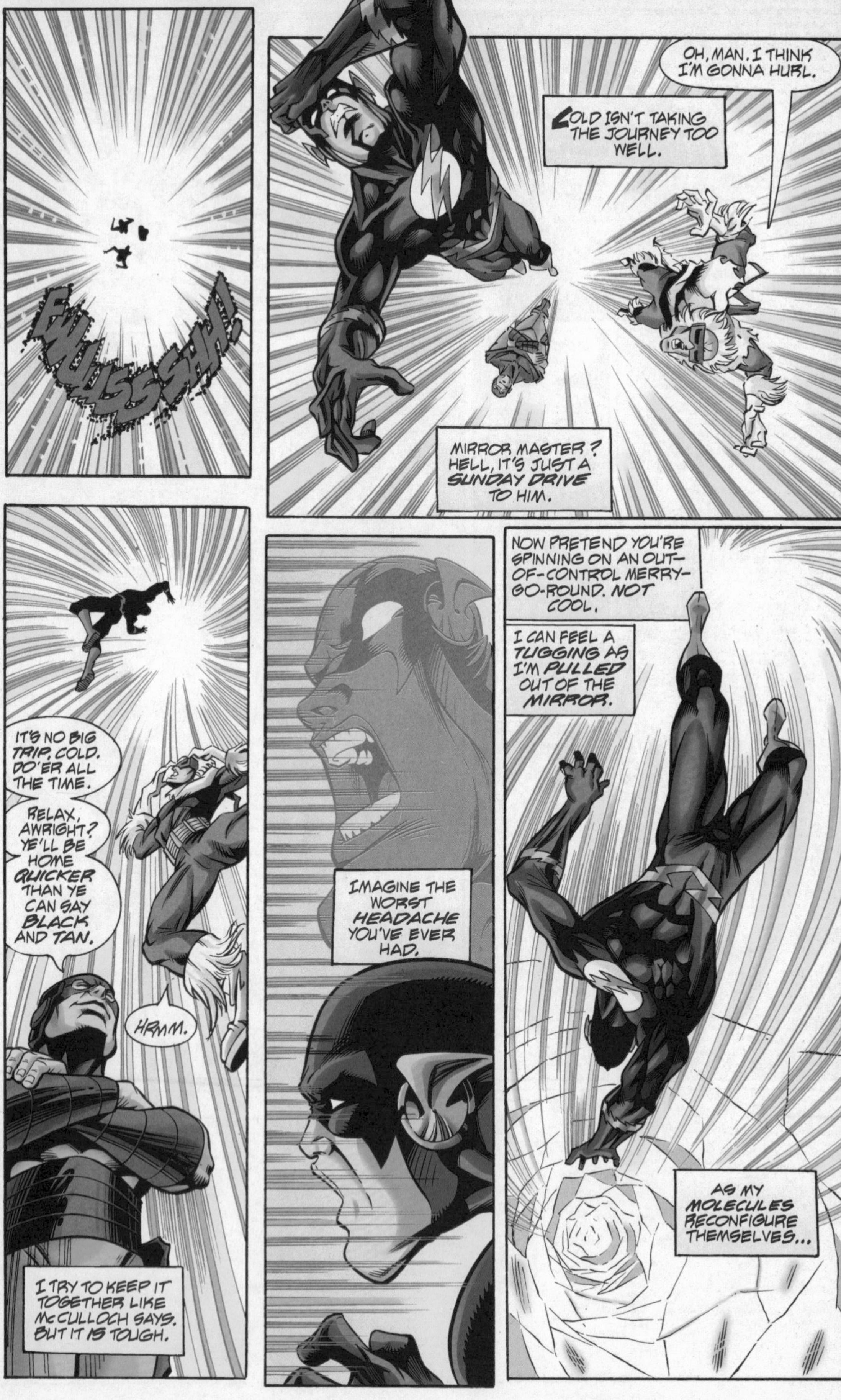
FWUSSSH!
OH, MAN. I THINK I'M GONNA HURL.
COLD ISN'T TAKING THE JOURNEY TOO WELL.
MIRROR MASTER? HELL, IT'S JUST A SUNDAY DRIVE TO HIM.
IT'S NO BIG TRIP, COLD. DO'ER ALL THE TIME.
RELAX, AWRIGHT? YE'LL BE HOME QUICKER THAN YE CAN SAY BLACK AND TAN.
HRMM.
I TRY TO KEEP IT TOGETHER LIKE McCULLOCH SAYS. BUT IT IS TOUGH.
IMAGINE THE WORST HEADACHE YOU'VE EVER HAD.
NOW PRETEND YOU'RE SPINNING ON AN OUT-OF-CONTROL MERRY-GO-ROUND. NOT COOL.
I CAN FEEL A TUGGING AS I'M PULLED OUT OF THE MIRROR.
AS MY MOLECULES RECONFIGURE THEMSELVES...

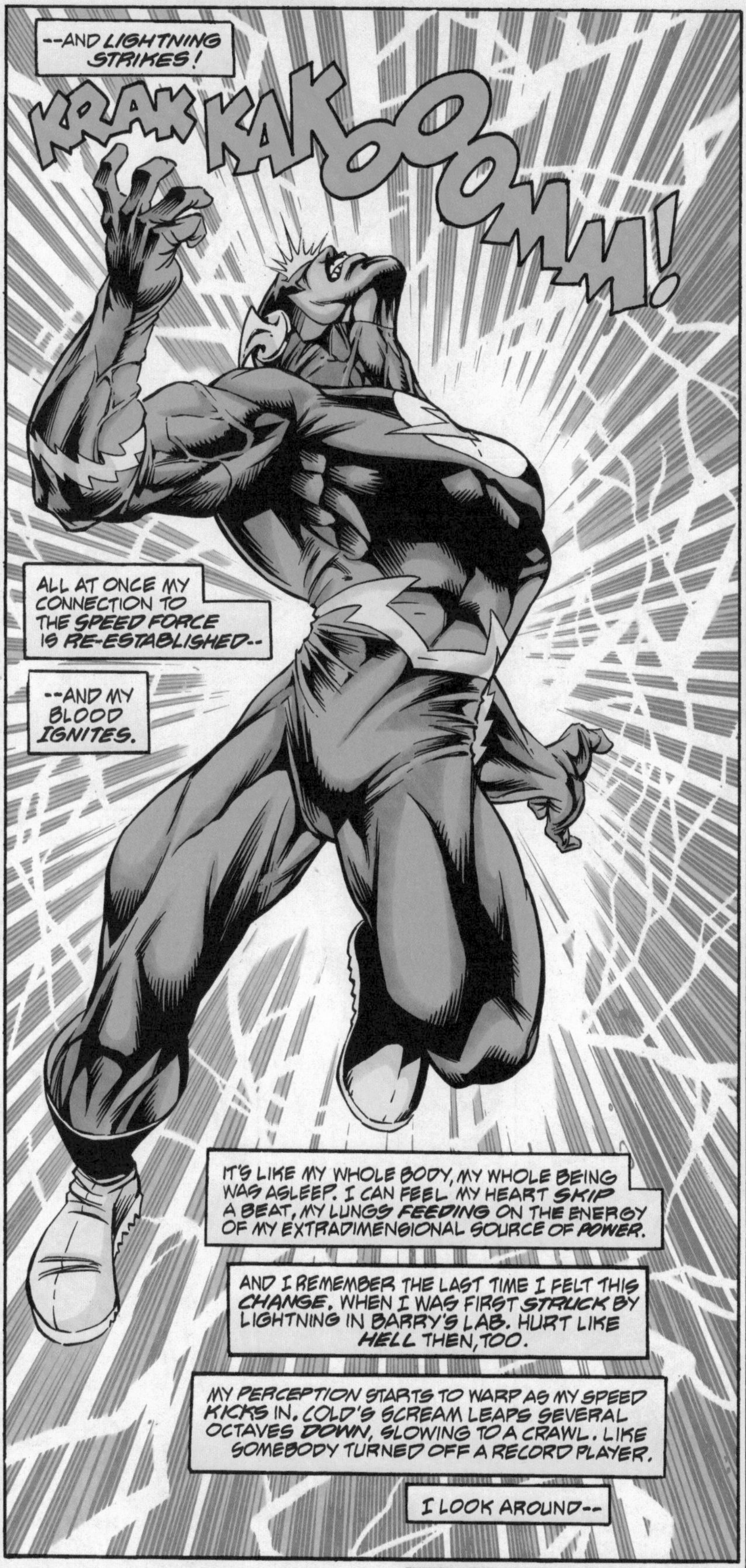
--AND LIGHTNING STRIKES!
KRAK KAKOOOOMM!
ALL AT ONCE MY CONNECTION TO THE SPEED FORCE IS RE-ESTABLISHED--
--AND MY BLOOD IGNITES.
IT'S LIKE MY WHOLE BODY, MY WHOLE BEING WAS ASLEEP. I CAN FEEL MY HEART SKIP A BEAT, MY LUNGS FEEDING ON THE ENERGY OF MY EXTRADIMENSIONAL SOURCE OF POWER.
AND I REMEMBER THE LAST TIME I FELT THIS CHANGE. WHEN I WAS FIRST STRUCK BY LIGHTNING IN BARRY'S LAB. HURT LIKE HELL THEN, TOO.
MY PERCEPTION STARTS TO WARP AS MY SPEED KICKS IN. COLD'S SCREAM LEAPS SEVERAL OCTAVES DOWN, SLOWING TO A CRAWL. LIKE SOMEBODY TURNED OFF A RECORD PLAYER.
I LOOK AROUND--
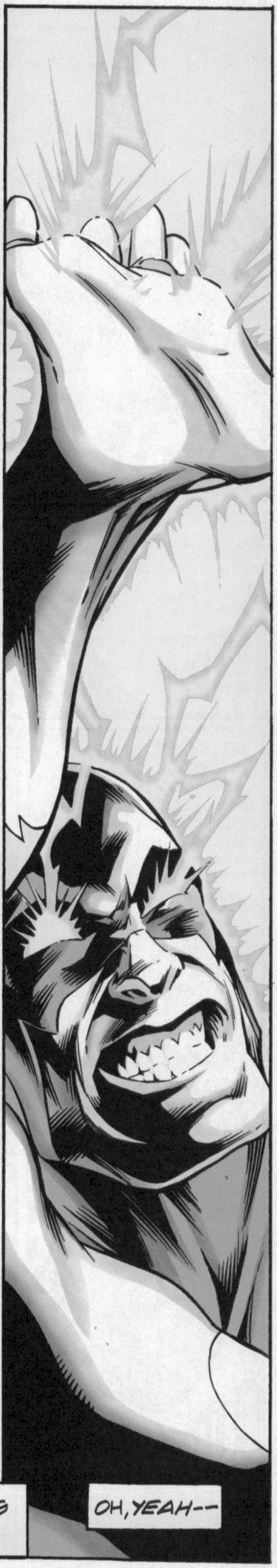
--AND I CAN SEE THE LIGHTNING STREAK--WATCH LIGHT TWIST AND TURN.
OH, YEAH--

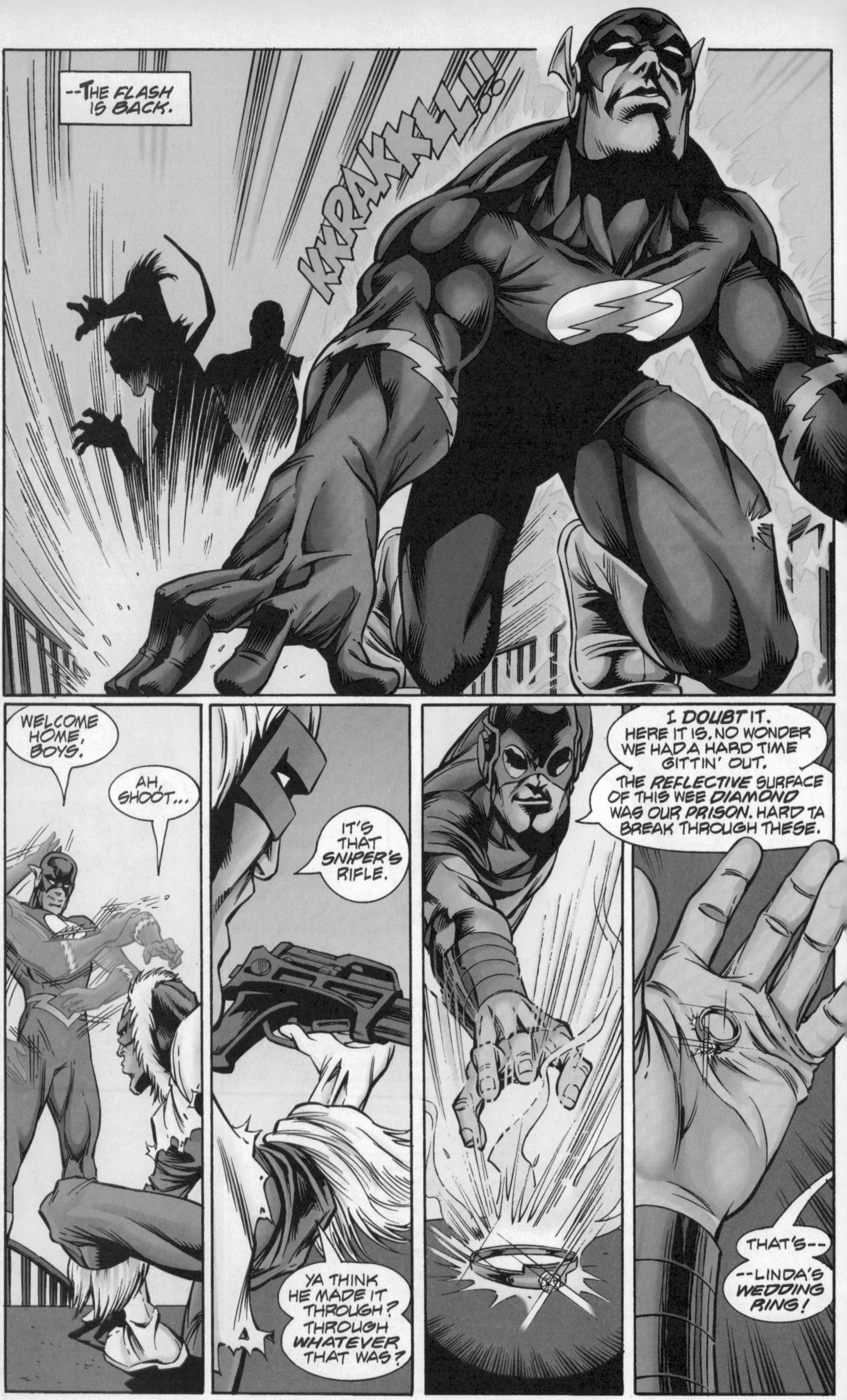
--THE FLASH IS BACK.
KKRAKKLL!!
WELCOME HOME, BOYS.
AH, SHOOT...
IT'S THAT SNIPER'S RIFLE.
YA THINK HE MADE IT THROUGH? THROUGH WHATEVER THAT WAS?
I DOUBT IT. HERE IT IS. NO WONDER WE HAD A HARD TIME GITTIN' OUT.
THE REFLECTIVE SURFACE OF THIS WEE DIAMOND WAS OUR PRISON. HARD TA BREAK THROUGH THESE.
THAT'S--
--LINDA'S WEDDING RING!

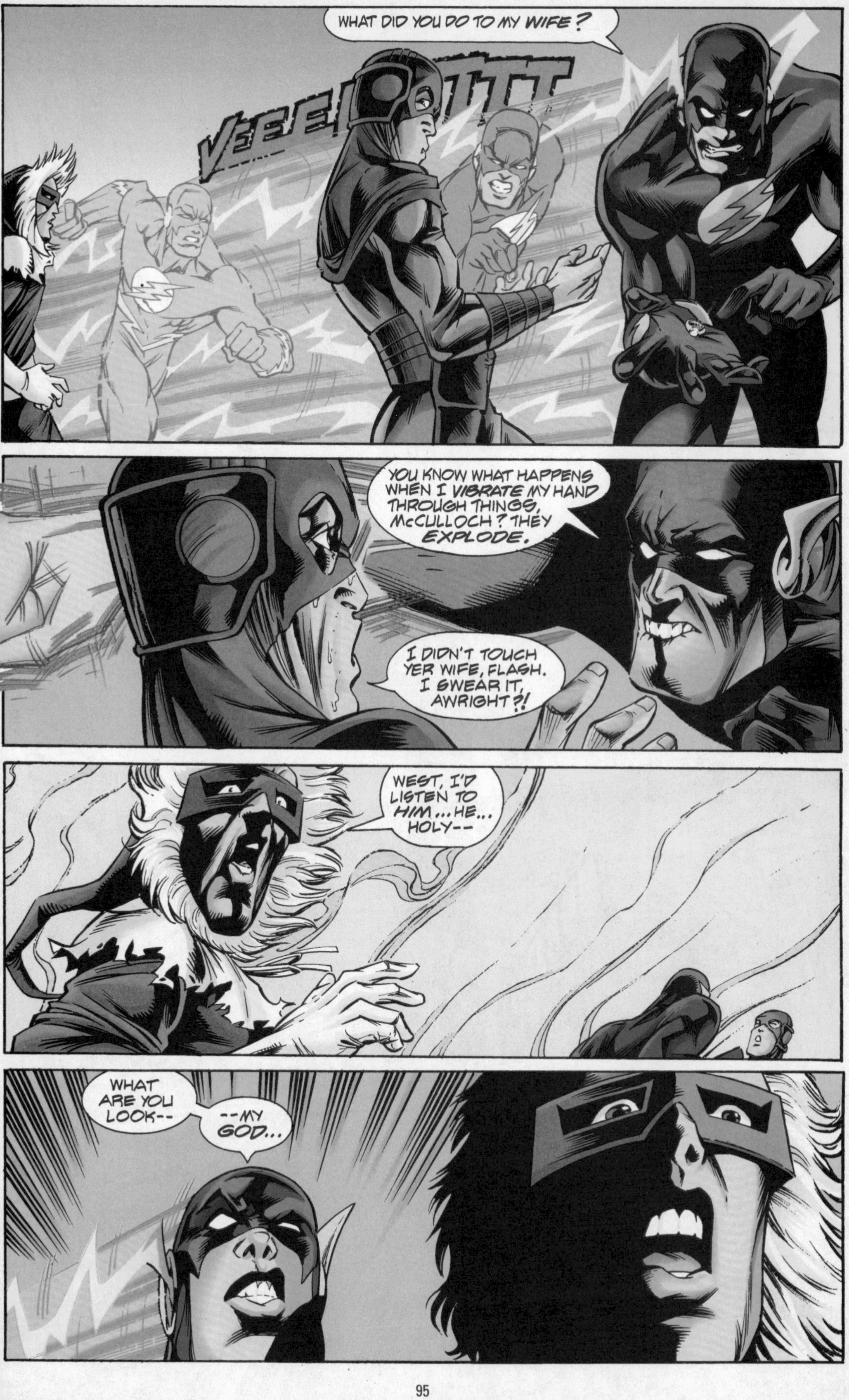

WHAT DID YOU DO TO MY WIFE?
VEEEOTTTT
YOU KNOW WHAT HAPPENS WHEN I VIBRATE MY HAND THROUGH THINGS, McCULLOCH? THEY EXPLODE.
I DIDN'T TOUCH YER WIFE, FLASH. I SWEAR IT, AWRIGHT?!
WEST, I'D LISTEN TO HIM... HE... HOLY--
WHAT ARE YOU LOOK--
--MY GOD...

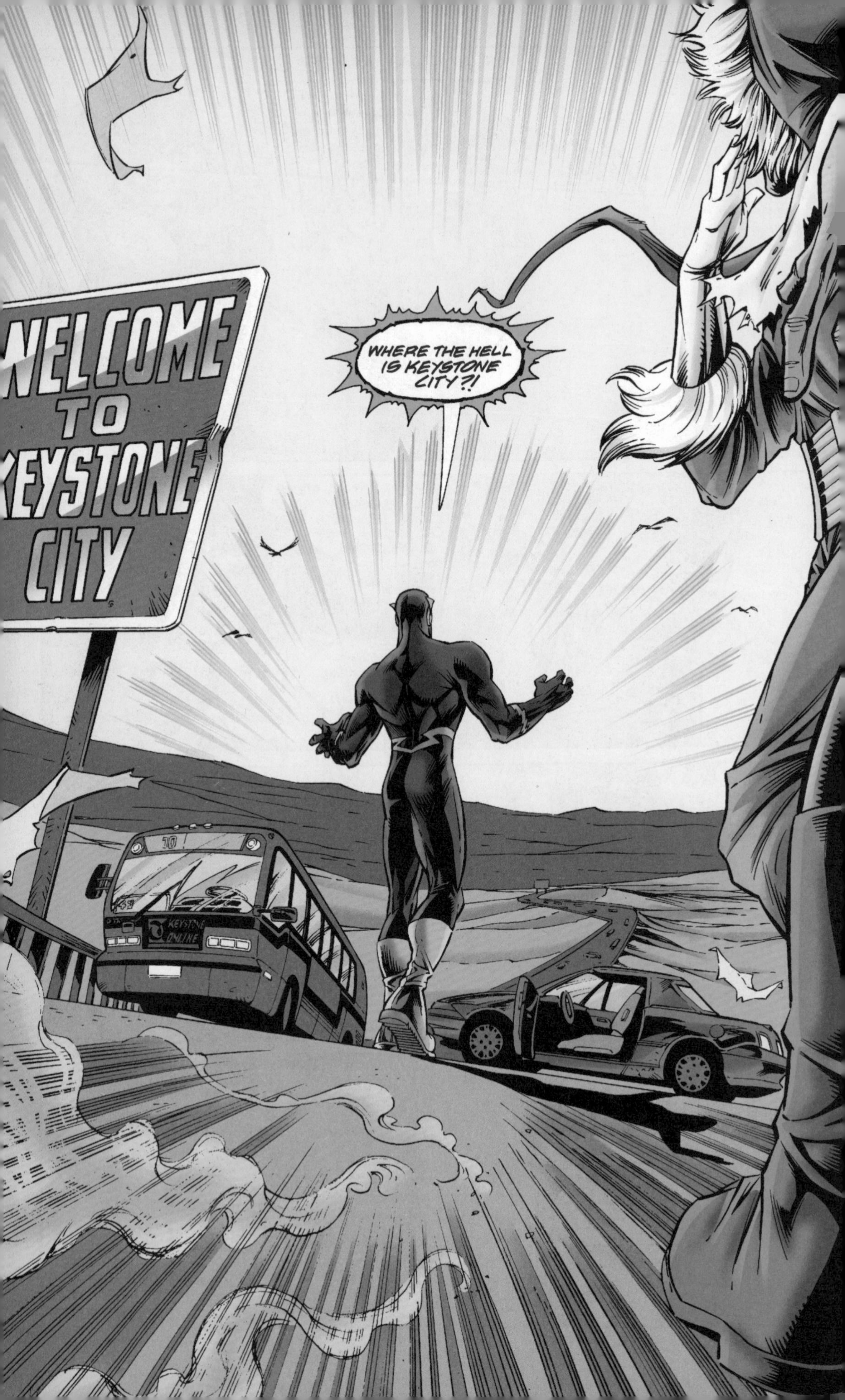
WELCOME TO KEYSTONE CITY
WHERE THE HELL IS KEYSTONE CITY?!
KEYSTONE ONLINE

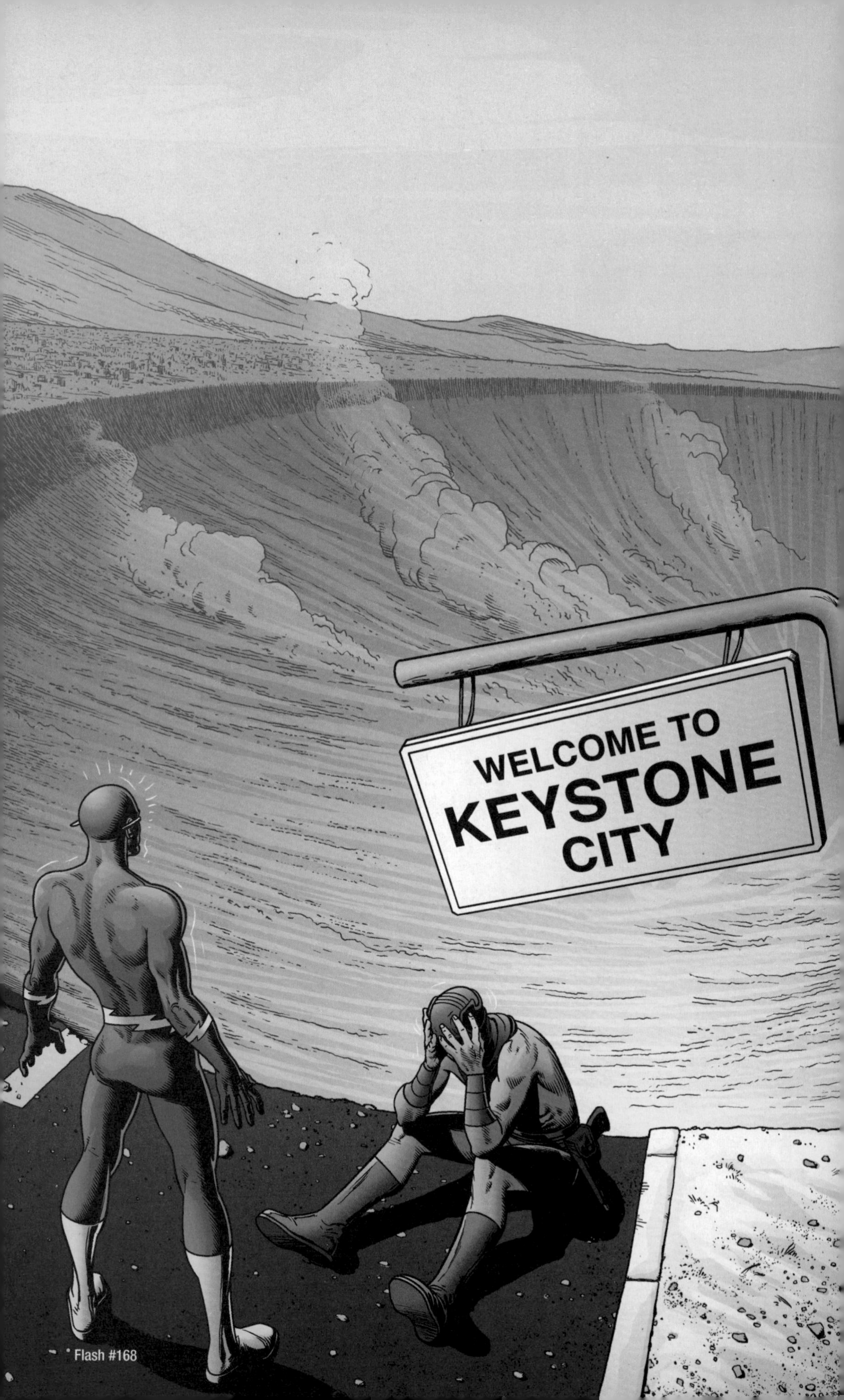
WELCOME TO
KEYSTONE
CITY

Flash #168

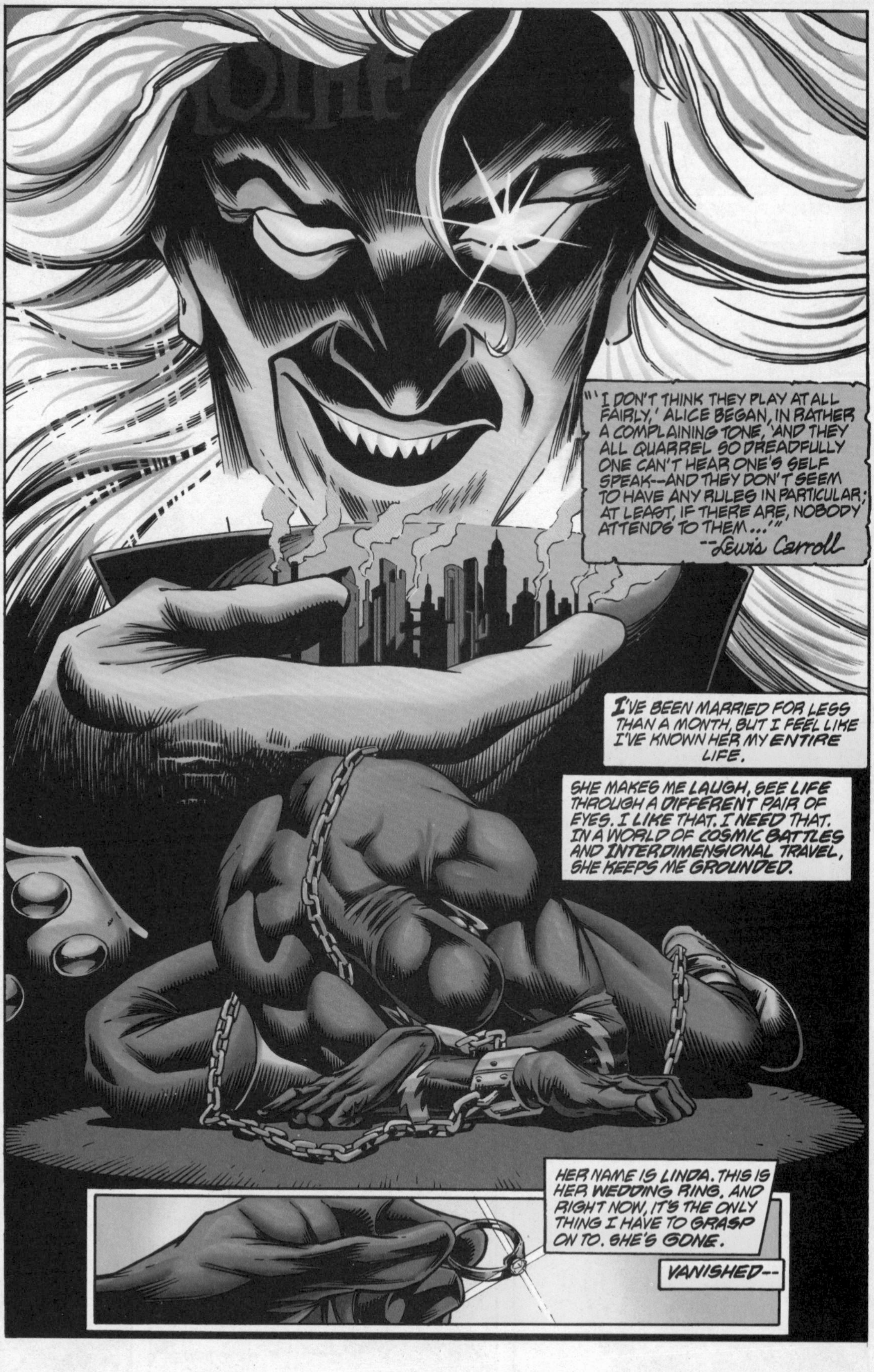
"'I DON'T THINK THEY PLAY AT ALL FAIRLY,' ALICE BEGAN, IN RATHER A COMPLAINING TONE, 'AND THEY ALL QUARREL SO DREADFULLY ONE CAN'T HEAR ONE'S SELF SPEAK--AND THEY DON'T SEEM TO HAVE ANY RULES IN PARTICULAR; AT LEAST, IF THERE ARE, NOBODY ATTENDS TO THEM...'" --Lewis Carroll
I'VE BEEN MARRIED FOR LESS THAN A MONTH, BUT I FEEL LIKE I'VE KNOWN HER MY ENTIRE LIFE.
SHE MAKES ME LAUGH, SEE LIFE THROUGH A DIFFERENT PAIR OF EYES. I LIKE THAT. I NEED THAT. IN A WORLD OF COSMIC BATTLES AND INTERDIMENSIONAL TRAVEL, SHE KEEPS ME GROUNDED.
HER NAME IS LINDA. THIS IS HER WEDDING RING. AND RIGHT NOW, IT'S THE ONLY THING I HAVE TO GRASP ON TO. SHE'S GONE.
VANISHED--

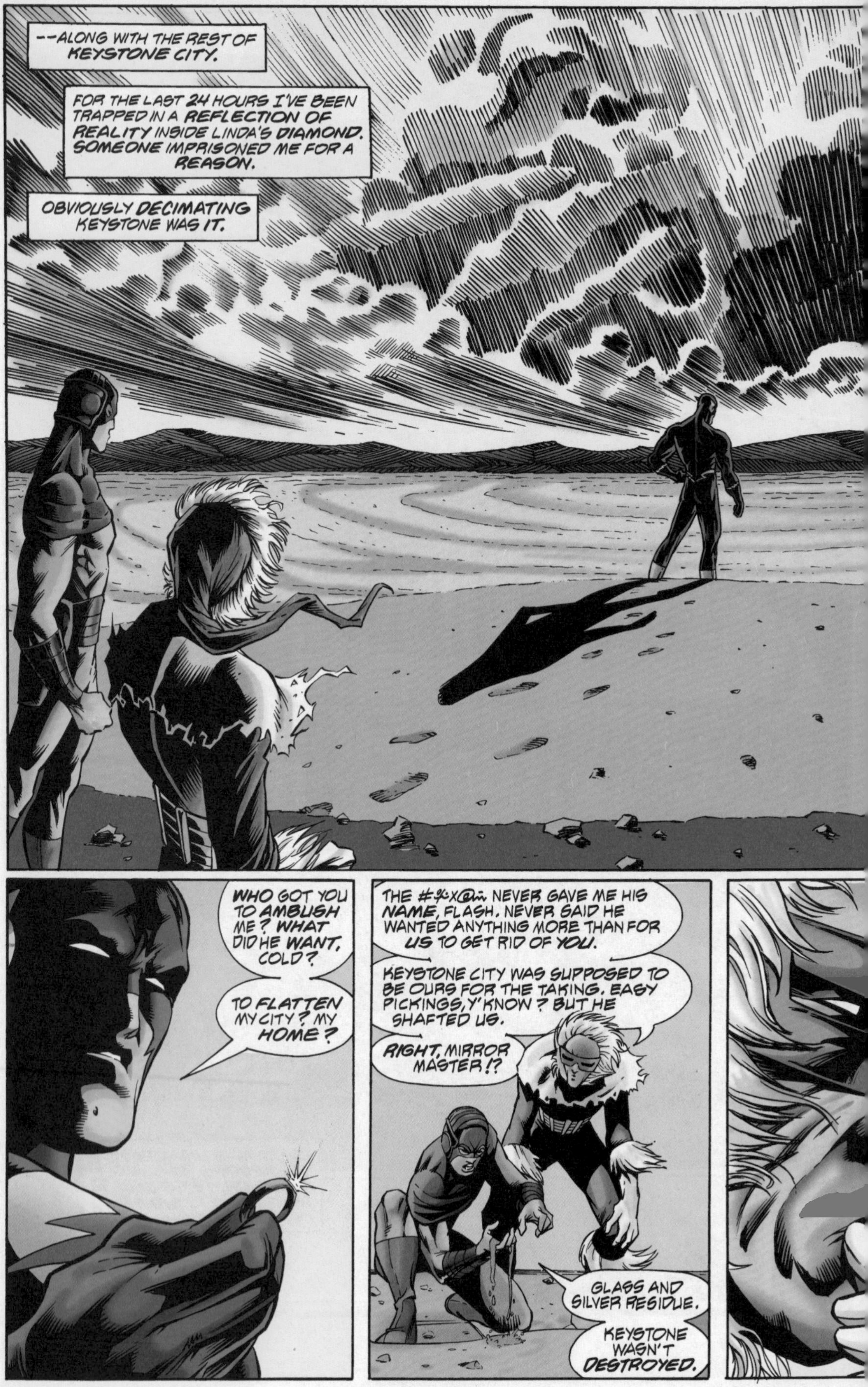

--ALONG WITH THE REST OF KEYSTONE CITY.
FOR THE LAST 24 HOURS I'VE BEEN TRAPPED IN A REFLECTION OF REALITY INSIDE LINDA'S DIAMOND. SOMEONE IMPRISONED ME FOR A REASON.
OBVIOUSLY DECIMATING KEYSTONE WAS IT.
WHO GOT YOU TO AMBUSH ME? WHAT DID HE WANT, COLD?
TO FLATTEN MY CITY? MY HOME?
THE #%x@! NEVER GAVE ME HIS NAME, FLASH. NEVER SAID HE WANTED ANYTHING MORE THAN FOR US TO GET RID OF YOU.
KEYSTONE CITY WAS SUPPOSED TO BE OURS FOR THE TAKING. EASY PICKINGS, Y'KNOW? BUT HE SHAFTED US.
RIGHT, MIRROR MASTER!?
GLASS AND SILVER RESIDUE.
KEYSTONE WASN'T DESTROYED.

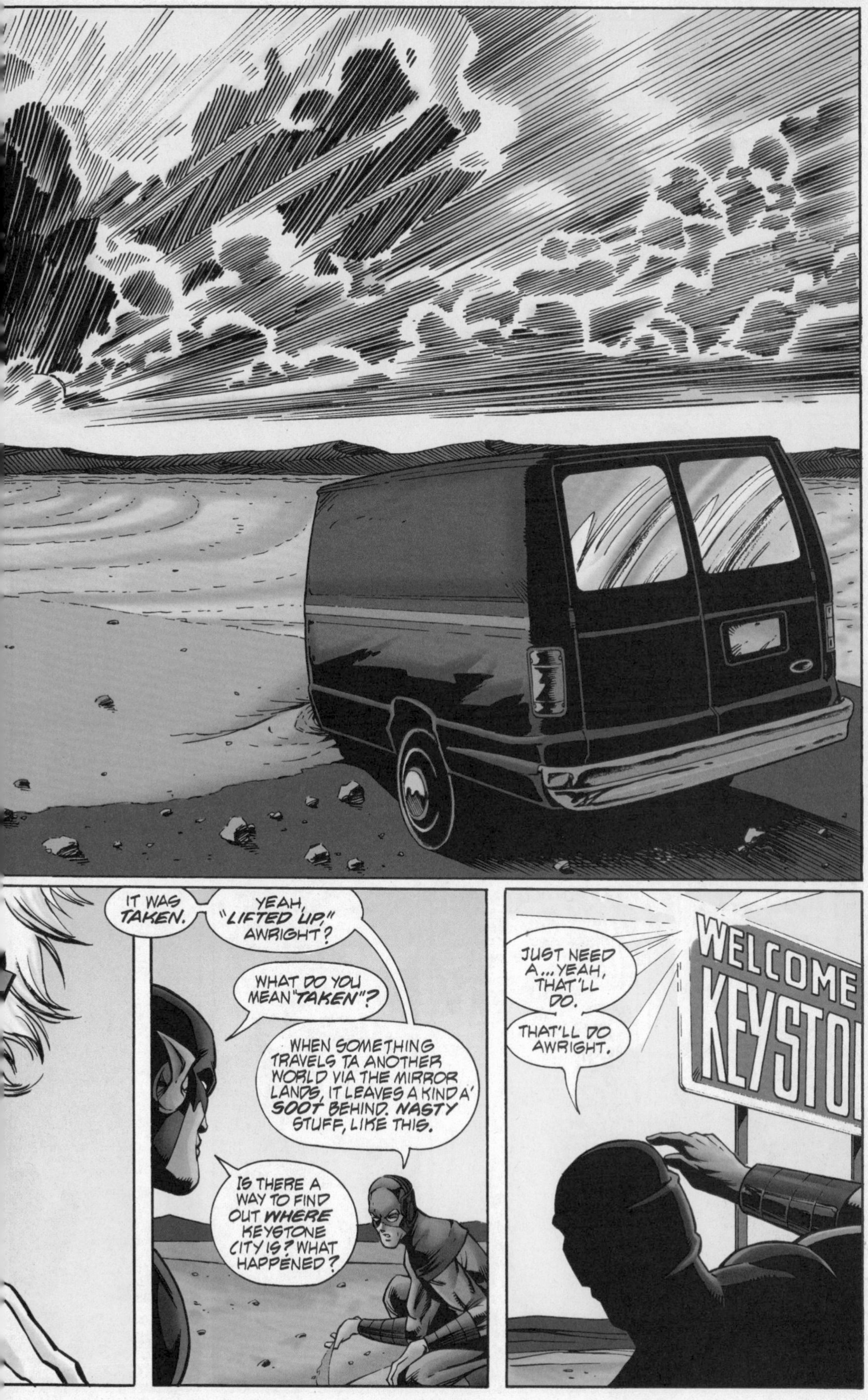
IT WAS TAKEN.
YEAH, "LIFTED UP," AWRIGHT?
WHAT DO YOU MEAN "TAKEN"?
WHEN SOMETHING TRAVELS TA ANOTHER WORLD VIA THE MIRROR LANDS, IT LEAVES A KIND A' SOOT BEHIND. NASTY STUFF, LIKE THIS.
IS THERE A WAY TO FIND OUT WHERE KEYSTONE CITY IS? WHAT HAPPENED?
JUST NEED A... YEAH, THAT'LL DO.
THAT'LL DO AWRIGHT.
WELCOME
KEYSTO

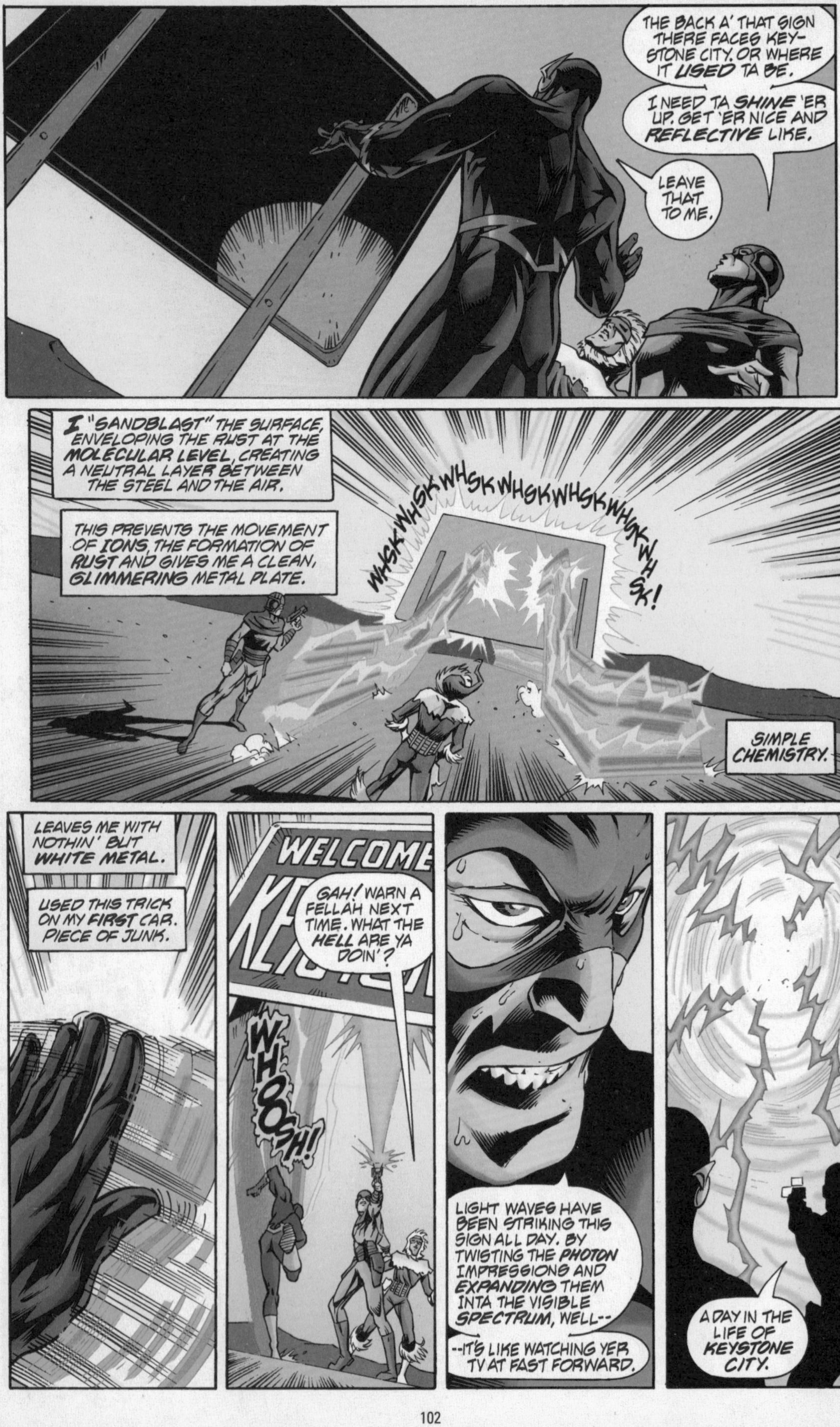
THE BACK A' THAT SIGN THERE FACES KEY-STONE CITY. OR WHERE IT USED TA BE.
I NEED TA SHINE 'ER UP. GET 'ER NICE AND REFLECTIVE LIKE.
LEAVE THAT TO ME.
I "SANDBLAST" THE SURFACE, ENVELOPING THE RUST AT THE MOLECULAR LEVEL, CREATING A NEUTRAL LAYER BETWEEN THE STEEL AND THE AIR.
THIS PREVENTS THE MOVEMENT OF IONS, THE FORMATION OF RUST AND GIVES ME A CLEAN, GLIMMERING METAL PLATE.
WHSK WHSK WHSK WHSK WHSK WHSK WHSK WHSK!
SIMPLE CHEMISTRY.
LEAVES ME WITH NOTHIN' BUT WHITE METAL.
USED THIS TRICK ON MY FIRST CAR. PIECE OF JUNK.
WELCOME
GAH! WARN A FELLAH NEXT TIME. WHAT THE HELL ARE YA DOIN'?
WHOOSH!
LIGHT WAVES HAVE BEEN STRIKING THIS SIGN ALL DAY. BY TWISTING THE PHOTON IMPRESSIONS AND EXPANDING THEM INTA THE VISIBLE SPECTRUM, WELL--
--IT'S LIKE WATCHING YER TV AT FAST FORWARD.
A DAY IN THE LIFE OF KEYSTONE CITY.

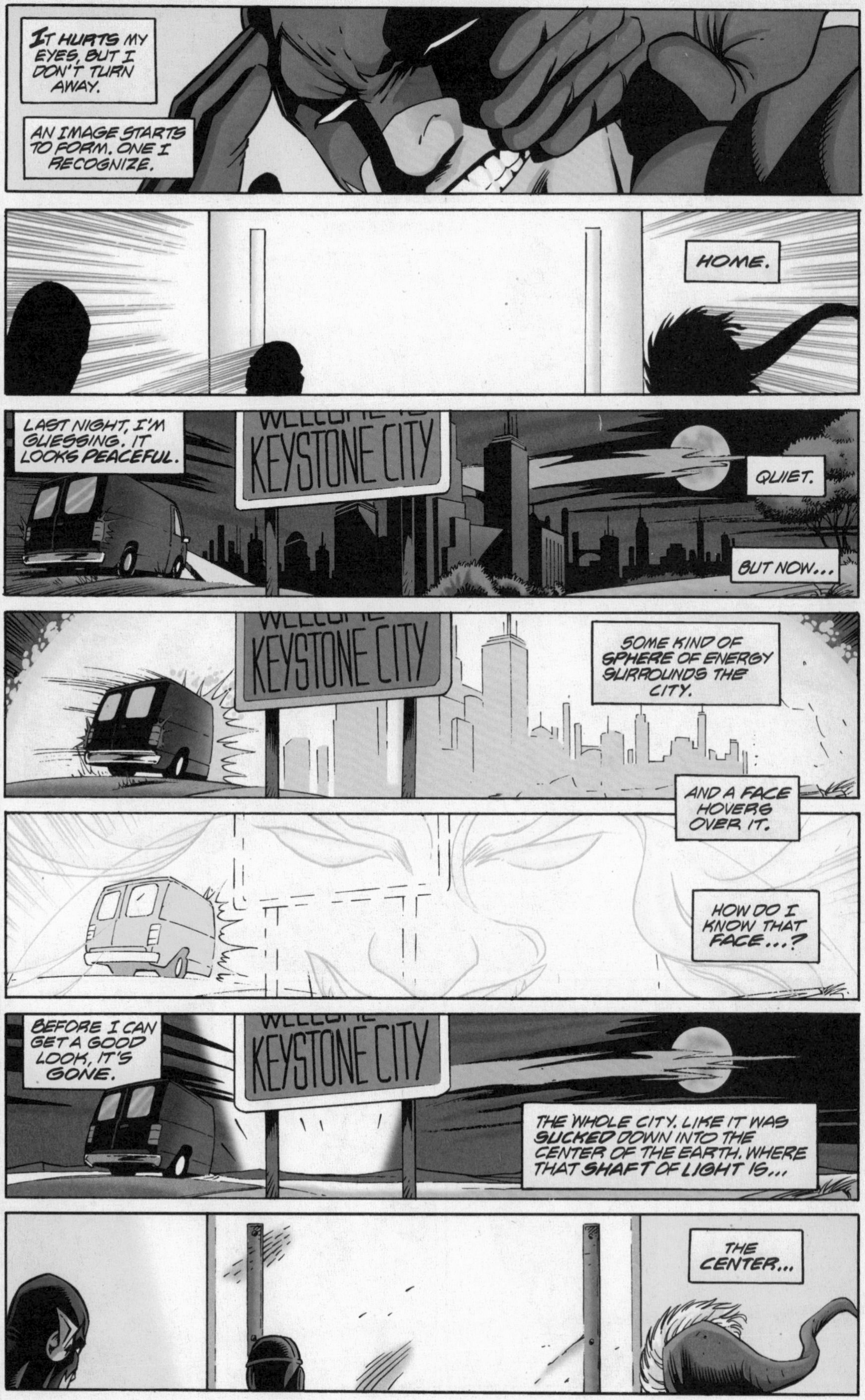
IT HURTS MY EYES, BUT I DON'T TURN AWAY.
AN IMAGE STARTS TO FORM. ONE I RECOGNIZE.
HOME.
LAST NIGHT, I'M GUESSING. IT LOOKS PEACEFUL.
KEYSTONE CITY
QUIET.
BUT NOW...
KEYSTONE CITY
SOME KIND OF SPHERE OF ENERGY SURROUNDS THE CITY.
AND A FACE HOVERS OVER IT.
HOW DO I KNOW THAT FACE...?
BEFORE I CAN GET A GOOD LOOK, IT'S GONE.
KEYSTONE CITY
THE WHOLE CITY. LIKE IT WAS SUCKED DOWN INTO THE CENTER OF THE EARTH. WHERE THAT SHAFT OF LIGHT IS...
THE CENTER...

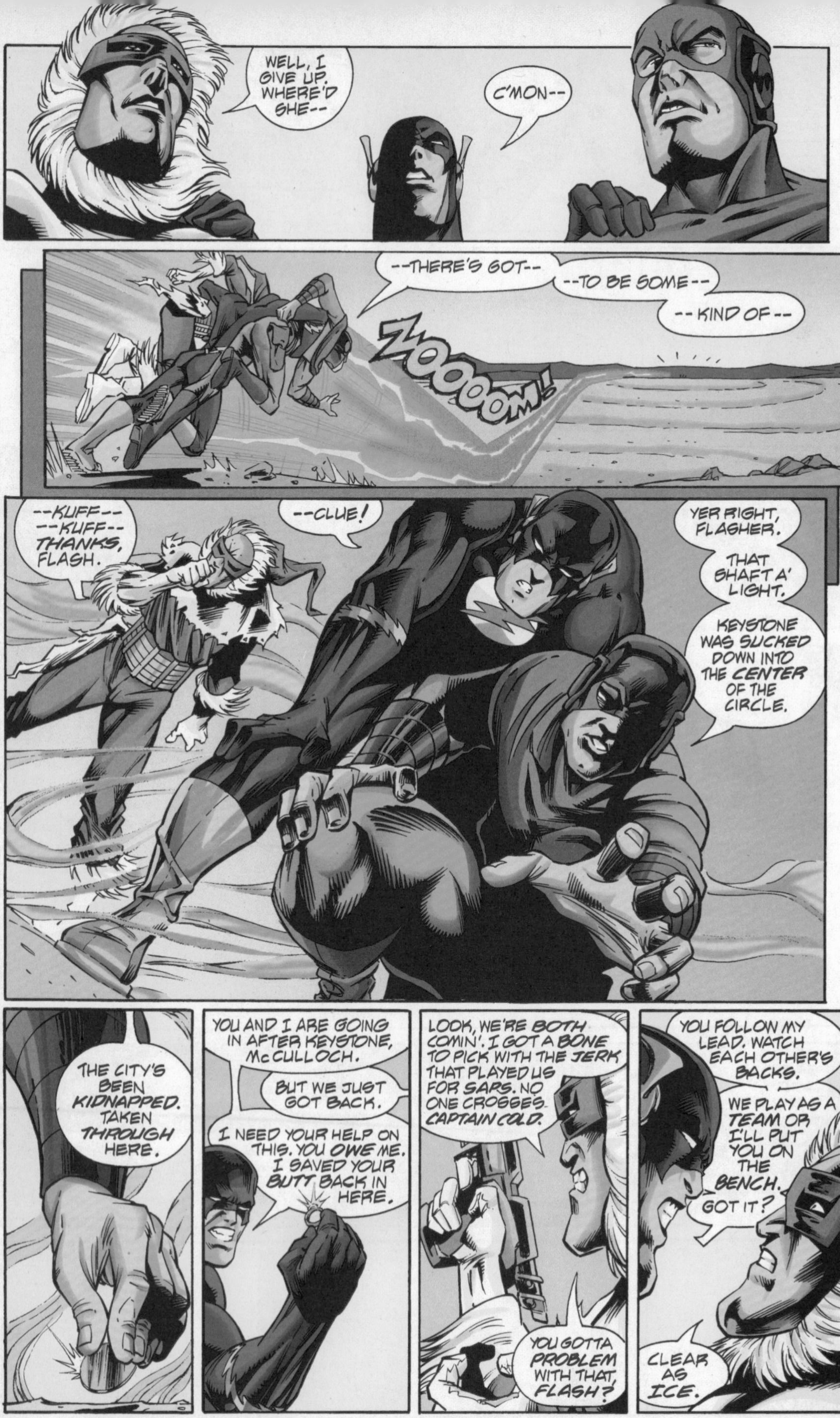
WELL, I GIVE UP. WHERE'D SHE--
C'MON--
--THERE'S GOT--
--TO BE SOME--
--KIND OF--
ZOOOOOM!
--KUFF-- --KUFF-- THANKS, FLASH.
--CLUE!
YER RIGHT, FLASHER.
THAT SHAFT A' LIGHT.
KEYSTONE WAS SUCKED DOWN INTO THE CENTER OF THE CIRCLE.
THE CITY'S BEEN KIDNAPPED. TAKEN THROUGH HERE.
YOU AND I ARE GOING IN AFTER KEYSTONE, McCULLOCH.
BUT WE JUST GOT BACK.
I NEED YOUR HELP ON THIS. YOU OWE ME. I SAVED YOUR BUTT BACK IN HERE.
LOOK, WE'RE BOTH COMIN'. I GOT A BONE TO PICK WITH THE JERK THAT PLAYED US FOR SAPS. NO ONE CROSSES CAPTAIN COLD.
YOU GOTTA PROBLEM WITH THAT, FLASH?
YOU FOLLOW MY LEAD. WATCH EACH OTHER'S BACKS.
WE PLAY AS A TEAM OR I'LL PUT YOU ON THE BENCH.
GOT IT?
CLEAR AS ICE.

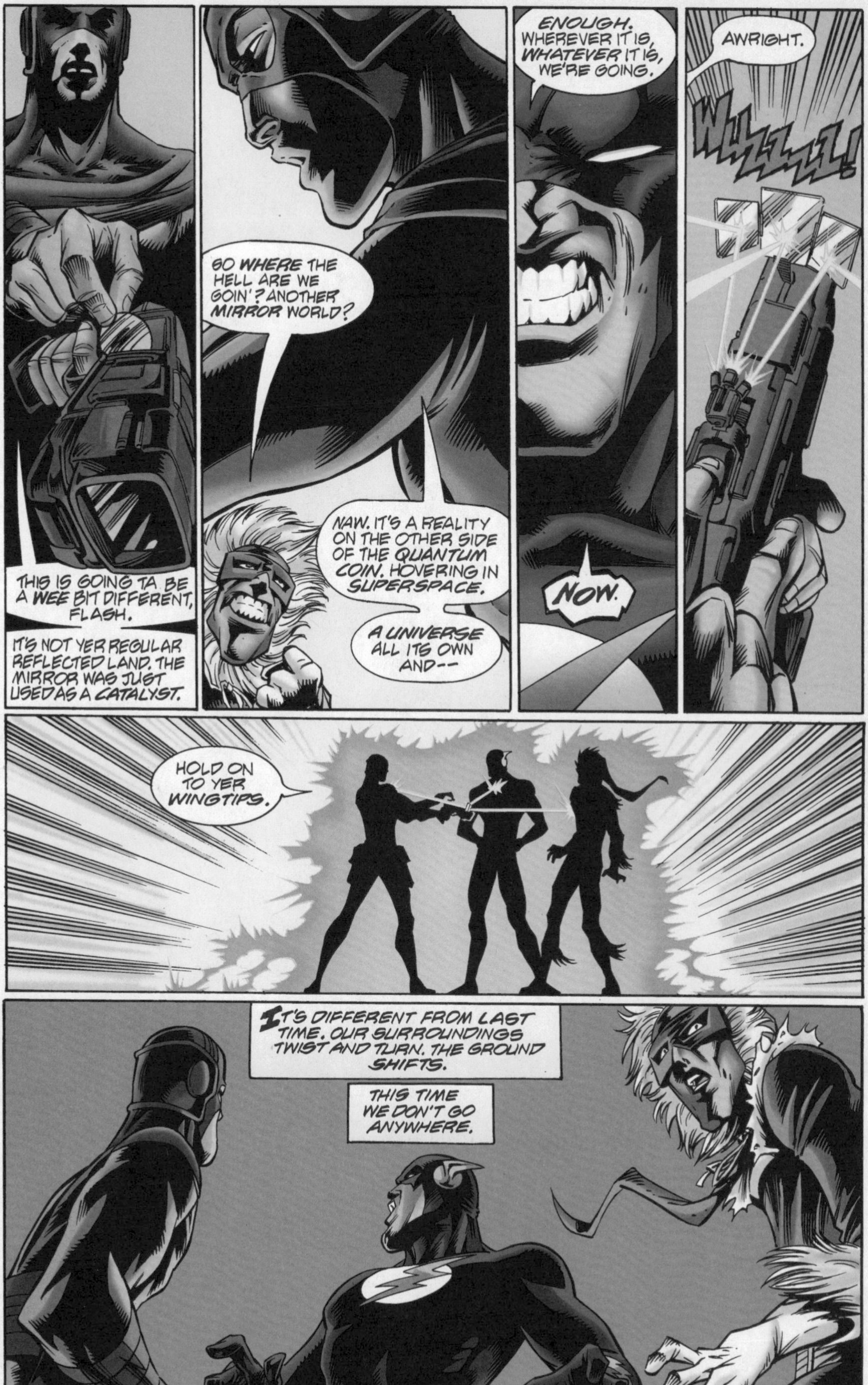
THIS IS GOING TA BE A WEE BIT DIFFERENT, FLASH.
IT'S NOT YER REGULAR REFLECTED LAND. THE MIRROR WAS JUST USED AS A CATALYST.
SO WHERE THE HELL ARE WE GOIN'? ANOTHER MIRROR WORLD?
NAW. IT'S A REALITY ON THE OTHER SIDE OF THE QUANTUM COIN. HOVERING IN SUPERSPACE.
A UNIVERSE ALL ITS OWN AND--
ENOUGH. WHEREVER IT IS, WHATEVER IT IS, WE'RE GOING.
NOW.
AWRIGHT.
WHZZZZT!
HOLD ON TO YER WINGTIPS.
IT'S DIFFERENT FROM LAST TIME. OUR SURROUNDINGS TWIST AND TURN. THE GROUND SHIFTS.
THIS TIME WE DON'T GO ANYWHERE.

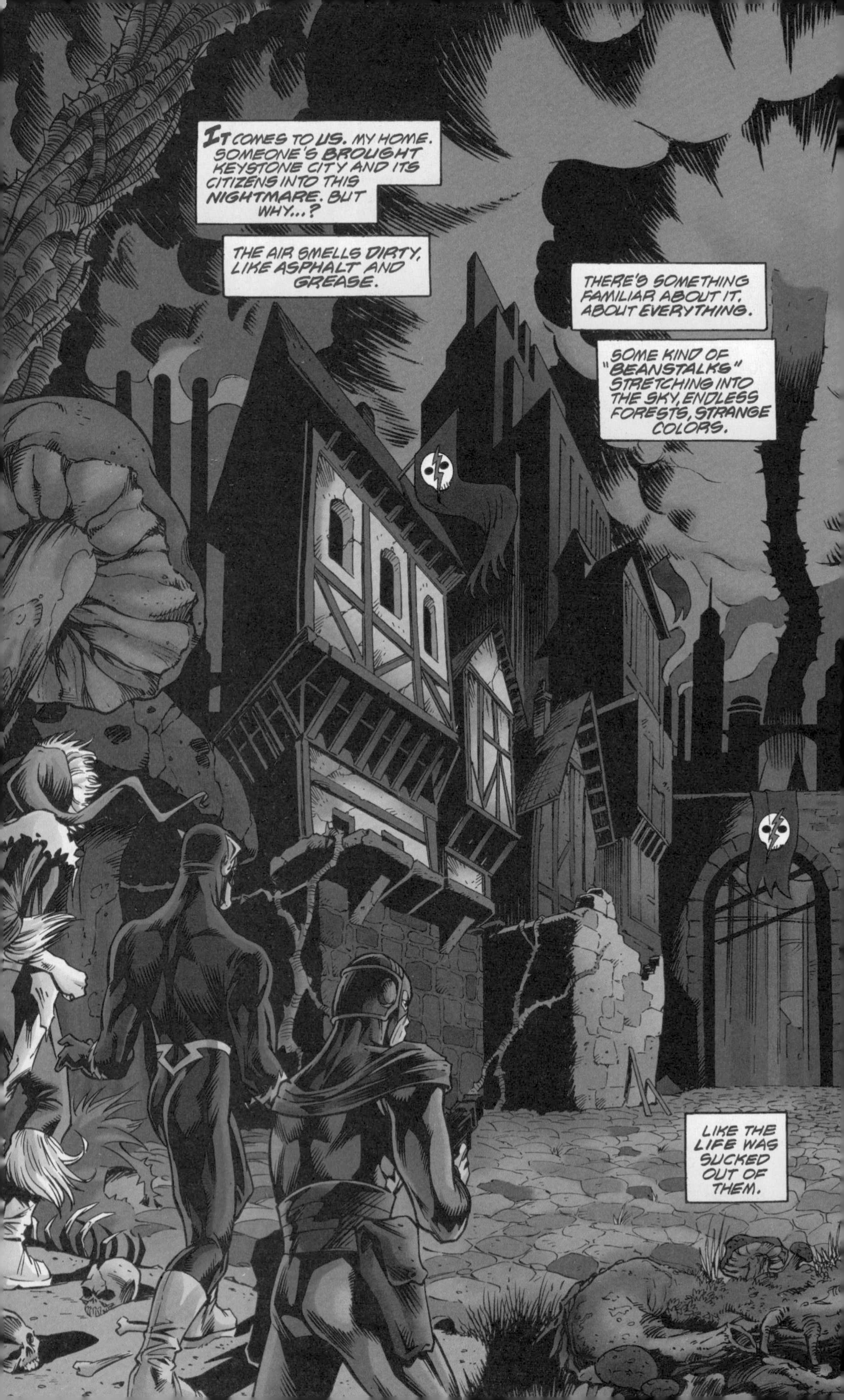
IT COMES TO US. MY HOME. SOMEONE'S BROUGHT KEYSTONE CITY AND ITS CITIZENS INTO THIS NIGHTMARE. BUT WHY...?
THE AIR SMELLS DIRTY, LIKE ASPHALT AND GREASE.
THERE'S SOMETHING FAMILIAR ABOUT IT, ABOUT EVERYTHING.
SOME KIND OF "BEANSTALKS" STRETCHING INTO THE SKY, ENDLESS FORESTS, STRANGE COLORS.
LIKE THE LIFE WAS SUCKED OUT OF THEM.

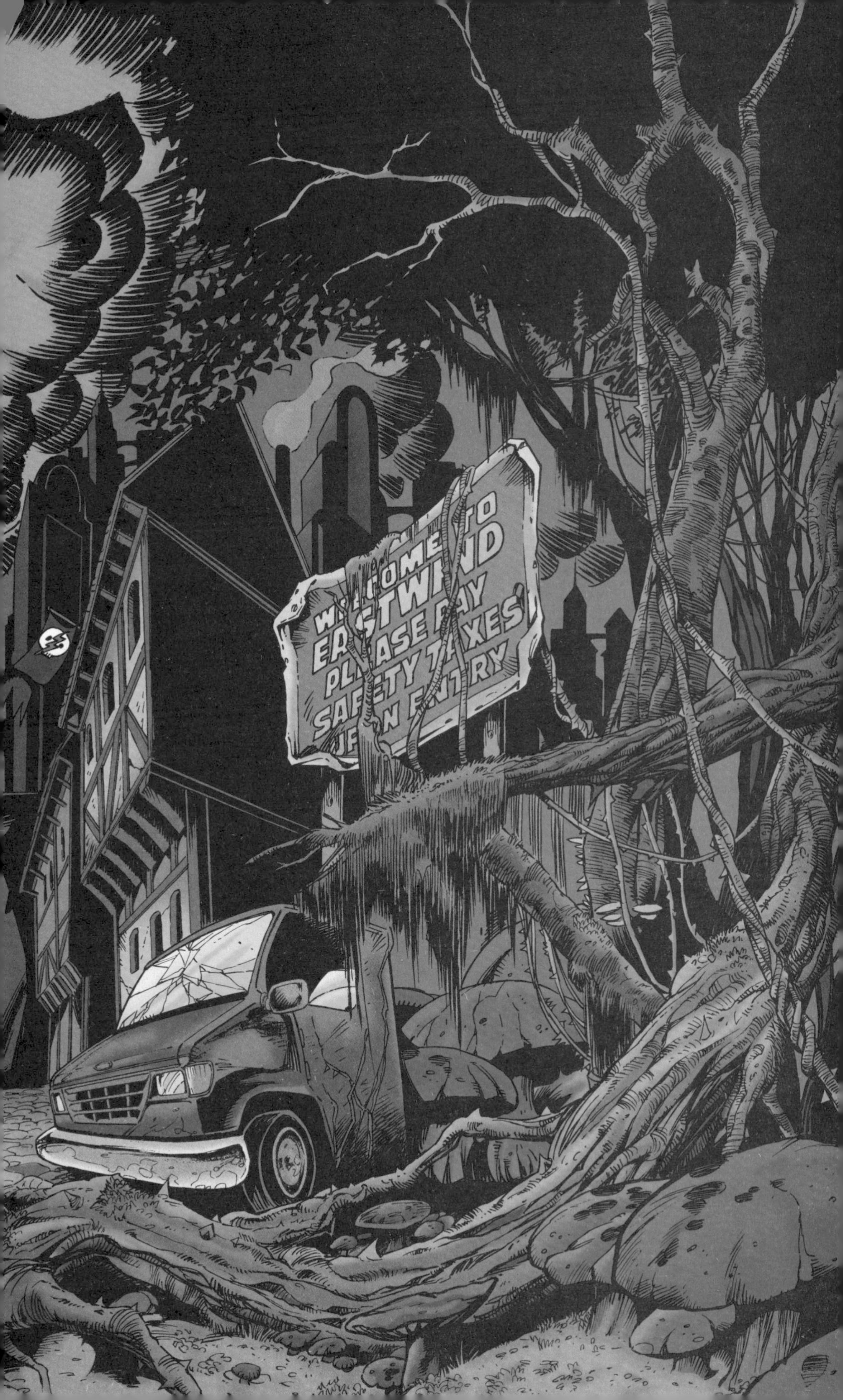
TO

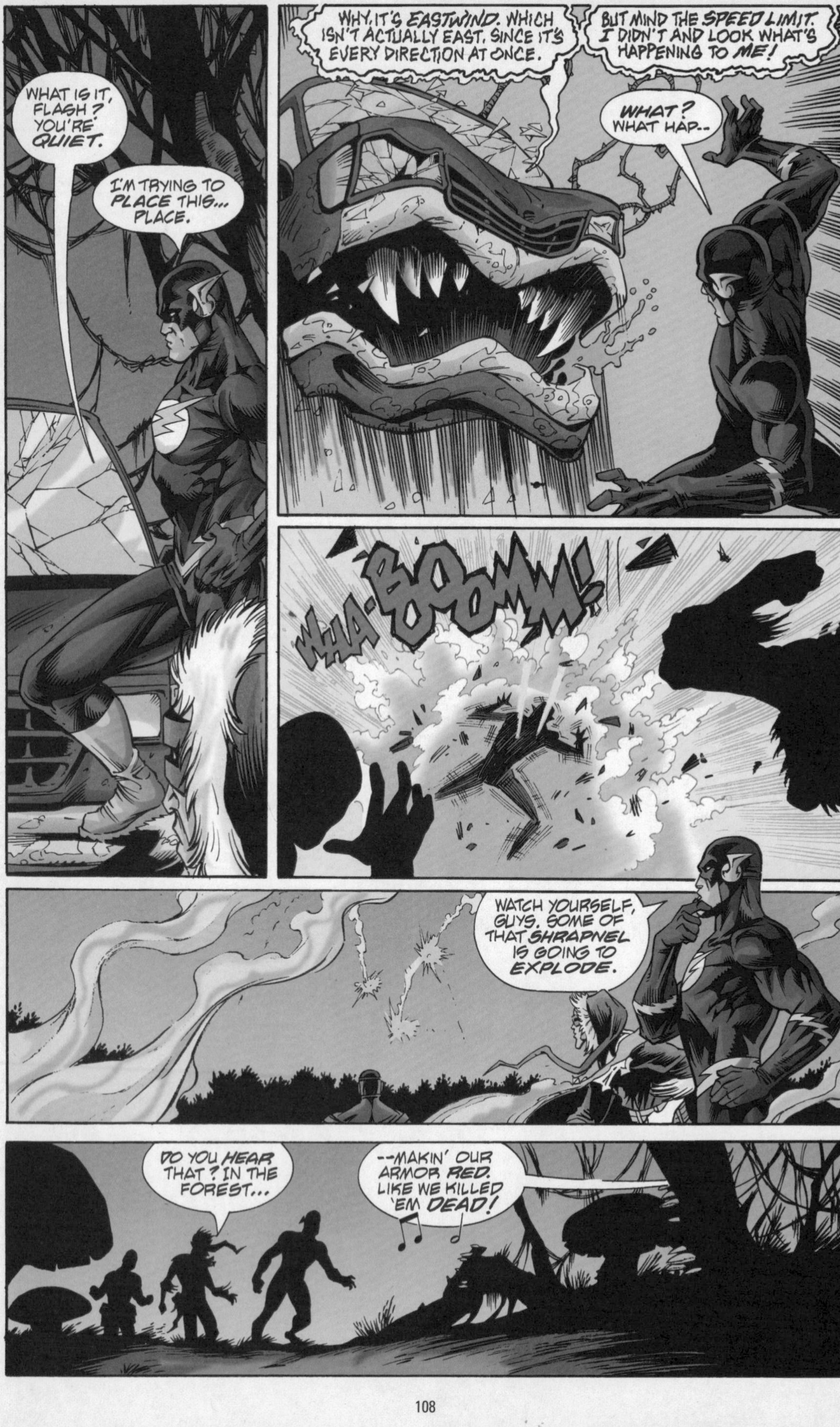
WHAT IS IT, FLASH? YOU'RE QUIET.
I'M TRYING TO PLACE THIS... PLACE.
WHY, IT'S EASTWIND. WHICH ISN'T ACTUALLY EAST. SINCE IT'S EVERY DIRECTION AT ONCE.
BUT MIND THE SPEED LIMIT. I DIDN'T AND LOOK WHAT'S HAPPENING TO ME!
WHAT? WHAT HAP--
WHA-BOOMM!
WATCH YOURSELF, GUYS. SOME OF THAT SHRAPNEL IS GOING TO EXPLODE.
DO YOU HEAR THAT? IN THE FOREST...
--MAKIN' OUR ARMOR RED. LIKE WE KILLED 'EM DEAD!

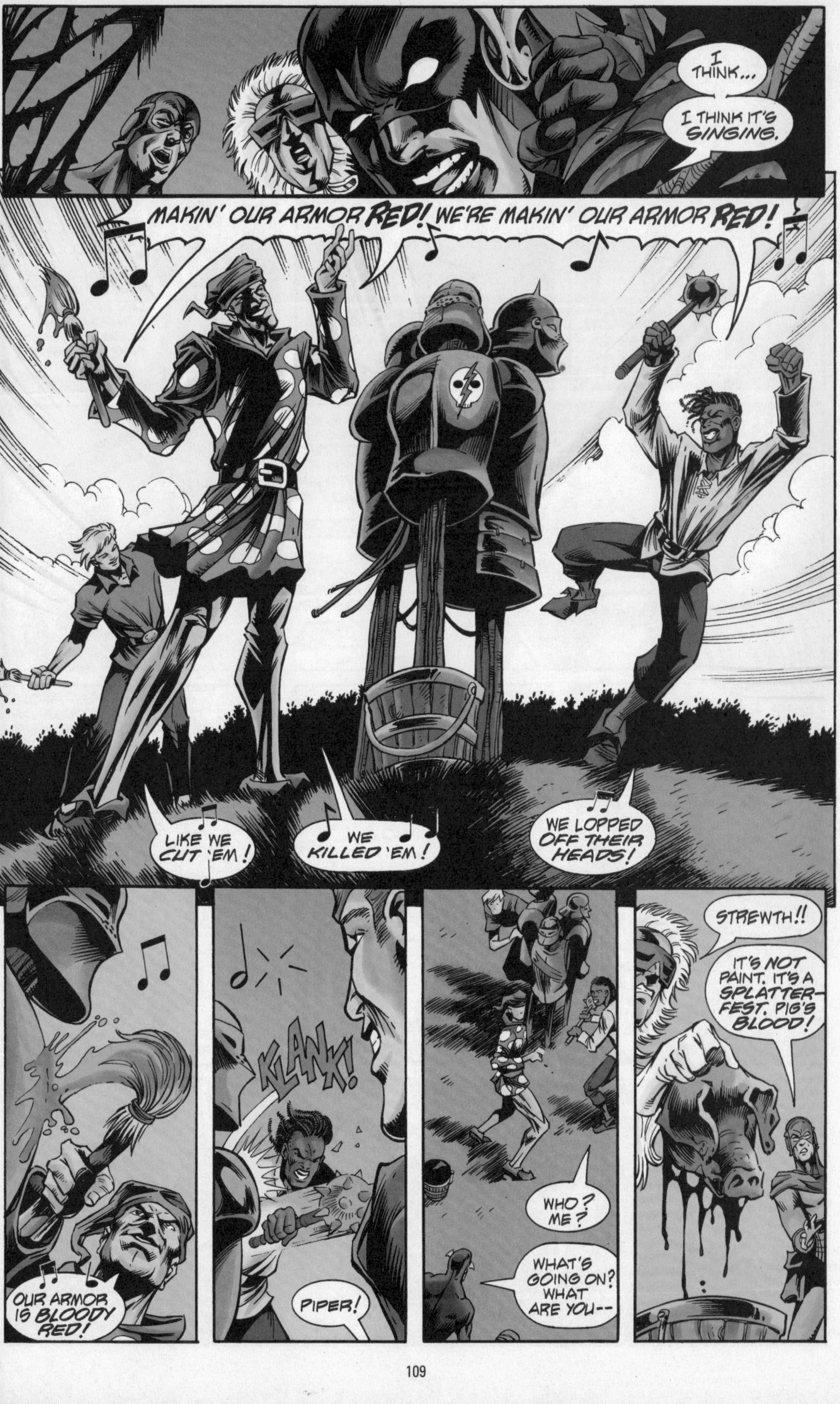
I THINK...
I THINK IT'S SINGING.
MAKIN' OUR ARMOR RED! WE'RE MAKIN' OUR ARMOR RED!
LIKE WE CUT 'EM!
WE KILLED 'EM!
WE LOPPED OFF THEIR HEADS!
OUR ARMOR IS BLOODY RED!
KLANK!
PIPER!
WHO? ME?
WHAT'S GOING ON? WHAT ARE YOU--
STREWTH!!
IT'S NOT PAINT. IT'S A SPLATTER-FEST. PIG'S BLOOD!

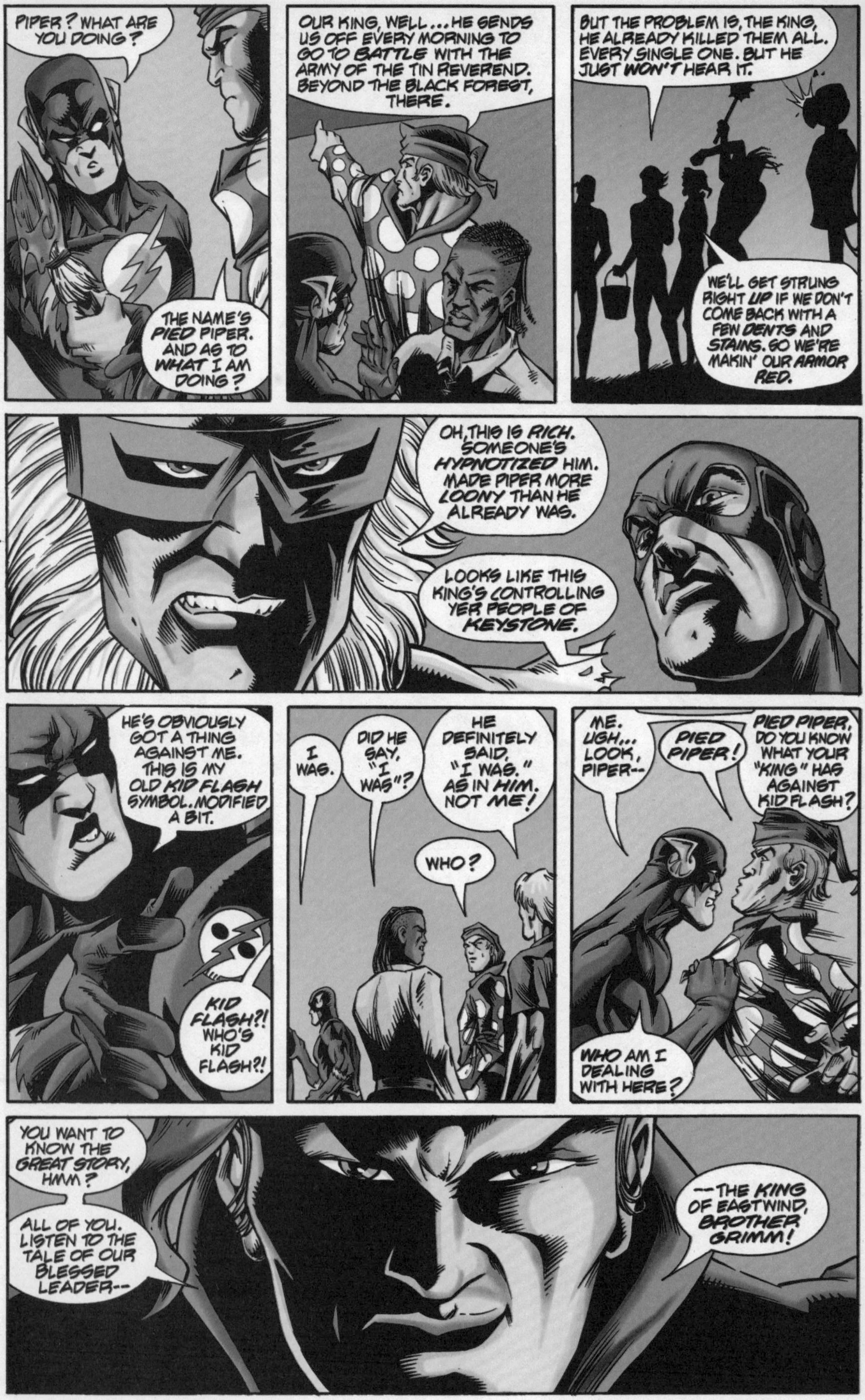
PIPER? WHAT ARE YOU DOING?
THE NAME'S PIED PIPER. AND AS TO WHAT I AM DOING?
OUR KING, WELL... HE SENDS US OFF EVERY MORNING TO GO TO BATTLE WITH THE ARMY OF THE TIN REVEREND. BEYOND THE BLACK FOREST, THERE.
BUT THE PROBLEM IS, THE KING, HE ALREADY KILLED THEM ALL. EVERY SINGLE ONE. BUT HE JUST WON'T HEAR IT.
WE'LL GET STRUNG RIGHT UP IF WE DON'T COME BACK WITH A FEW DENTS AND STAINS. SO WE'RE MAKIN' OUR ARMOR RED.
OH, THIS IS RICH. SOMEONE'S HYPNOTIZED HIM. MADE PIPER MORE LOONY THAN HE ALREADY WAS.
LOOKS LIKE THIS KING'S CONTROLLING YER PEOPLE OF KEYSTONE.
HE'S OBVIOUSLY GOT A THING AGAINST ME. THIS IS MY OLD KID FLASH SYMBOL. MODIFIED A BIT.
KID FLASH?! WHO'S KID FLASH?!
I WAS.
DID HE SAY, "I WAS"?
HE DEFINITELY SAID, "I WAS." AS IN HIM. NOT ME!
WHO?
ME. UGH... LOOK, PIPER--
PIED PIPER!
PIED PIPER, DO YOU KNOW WHAT YOUR "KING" HAS AGAINST KID FLASH?
WHO AM I DEALING WITH HERE?
YOU WANT TO KNOW THE GREAT STORY, HMM?
ALL OF YOU. LISTEN TO THE TALE OF OUR BLESSED LEADER--
--THE KING OF EASTWIND, BROTHER GRIMM!

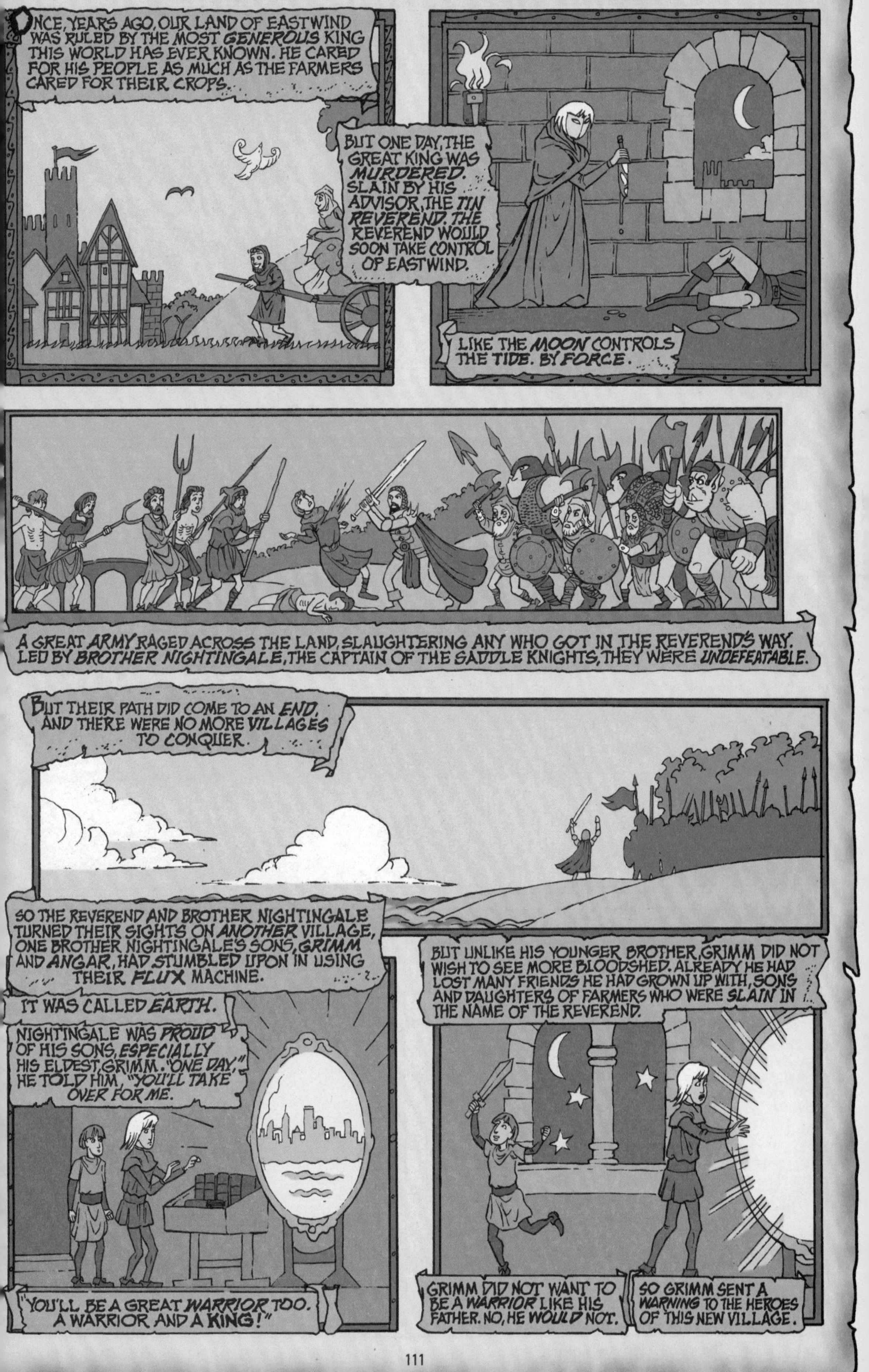
ONCE, YEARS AGO, OUR LAND OF EASTWIND WAS RULED BY THE MOST GENEROUS KING THIS WORLD HAS EVER KNOWN. HE CARED FOR HIS PEOPLE AS MUCH AS THE FARMERS CARED FOR THEIR CROPS.
BUT ONE DAY, THE GREAT KING WAS MURDERED. SLAIN BY HIS ADVISOR, THE TIN REVEREND. THE REVEREND WOULD SOON TAKE CONTROL OF EASTWIND.
LIKE THE MOON CONTROLS THE TIDE. BY FORCE.
A GREAT ARMY RAGED ACROSS THE LAND, SLAUGHTERING ANY WHO GOT IN THE REVEREND'S WAY. LED BY BROTHER NIGHTINGALE, THE CAPTAIN OF THE SADDLE KNIGHTS, THEY WERE UNDEFEATABLE.
BUT THEIR PATH DID COME TO AN END, AND THERE WERE NO MORE VILLAGES TO CONQUER.
SO THE REVEREND AND BROTHER NIGHTINGALE TURNED THEIR SIGHTS ON ANOTHER VILLAGE, ONE BROTHER NIGHTINGALE'S SONS, GRIMM AND ANGAR, HAD STUMBLED UPON IN USING THEIR FLUX MACHINE.
IT WAS CALLED EARTH.
NIGHTINGALE WAS PROUD OF HIS SONS, ESPECIALLY HIS ELDEST, GRIMM. "ONE DAY," HE TOLD HIM, "YOU'LL TAKE OVER FOR ME.
"YOU'LL BE A GREAT WARRIOR TOO. A WARRIOR AND A KING!"
BUT UNLIKE HIS YOUNGER BROTHER, GRIMM DID NOT WISH TO SEE MORE BLOODSHED. ALREADY HE HAD LOST MANY FRIENDS HE HAD GROWN UP WITH, SONS AND DAUGHTERS OF FARMERS WHO WERE SLAIN IN THE NAME OF THE REVEREND.
GRIMM DID NOT WANT TO BE A WARRIOR LIKE HIS FATHER. NO, HE WOULD NOT.
SO GRIMM SENT A WARNING TO THE HEROES OF THIS NEW VILLAGE.

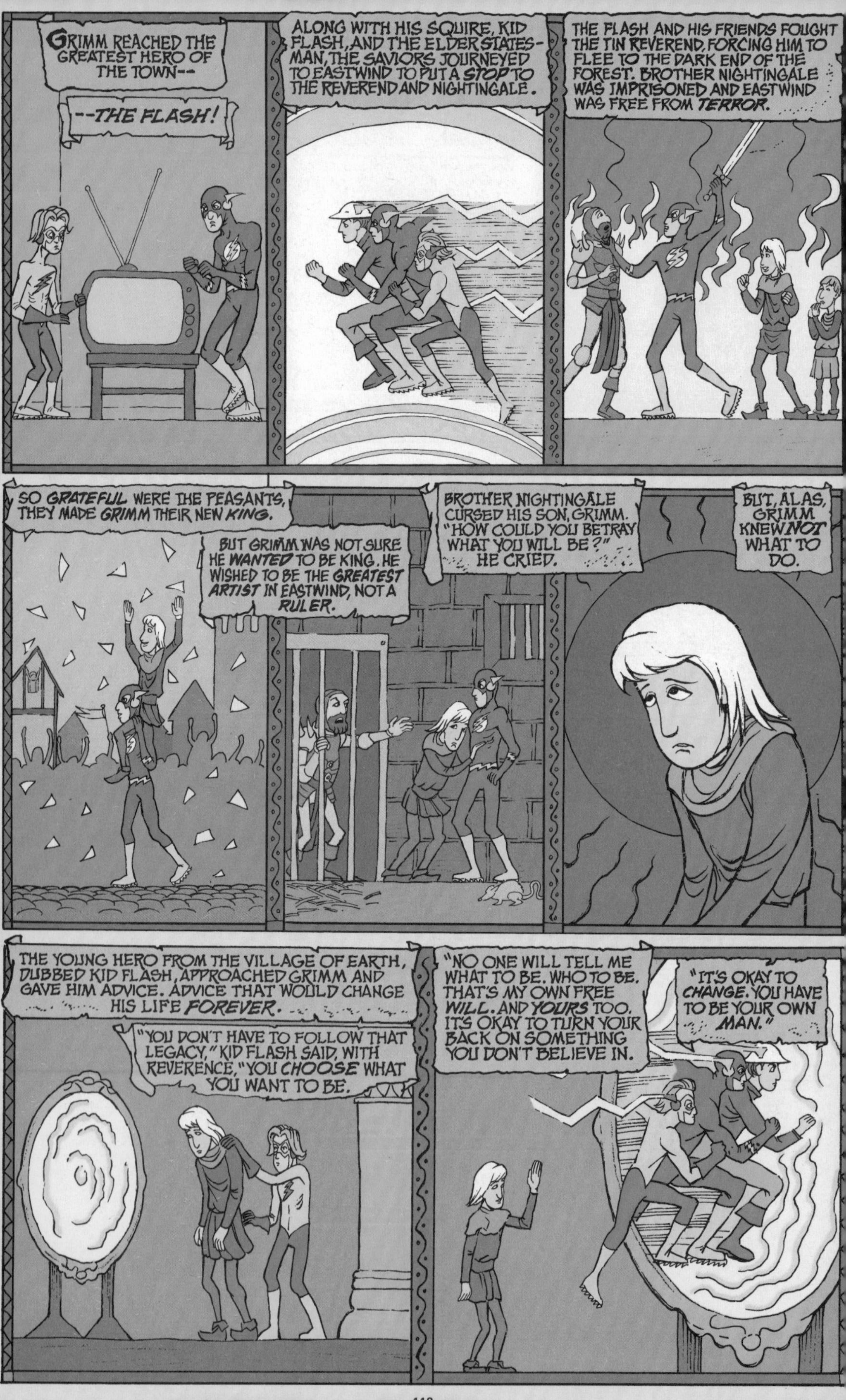
GRIMM REACHED THE GREATEST HERO OF THE TOWN--
--THE FLASH!
ALONG WITH HIS SQUIRE, KID FLASH, AND THE ELDER STATESMAN, THE SAVIORS JOURNEYED TO EASTWIND TO PUT A STOP TO THE REVEREND AND NIGHTINGALE.
THE FLASH AND HIS FRIENDS FOUGHT THE TIN REVEREND, FORCING HIM TO FLEE TO THE DARK END OF THE FOREST. BROTHER NIGHTINGALE WAS IMPRISONED AND EASTWIND WAS FREE FROM TERROR.
SO GRATEFUL WERE THE PEASANTS, THEY MADE GRIMM THEIR NEW KING.
BUT GRIMM WAS NOT SURE HE WANTED TO BE KING. HE WISHED TO BE THE GREATEST ARTIST IN EASTWIND, NOT A RULER.
BROTHER NIGHTINGALE CURSED HIS SON, GRIMM. "HOW COULD YOU BETRAY WHAT YOU WILL BE?" HE CRIED.
BUT, ALAS, GRIMM KNEW NOT WHAT TO DO.
THE YOUNG HERO FROM THE VILLAGE OF EARTH, DUBBED KID FLASH, APPROACHED GRIMM AND GAVE HIM ADVICE. ADVICE THAT WOULD CHANGE HIS LIFE FOREVER.
"YOU DON'T HAVE TO FOLLOW THAT LEGACY," KID FLASH SAID, WITH REVERENCE, "YOU CHOOSE WHAT YOU WANT TO BE.
"NO ONE WILL TELL ME WHAT TO BE. WHO TO BE. THAT'S MY OWN FREE WILL. AND YOURS TOO. IT'S OKAY TO TURN YOUR BACK ON SOMETHING YOU DON'T BELIEVE IN.
"IT'S OKAY TO CHANGE. YOU HAVE TO BE YOUR OWN MAN."

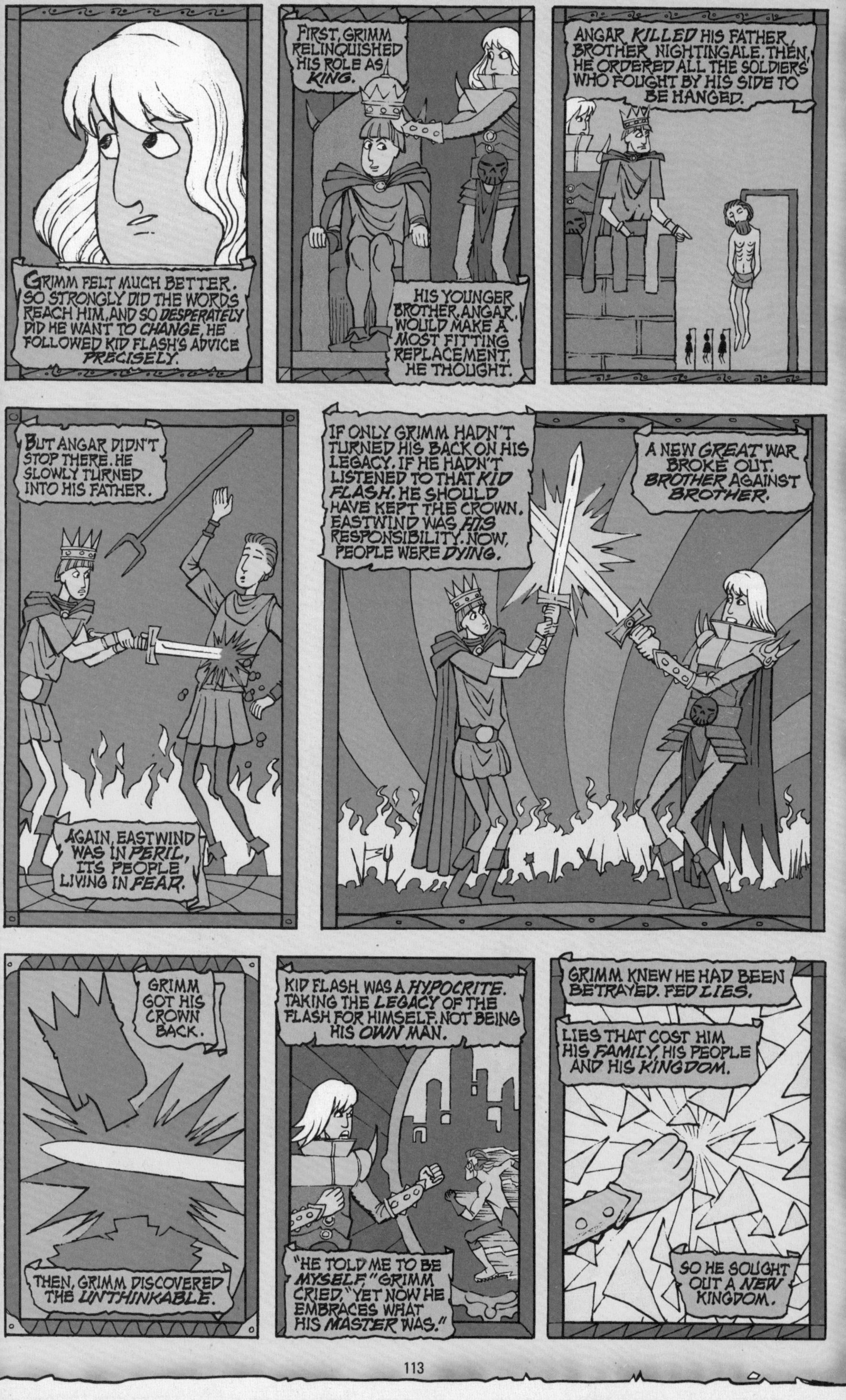
GRIMM FELT MUCH BETTER. SO STRONGLY DID THE WORDS REACH HIM, AND SO DESPERATELY DID HE WANT TO CHANGE, HE FOLLOWED KID FLASH'S ADVICE PRECISELY.
FIRST, GRIMM RELINQUISHED HIS ROLE AS KING.
HIS YOUNGER BROTHER, ANGAR, WOULD MAKE A MOST FITTING REPLACEMENT, HE THOUGHT.
ANGAR KILLED HIS FATHER, BROTHER NIGHTINGALE. THEN, HE ORDERED ALL THE SOLDIERS WHO FOUGHT BY HIS SIDE TO BE HANGED.
BUT ANGAR DIDN'T STOP THERE. HE SLOWLY TURNED INTO HIS FATHER.
AGAIN, EASTWIND WAS IN PERIL, ITS PEOPLE LIVING IN FEAR.
IF ONLY GRIMM HADN'T TURNED HIS BACK ON HIS LEGACY. IF HE HADN'T LISTENED TO THAT KID FLASH. HE SHOULD HAVE KEPT THE CROWN. EASTWIND WAS HIS RESPONSIBILITY. NOW, PEOPLE WERE DYING.
A NEW GREAT WAR BROKE OUT. BROTHER AGAINST BROTHER.
GRIMM GOT HIS CROWN BACK.
THEN, GRIMM DISCOVERED THE UNTHINKABLE.
KID FLASH WAS A HYPOCRITE. TAKING THE LEGACY OF THE FLASH FOR HIMSELF. NOT BEING HIS OWN MAN.
"HE TOLD ME TO BE MYSELF," GRIMM CRIED, "YET NOW HE EMBRACES WHAT HIS MASTER WAS."
GRIMM KNEW HE HAD BEEN BETRAYED. FED LIES.
LIES THAT COST HIM HIS FAMILY, HIS PEOPLE AND HIS KINGDOM.
SO HE SOUGHT OUT A NEW KINGDOM.

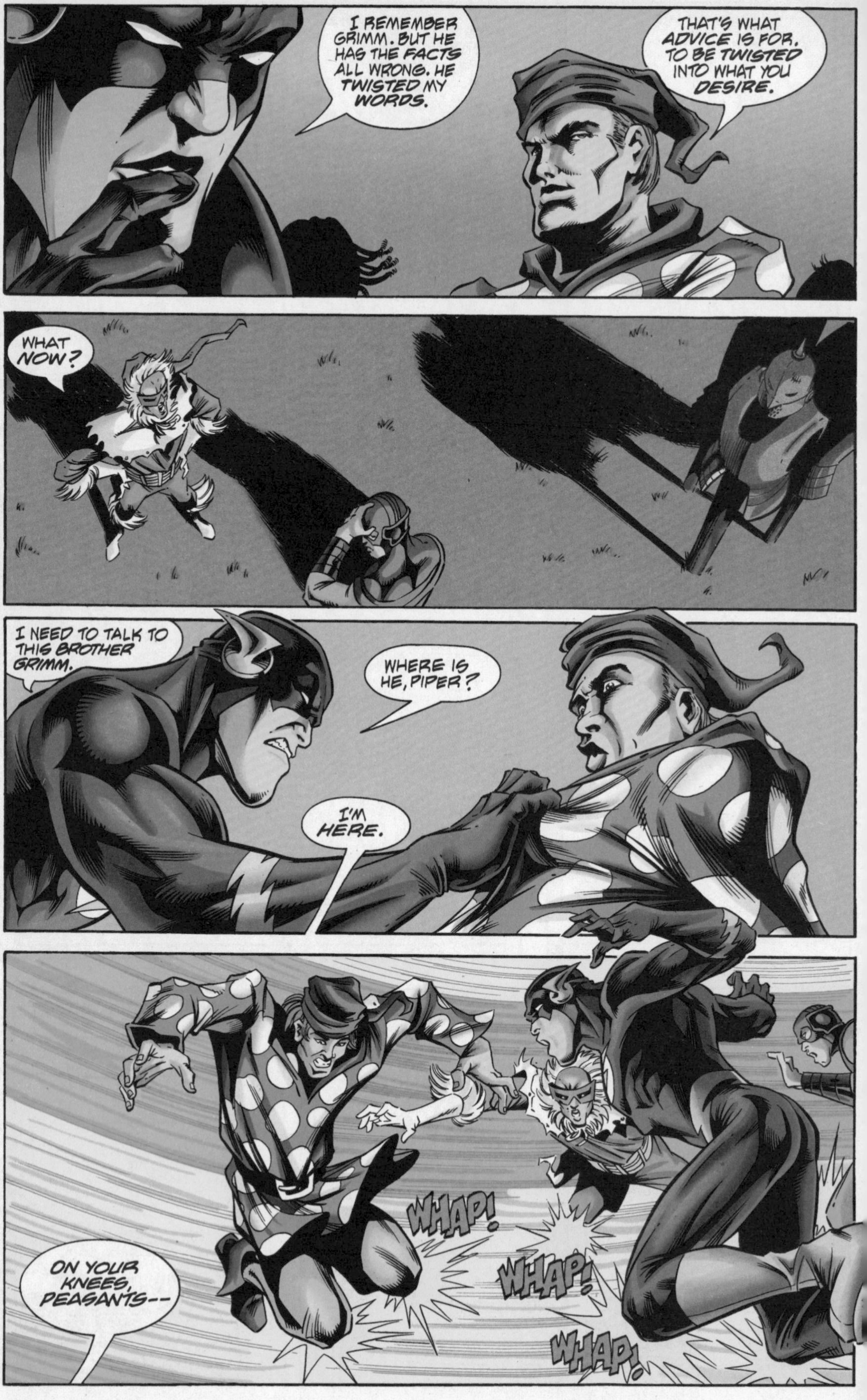
I REMEMBER GRIMM. BUT HE HAS THE FACTS ALL WRONG. HE TWISTED MY WORDS.
THAT'S WHAT ADVICE IS FOR. TO BE TWISTED INTO WHAT YOU DESIRE.
WHAT NOW?
I NEED TO TALK TO THIS BROTHER GRIMM.
WHERE IS HE, PIPER?
I'M HERE.
ON YOUR KNEES, PEASANTS--
WHAP!
WHAP!
WHAP!

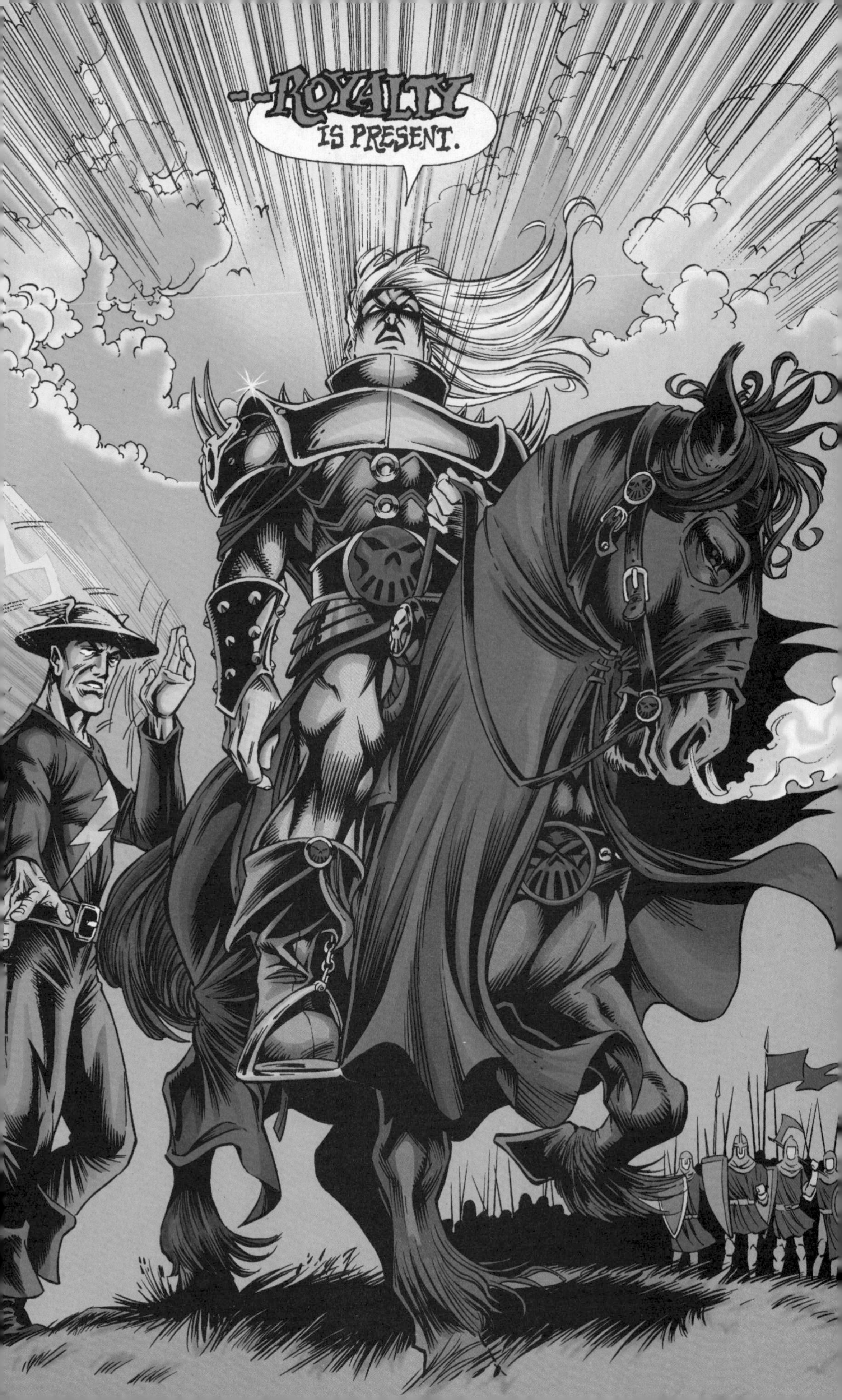
--ROYALTY IS PRESENT.

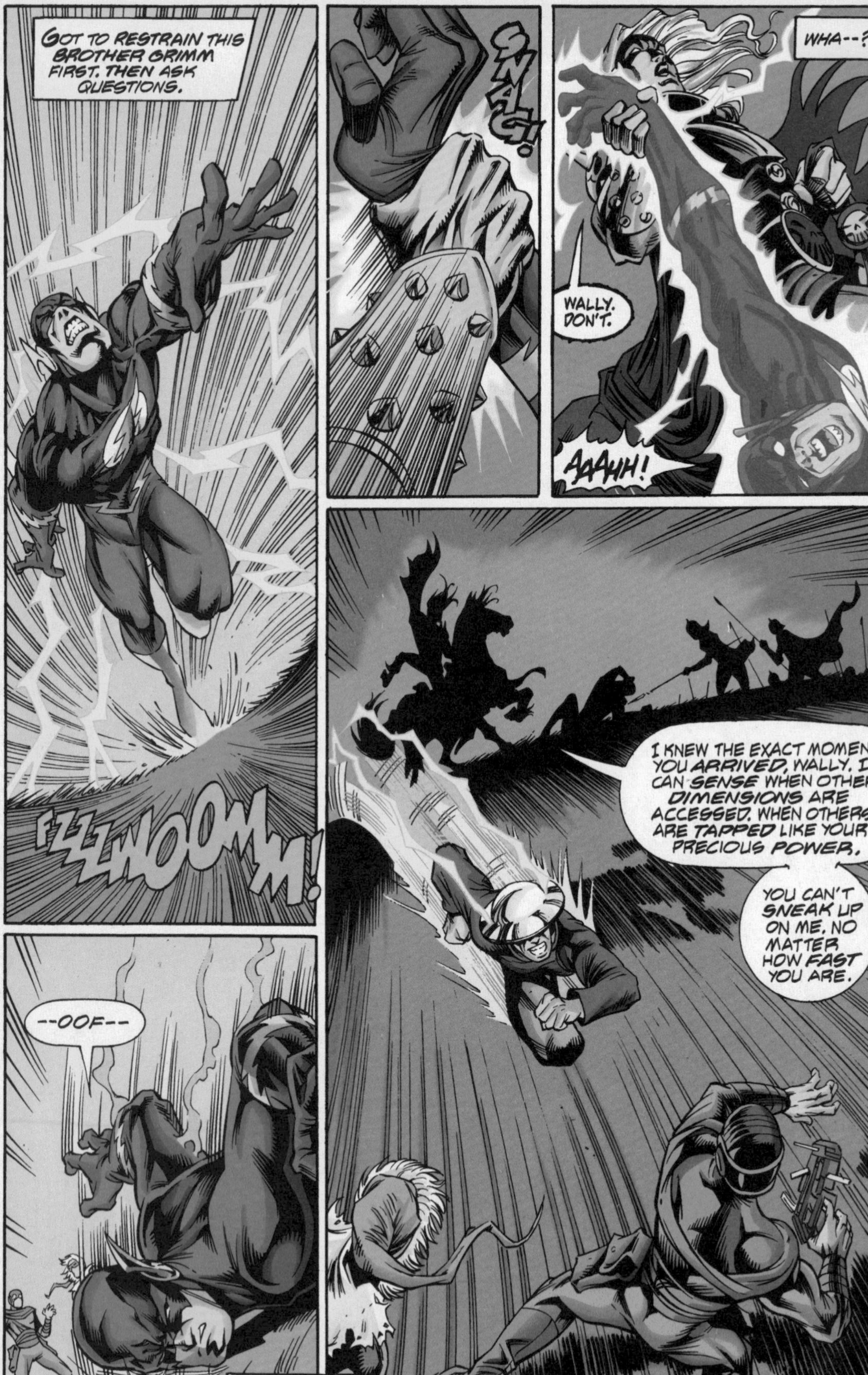
GOT TO RESTRAIN THIS BROTHER GRIMM FIRST. THEN ASK QUESTIONS.
FZZWOOMM!
SNAG!
WHA--?
WALLY. DON'T.
AAAHH!
--OOF--
WHAT'D HE DO TO ME...? HOW?
I KNEW THE EXACT MOMENT YOU ARRIVED, WALLY. I CAN SENSE WHEN OTHER DIMENSIONS ARE ACCESSED. WHEN OTHERS ARE TAPPED LIKE YOUR PRECIOUS POWER.
YOU CAN'T SNEAK UP ON ME. NO MATTER HOW FAST YOU ARE.

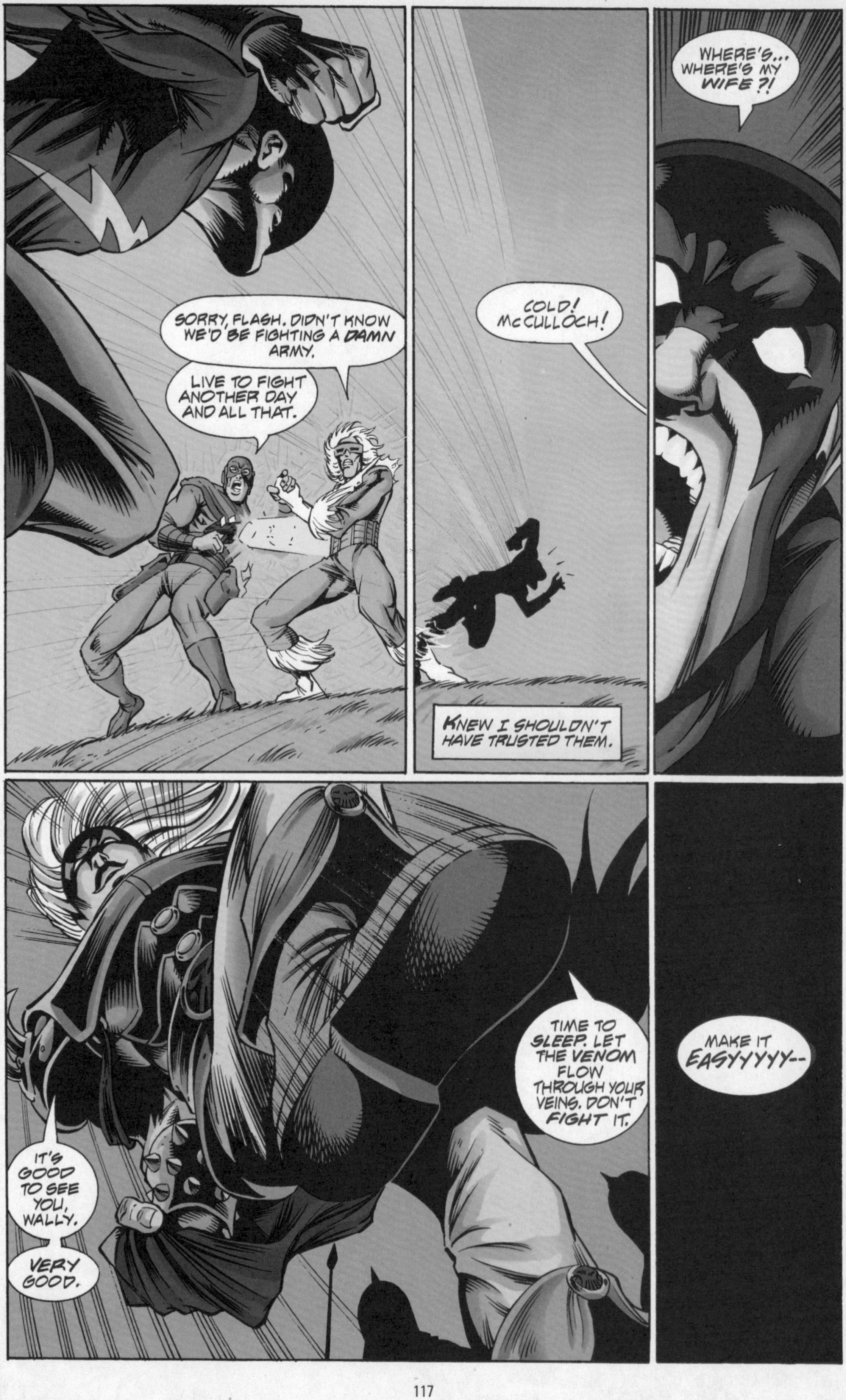
SORRY, FLASH. DIDN'T KNOW WE'D BE FIGHTING A DAMN ARMY.
LIVE TO FIGHT ANOTHER DAY AND ALL THAT.
COLD! McCULLOCH!
KNEW I SHOULDN'T HAVE TRUSTED THEM.
WHERE'S... WHERE'S MY WIFE?!
IT'S GOOD TO SEE YOU, WALLY.
VERY GOOD.
TIME TO SLEEP. LET THE VENOM FLOW THROUGH YOUR VEINS. DON'T FIGHT IT.
MAKE IT EASYYYYY--

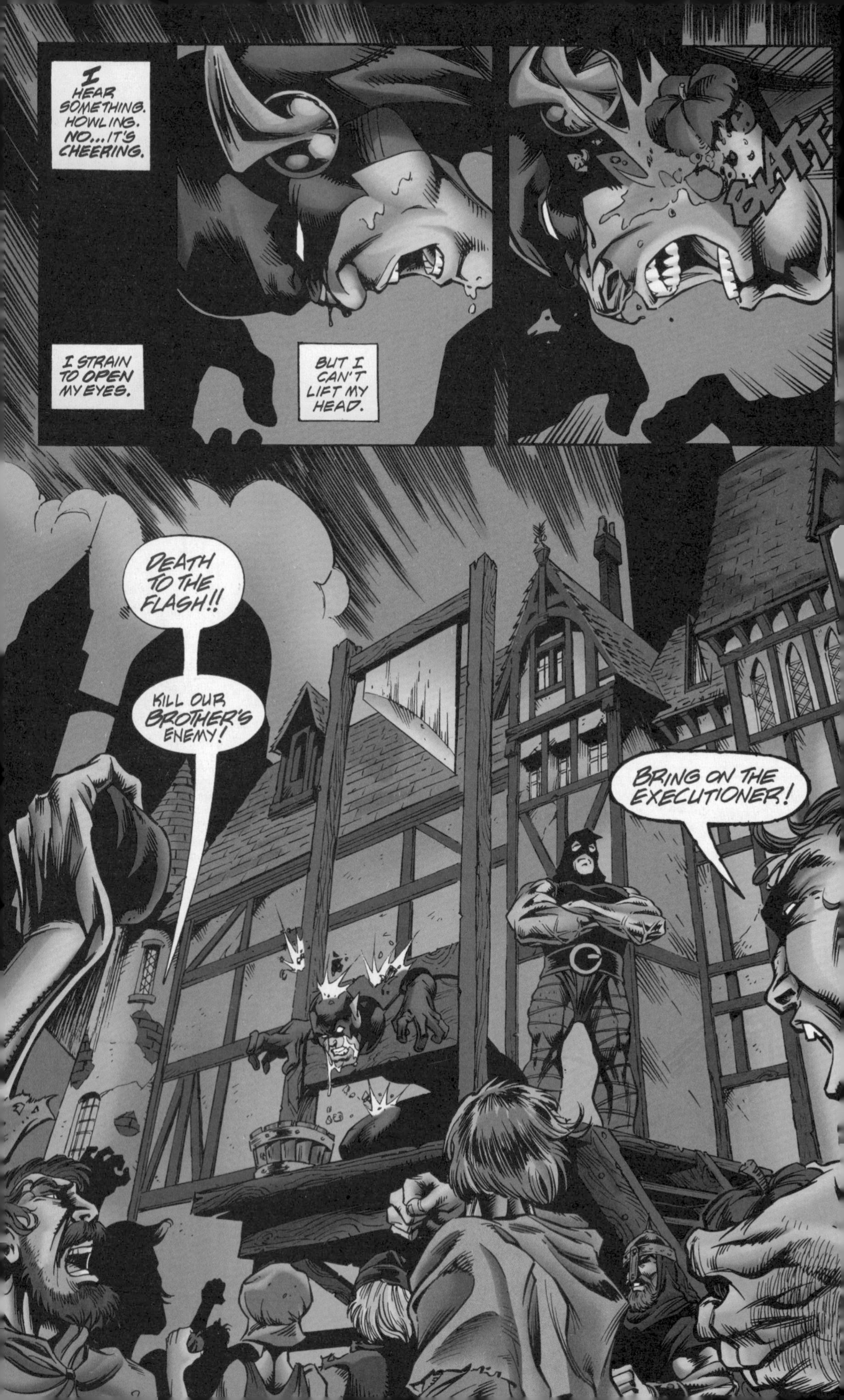

I HEAR SOMETHING. HOWLING. NO...IT'S CHEERING.
I STRAIN TO OPEN MY EYES.
BUT I CAN'T LIFT MY HEAD.
BLATT
DEATH TO THE FLASH!!
KILL OUR BROTHER'S ENEMY!
BRING ON THE EXECUTIONER!

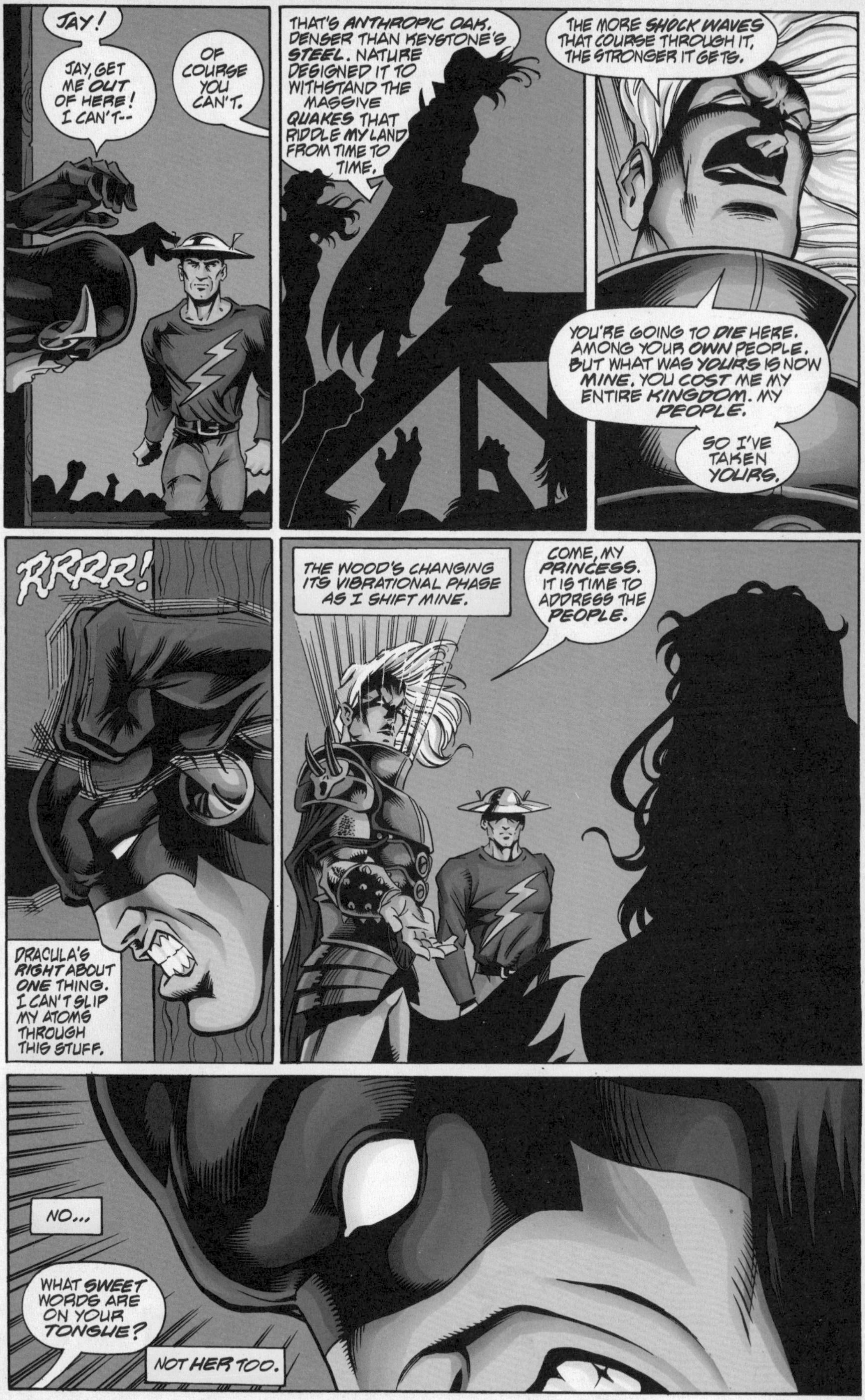
JAY!
JAY, GET ME OUT OF HERE! I CAN'T--
OF COURSE YOU CAN'T.
THAT'S ANTHROPIC OAK. DENSER THAN KEYSTONE'S STEEL. NATURE DESIGNED IT TO WITHSTAND THE MASSIVE QUAKES THAT RIDDLE MY LAND FROM TIME TO TIME.
THE MORE SHOCK WAVES THAT COURSE THROUGH IT, THE STRONGER IT GETS.
YOU'RE GOING TO DIE HERE. AMONG YOUR OWN PEOPLE. BUT WHAT WAS YOURS IS NOW MINE. YOU COST ME MY ENTIRE KINGDOM. MY PEOPLE.
SO I'VE TAKEN YOURS.
RRRR!
DRACULA'S RIGHT ABOUT ONE THING. I CAN'T SLIP MY ATOMS THROUGH THIS STUFF.
THE WOOD'S CHANGING ITS VIBRATIONAL PHASE AS I SHIFT MINE.
COME, MY PRINCESS. IT IS TIME TO ADDRESS THE PEOPLE.
NO...
WHAT SWEET WORDS ARE ON YOUR TONGUE?
NOT HER TOO.

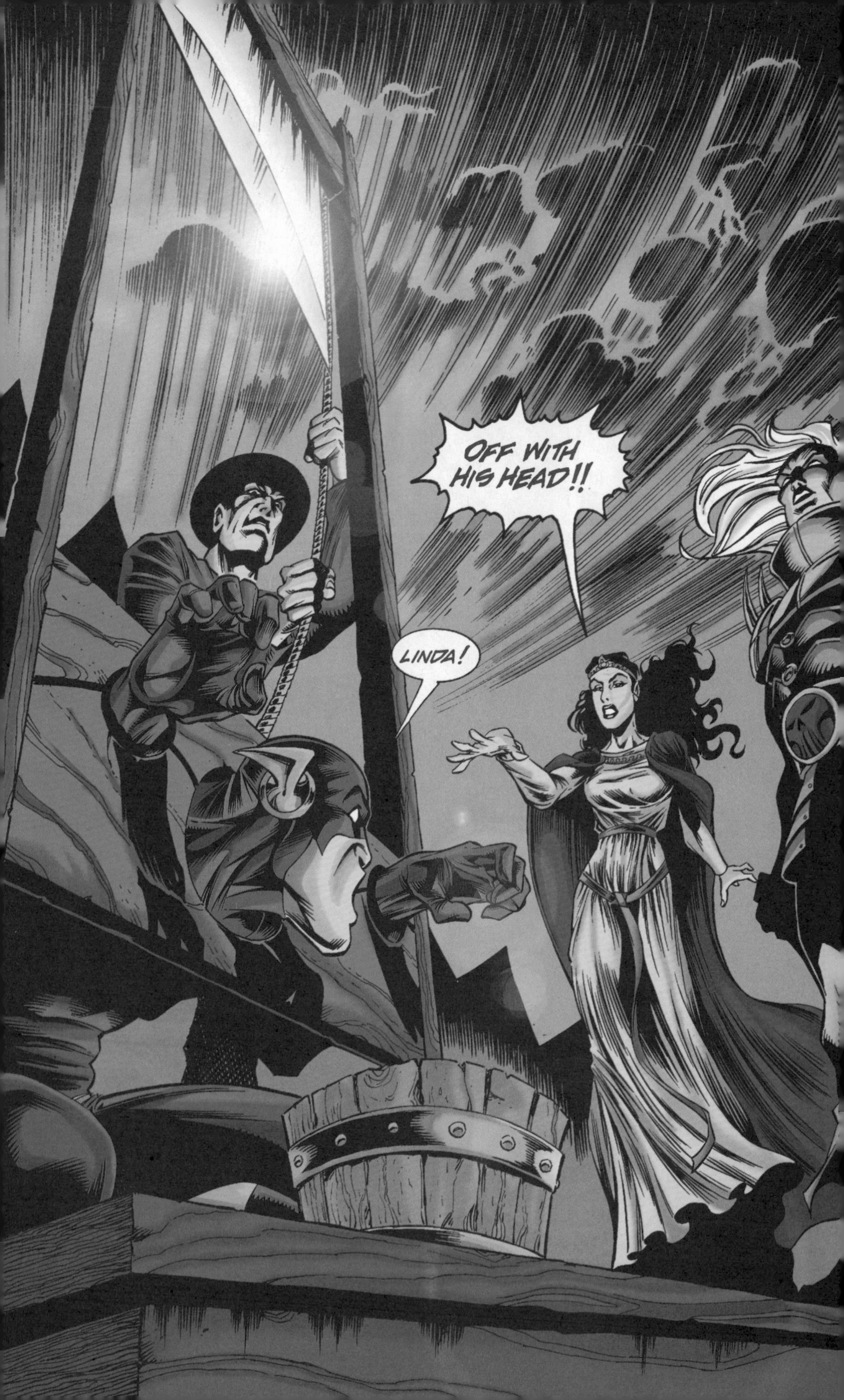
OFF WITH HIS HEAD!!
LINDA!

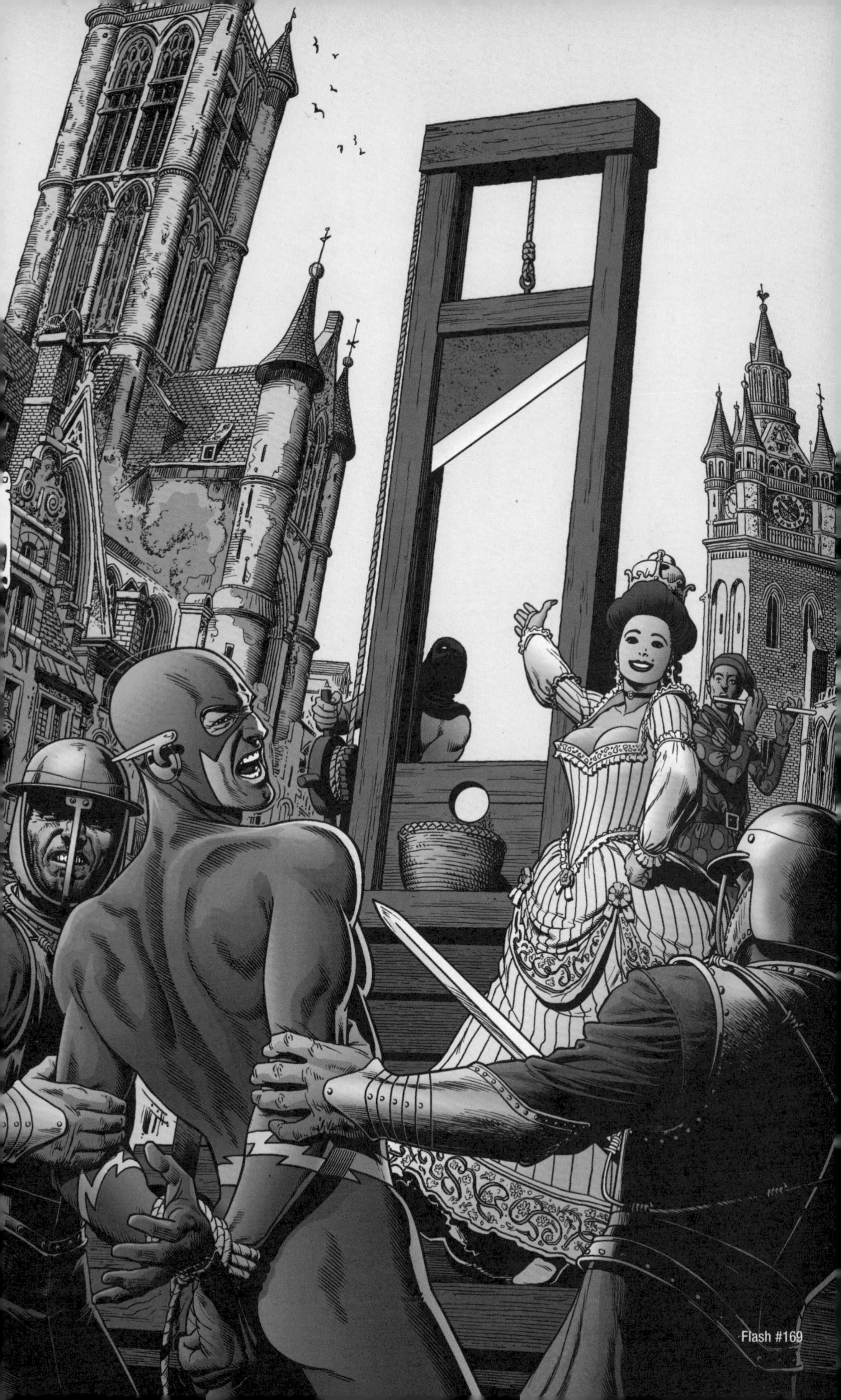

Flash #169

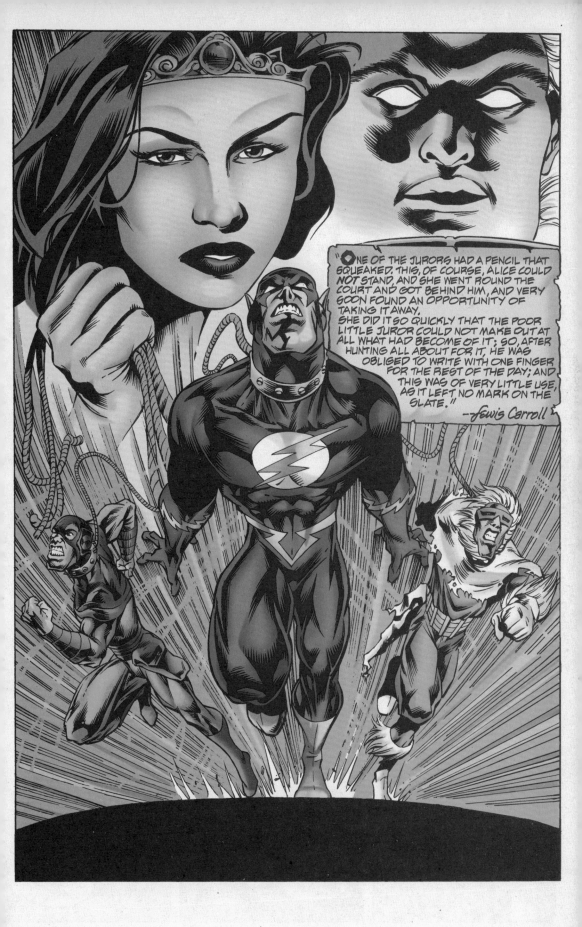

"ONE OF THE JURORS HAD A PENCIL THAT SQUEAKED. THIS, OF COURSE, ALICE COULD NOT STAND, AND SHE WENT ROUND THE COURT AND GOT BEHIND HIM, AND VERY SOON FOUND AN OPPORTUNITY OF TAKING IT AWAY.
SHE DID IT SO QUICKLY THAT THE POOR LITTLE JUROR COULD NOT MAKE OUT AT ALL WHAT HAD BECOME OF IT; SO, AFTER HUNTING ALL ABOUT FOR IT, HE WAS OBLIGED TO WRITE WITH ONE FINGER FOR THE REST OF THE DAY; AND THIS WAS OF VERY LITTLE USE, AS IT LEFT NO MARK ON THE SLATE."

—Lewis Carroll

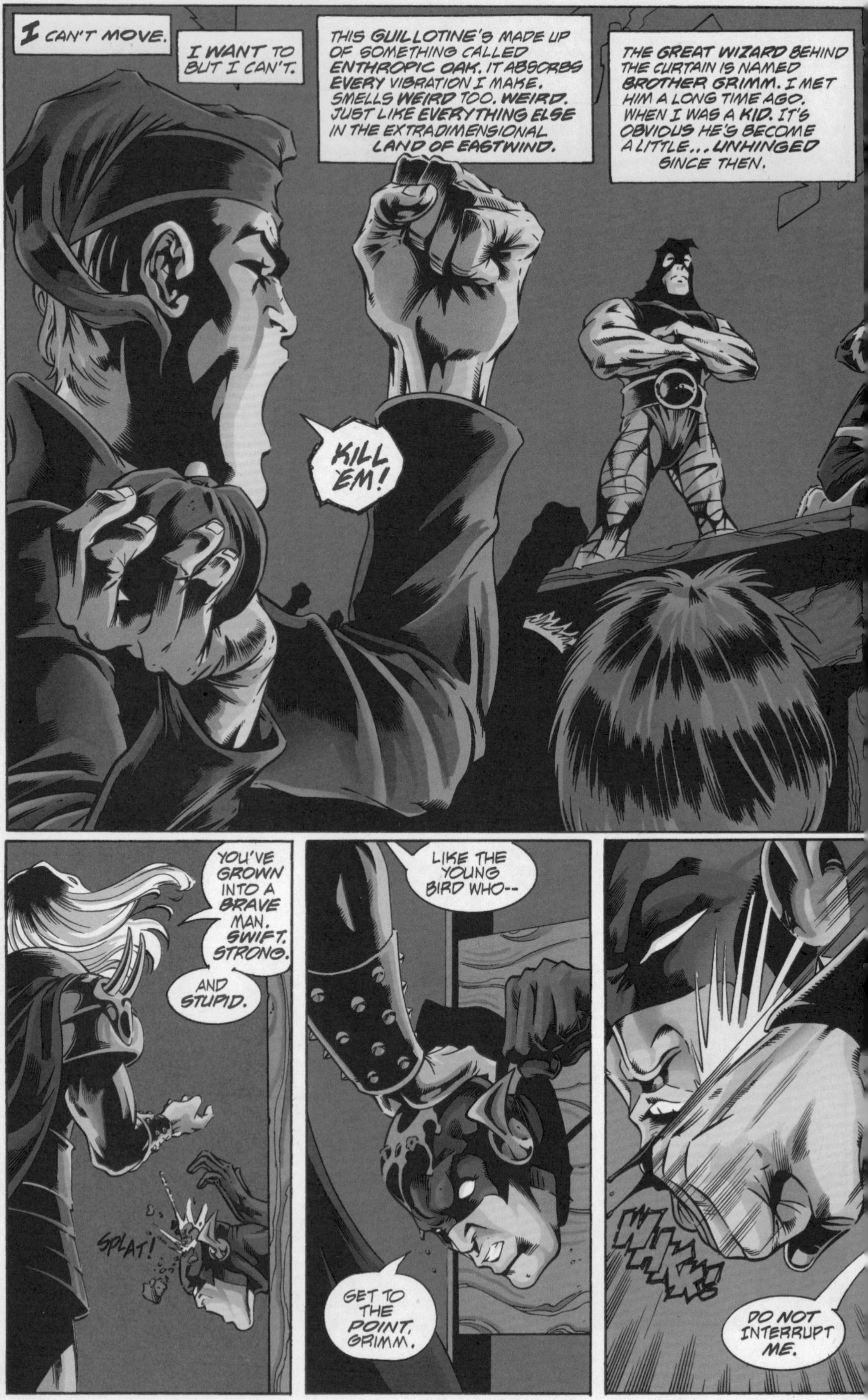

I CAN'T MOVE.
I WANT TO BUT I CAN'T.
THIS GUILLOTINE'S MADE UP OF SOMETHING CALLED ENTHROPIC OAK. IT ABSORBS EVERY VIBRATION I MAKE. SMELLS WEIRD TOO. WEIRD. JUST LIKE EVERYTHING ELSE IN THE EXTRADIMENSIONAL LAND OF EASTWIND.
THE GREAT WIZARD BEHIND THE CURTAIN IS NAMED BROTHER GRIMM. I MET HIM A LONG TIME AGO. WHEN I WAS A KID. IT'S OBVIOUS HE'S BECOME A LITTLE... UNHINGED SINCE THEN.
KILL 'EM!
YOU'VE GROWN INTO A BRAVE MAN. SWIFT. STRONG.
AND STUPID.
SPLAT!
LIKE THE YOUNG BIRD WHO--
GET TO THE POINT, GRIMM.
WHAKK!
DO NOT INTERRUPT ME.

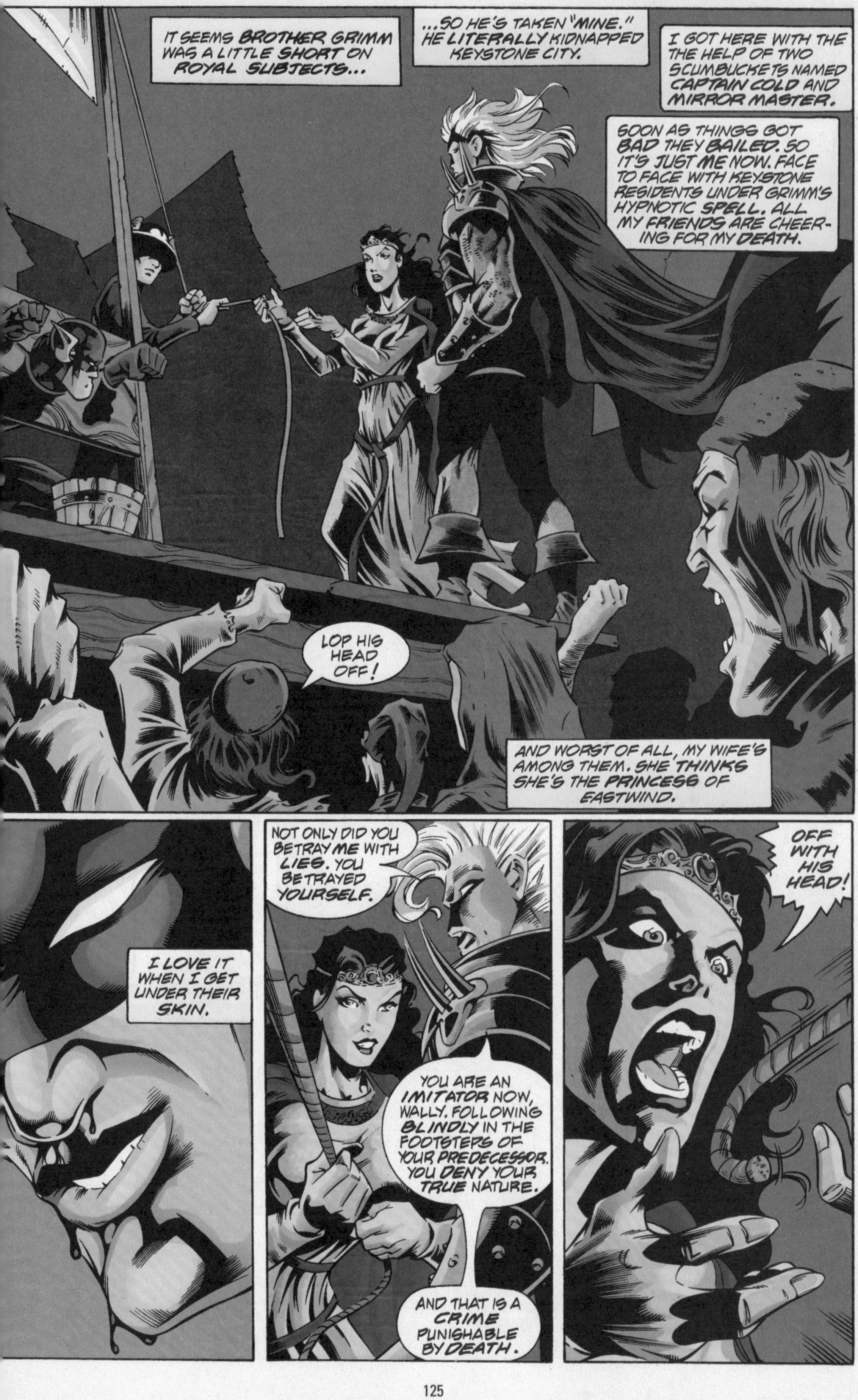

IT SEEMS BROTHER GRIMM WAS A LITTLE SHORT ON ROYAL SUBJECTS...
...SO HE'S TAKEN "MINE." HE LITERALLY KIDNAPPED KEYSTONE CITY.
I GOT HERE WITH THE THE HELP OF TWO SCUMBUCKETS NAMED CAPTAIN COLD AND MIRROR MASTER.
SOON AS THINGS GOT BAD THEY BAILED. SO IT'S JUST ME NOW. FACE TO FACE WITH KEYSTONE RESIDENTS UNDER GRIMM'S HYPNOTIC SPELL. ALL MY FRIENDS ARE CHEERING FOR MY DEATH.
LOP HIS HEAD OFF!
AND WORST OF ALL, MY WIFE'S AMONG THEM. SHE THINKS SHE'S THE PRINCESS OF EASTWIND.
I LOVE IT WHEN I GET UNDER THEIR SKIN.
NOT ONLY DID YOU BETRAY ME WITH LIES. YOU BETRAYED YOURSELF.
YOU ARE AN IMITATOR NOW, WALLY. FOLLOWING BLINDLY IN THE FOOTSTEPS OF YOUR PREDECESSOR. YOU DENY YOUR TRUE NATURE.
AND THAT IS A CRIME PUNISHABLE BY DEATH.
OFF WITH HIS HEAD!

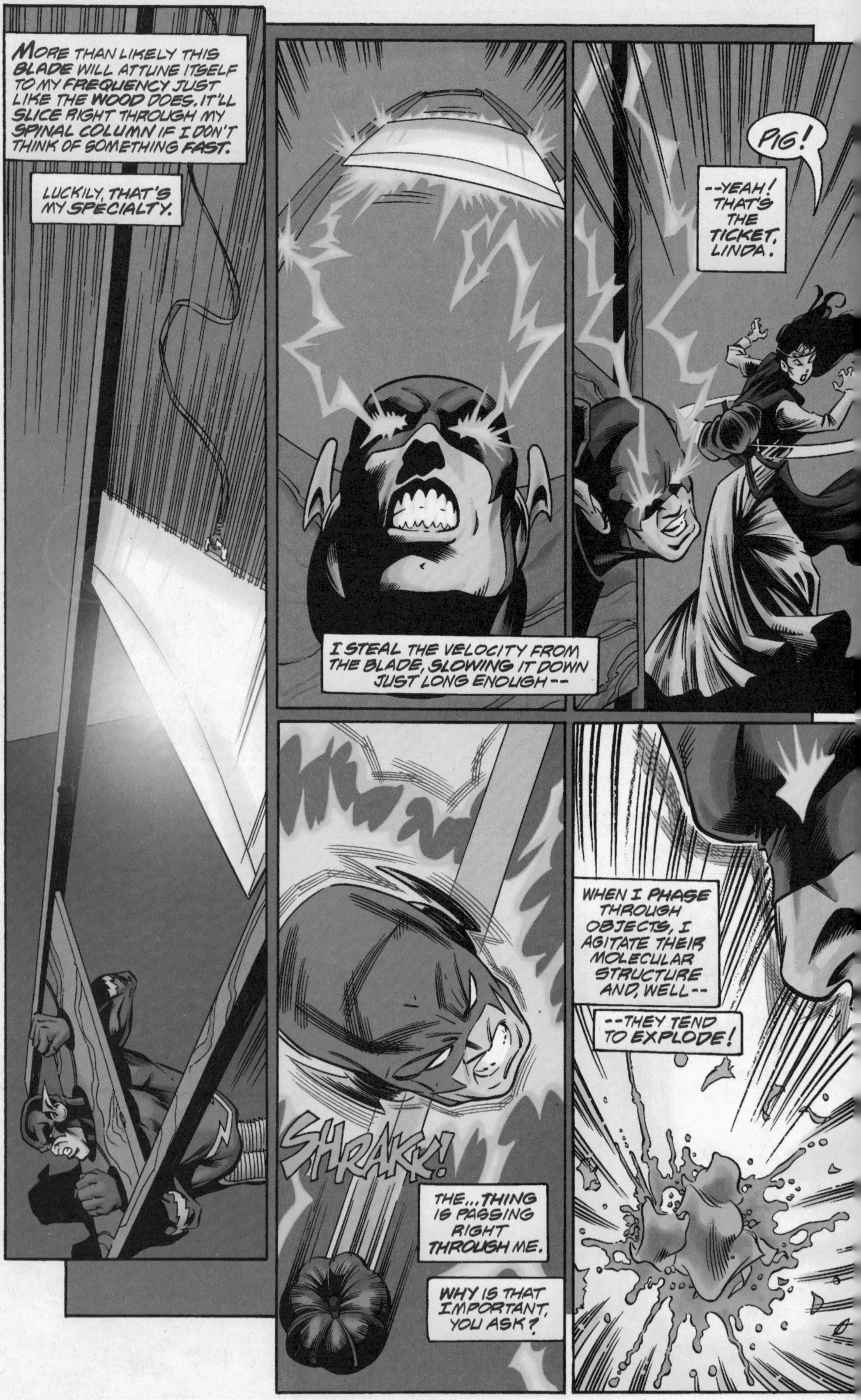

MORE THAN LIKELY THIS BLADE WILL ATTUNE ITSELF TO MY FREQUENCY JUST LIKE THE WOOD DOES. IT'LL SLICE RIGHT THROUGH MY SPINAL COLUMN IF I DON'T THINK OF SOMETHING FAST.
LUCKILY, THAT'S MY SPECIALTY.
I STEAL THE VELOCITY FROM THE BLADE, SLOWING IT DOWN JUST LONG ENOUGH--
PIG!
--YEAH! THAT'S THE TICKET, LINDA.
SHRAKK!
THE...THING IS PASSING RIGHT THROUGH ME.
WHY IS THAT IMPORTANT, YOU ASK?
WHEN I PHASE THROUGH OBJECTS, I AGITATE THEIR MOLECULAR STRUCTURE AND, WELL--
--THEY TEND TO EXPLODE!

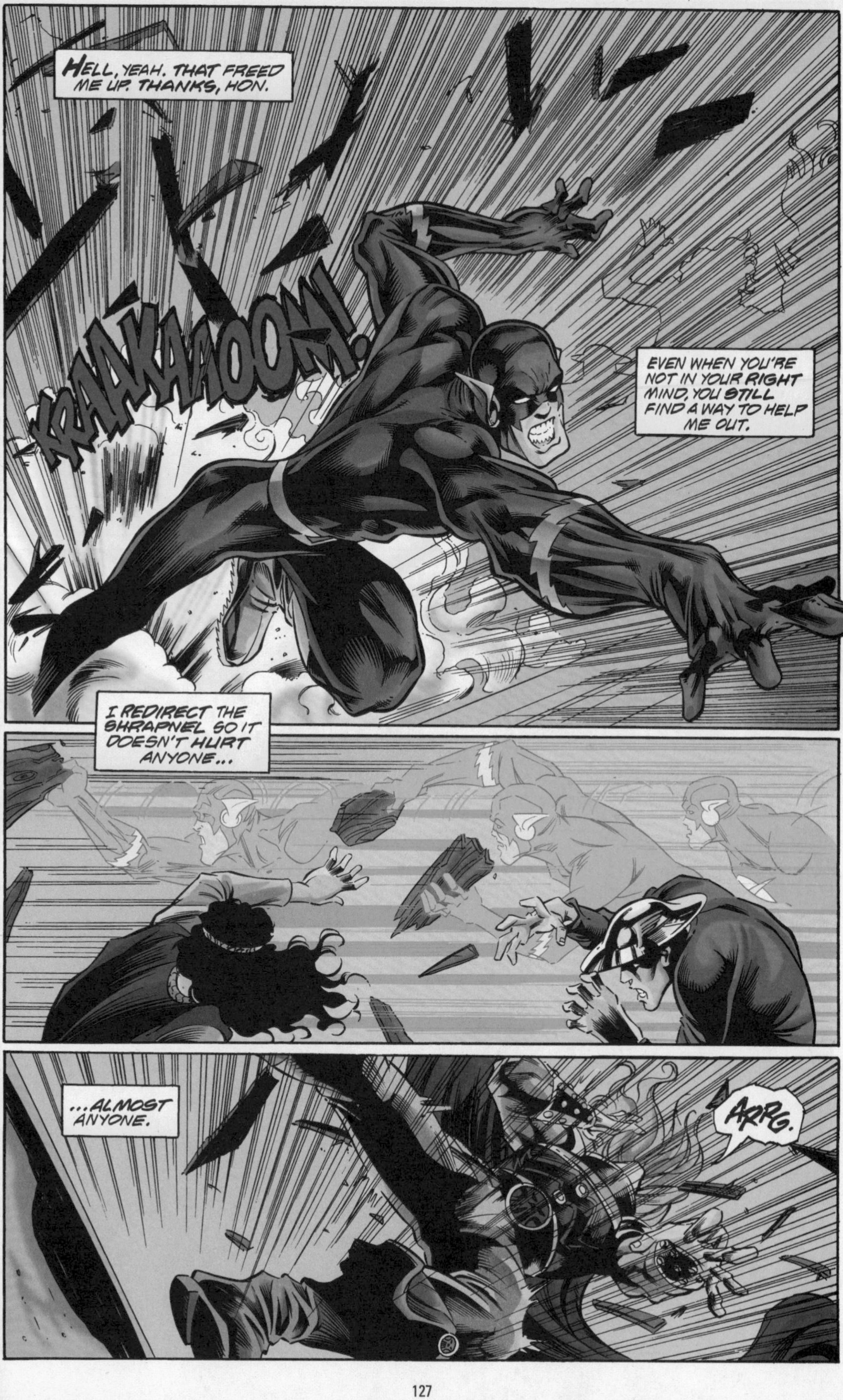
HELL, YEAH. THAT FREED ME UP. THANKS, HON.
KRAAKAAOOM!
EVEN WHEN YOU'RE NOT IN YOUR RIGHT MIND, YOU STILL FIND A WAY TO HELP ME OUT.
I REDIRECT THE SHRAPNEL SO IT DOESN'T HURT ANYONE...
...ALMOST ANYONE.
ARRG.

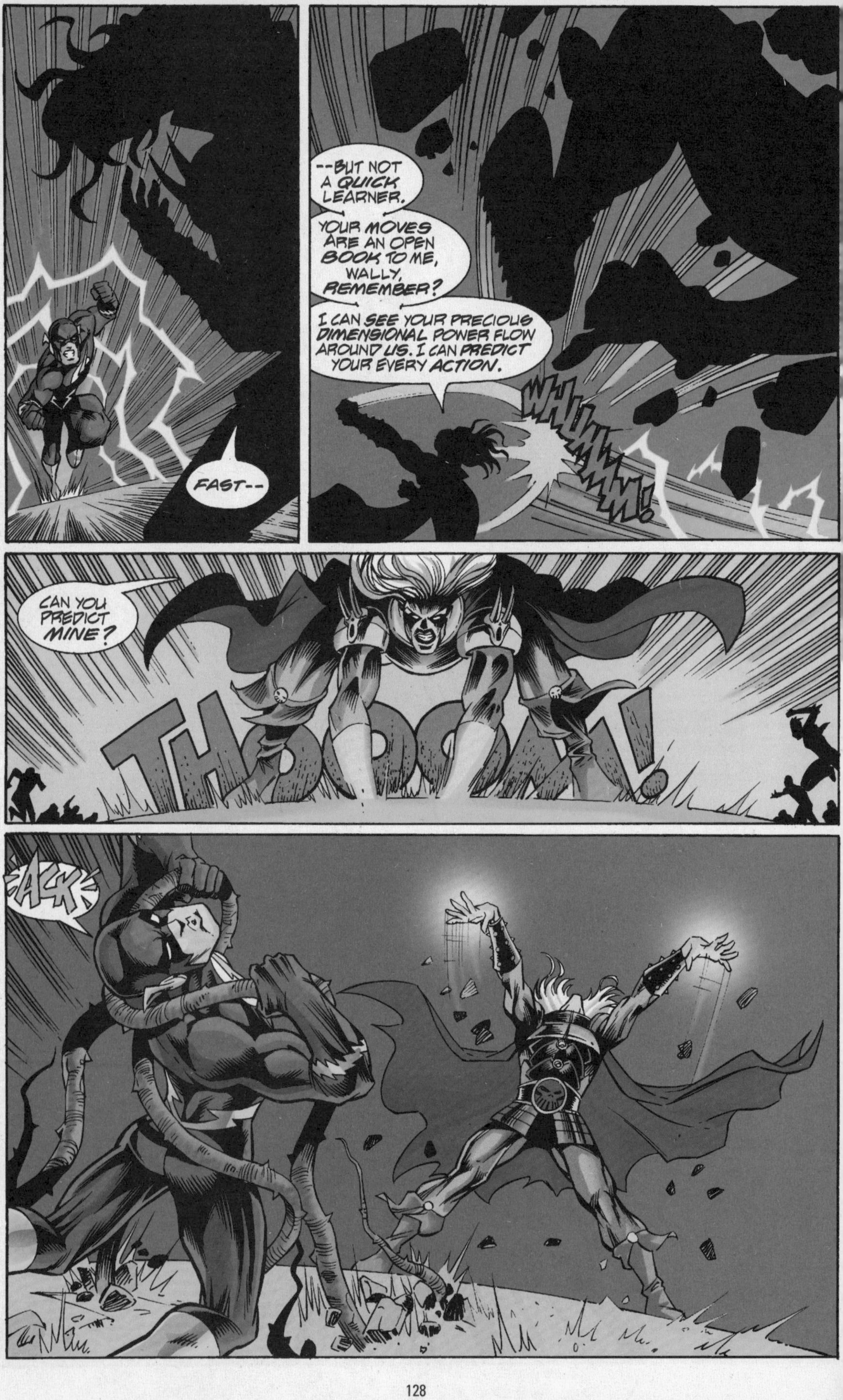
FAST--
--BUT NOT A QUICK LEARNER.
YOUR MOVES ARE AN OPEN BOOK TO ME, WALLY, REMEMBER?
I CAN SEE YOUR PRECIOUS DIMENSIONAL POWER FLOW AROUND US. I CAN PREDICT YOUR EVERY ACTION.
WHUMMM!
CAN YOU PREDICT MINE?
THOOOM!
ACK

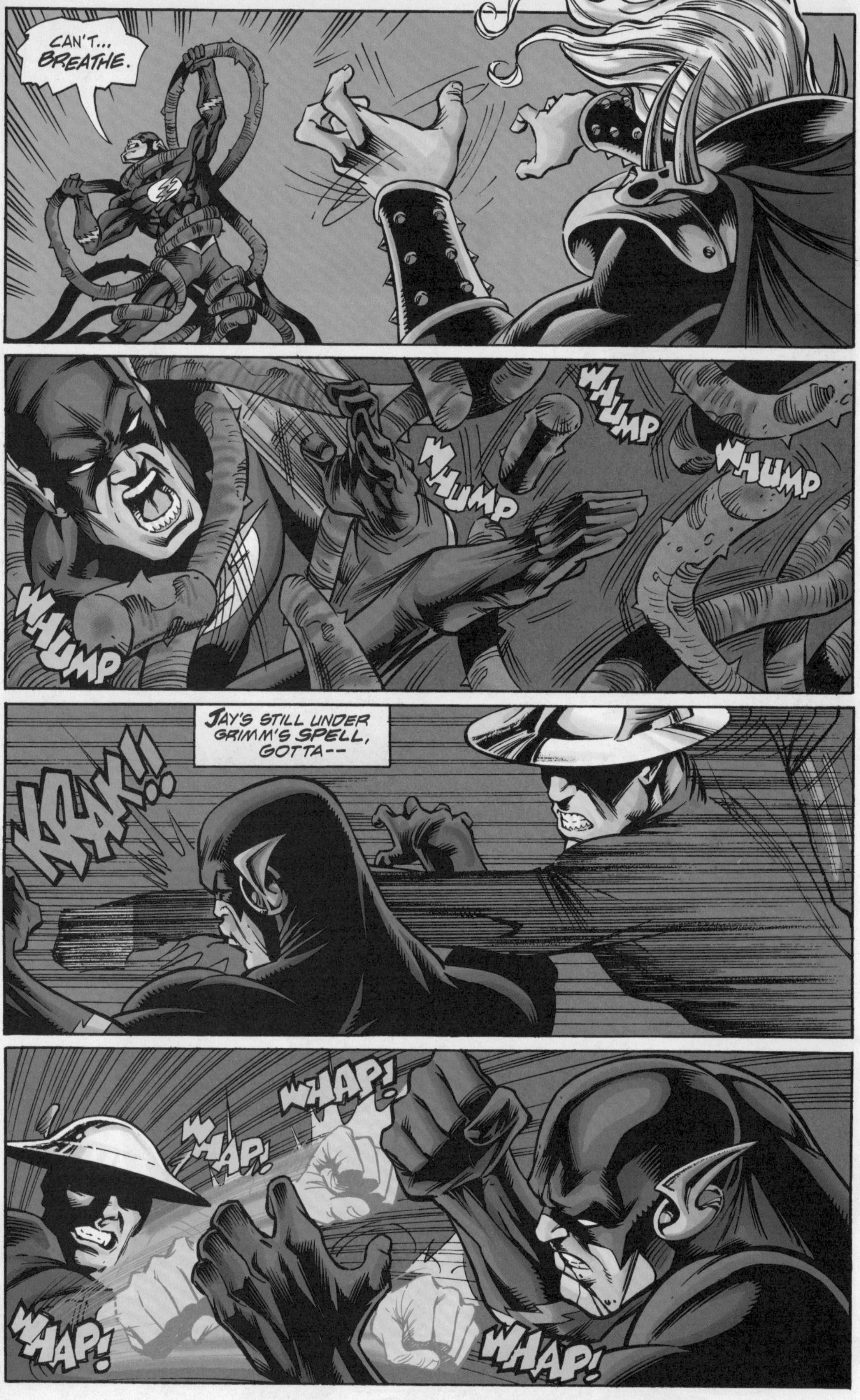
CAN'T... BREATHE.
WHUMP
WHUMP
WHUMP
WHUMP
JAY'S STILL UNDER GRIMM'S SPELL, GOTTA--
KRAK!!
WHAP!
WHAP!
WHAP!
WHAP!

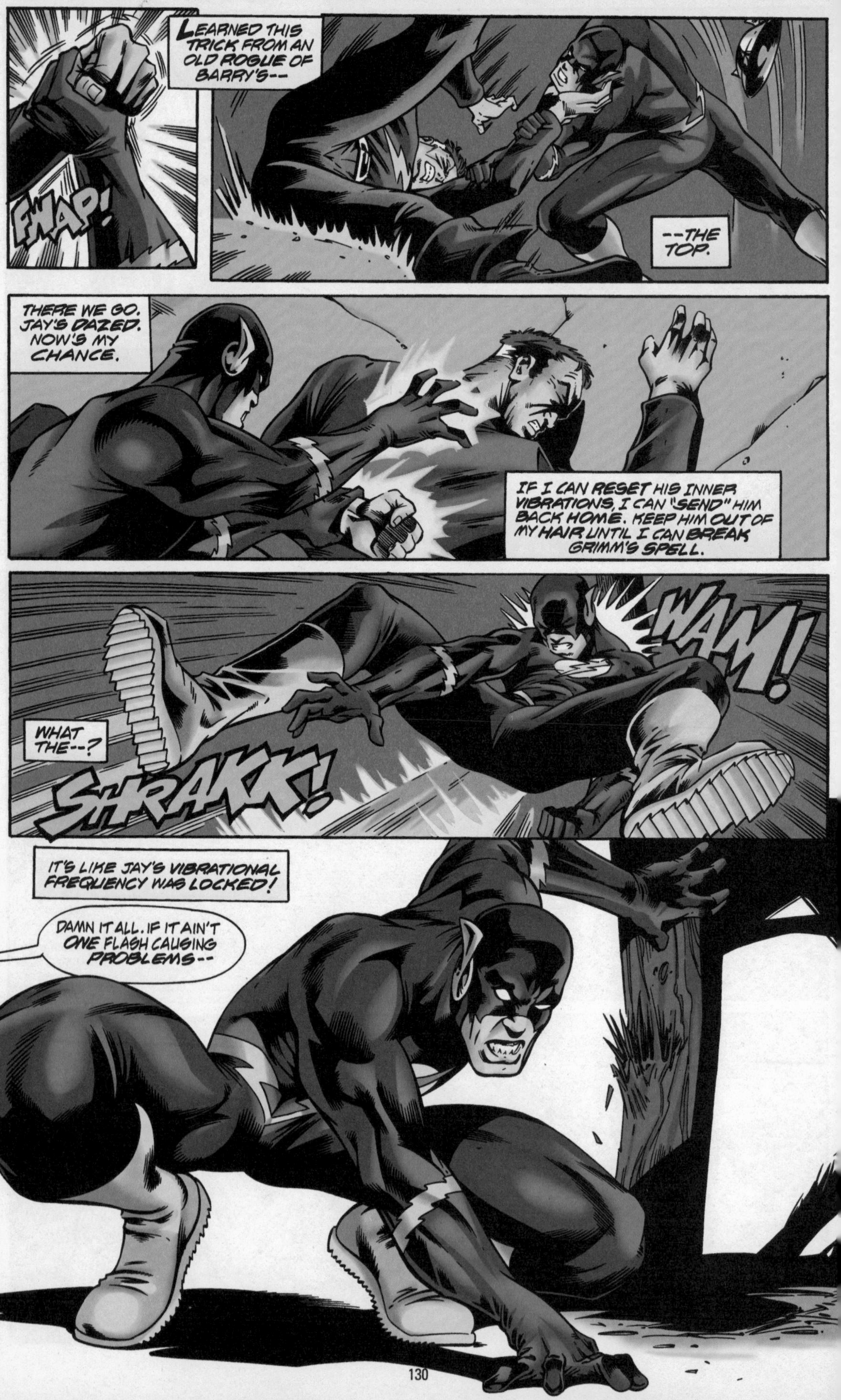
FWAP!
LEARNED THIS TRICK FROM AN OLD ROGUE OF BARRY'S--
--THE TOP.
THERE WE GO. JAY'S DAZED. NOW'S MY CHANCE.
IF I CAN RESET HIS INNER VIBRATIONS, I CAN "SEND" HIM BACK HOME. KEEP HIM OUT OF MY HAIR UNTIL I CAN BREAK GRIMM'S SPELL.
WAM!
WHAT THE--?
SHRAKK!
IT'S LIKE JAY'S VIBRATIONAL FREQUENCY WAS LOCKED!
DAMN IT ALL. IF IT AIN'T ONE FLASH CAUSING PROBLEMS--

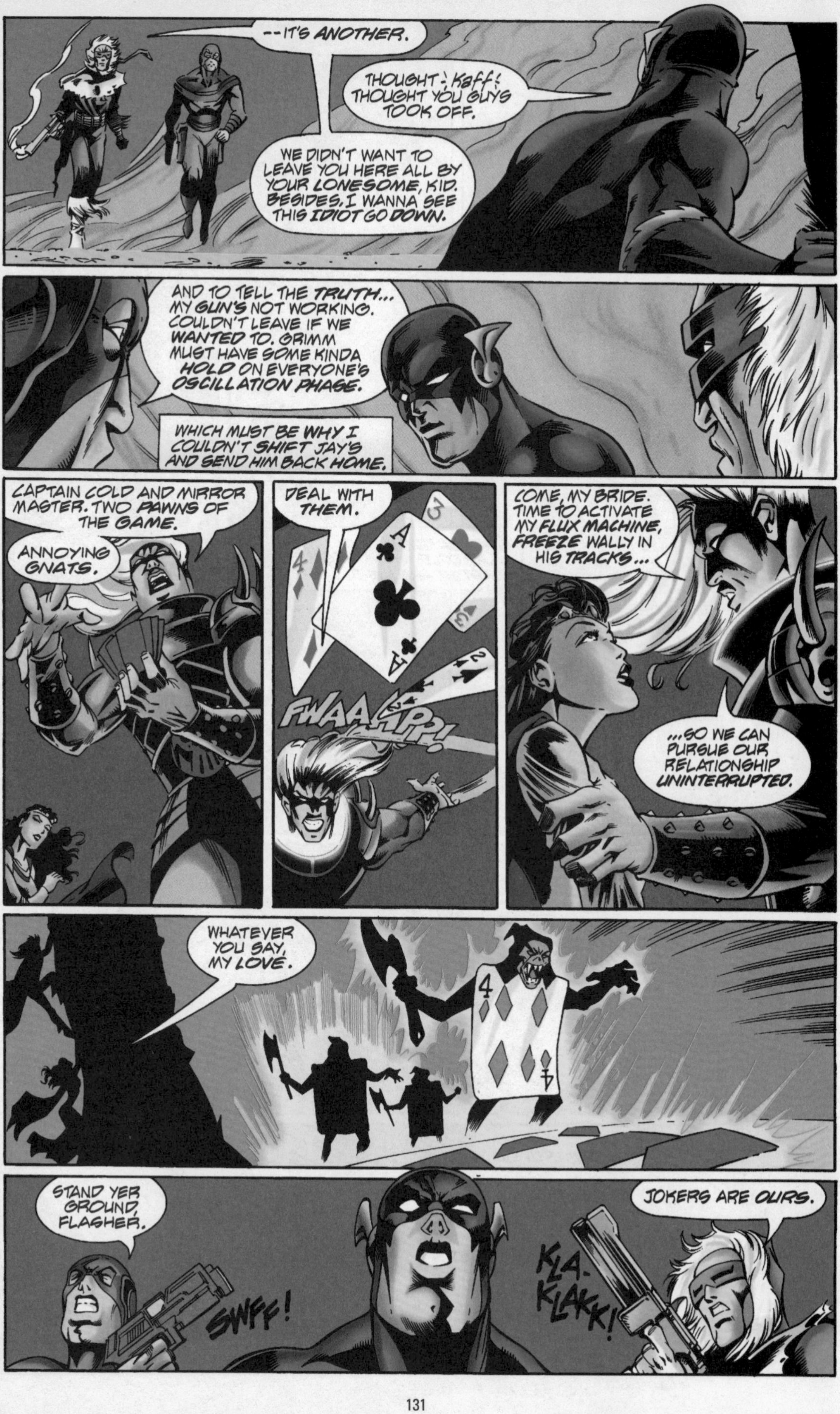
--IT'S ANOTHER.
THOUGHT--Kaff!--THOUGHT YOU GUYS TOOK OFF.
WE DIDN'T WANT TO LEAVE YOU HERE ALL BY YOUR LONESOME, KID. BESIDES, I WANNA SEE THIS IDIOT GO DOWN.
AND TO TELL THE TRUTH... MY GUN'S NOT WORKING. COULDN'T LEAVE IF WE WANTED TO. GRIMM MUST HAVE SOME KINDA HOLD ON EVERYONE'S OSCILLATION PHASE.
WHICH MUST BE WHY I COULDN'T SHIFT JAY'S AND SEND HIM BACK HOME.
CAPTAIN COLD AND MIRROR MASTER. TWO PAWNS OF THE GAME.
ANNOYING GNATS.
DEAL WITH THEM.
FWAASHPP!
COME, MY BRIDE. TIME TO ACTIVATE MY FLUX MACHINE, FREEZE WALLY IN HIS TRACKS...
...SO WE CAN PURSUE OUR RELATIONSHIP UNINTERRUPTED.
WHATEVER YOU SAY, MY LOVE.
STAND YER GROUND, FLASHER.
JOKERS ARE OURS.
SWFF!
KLA-KLAKK!

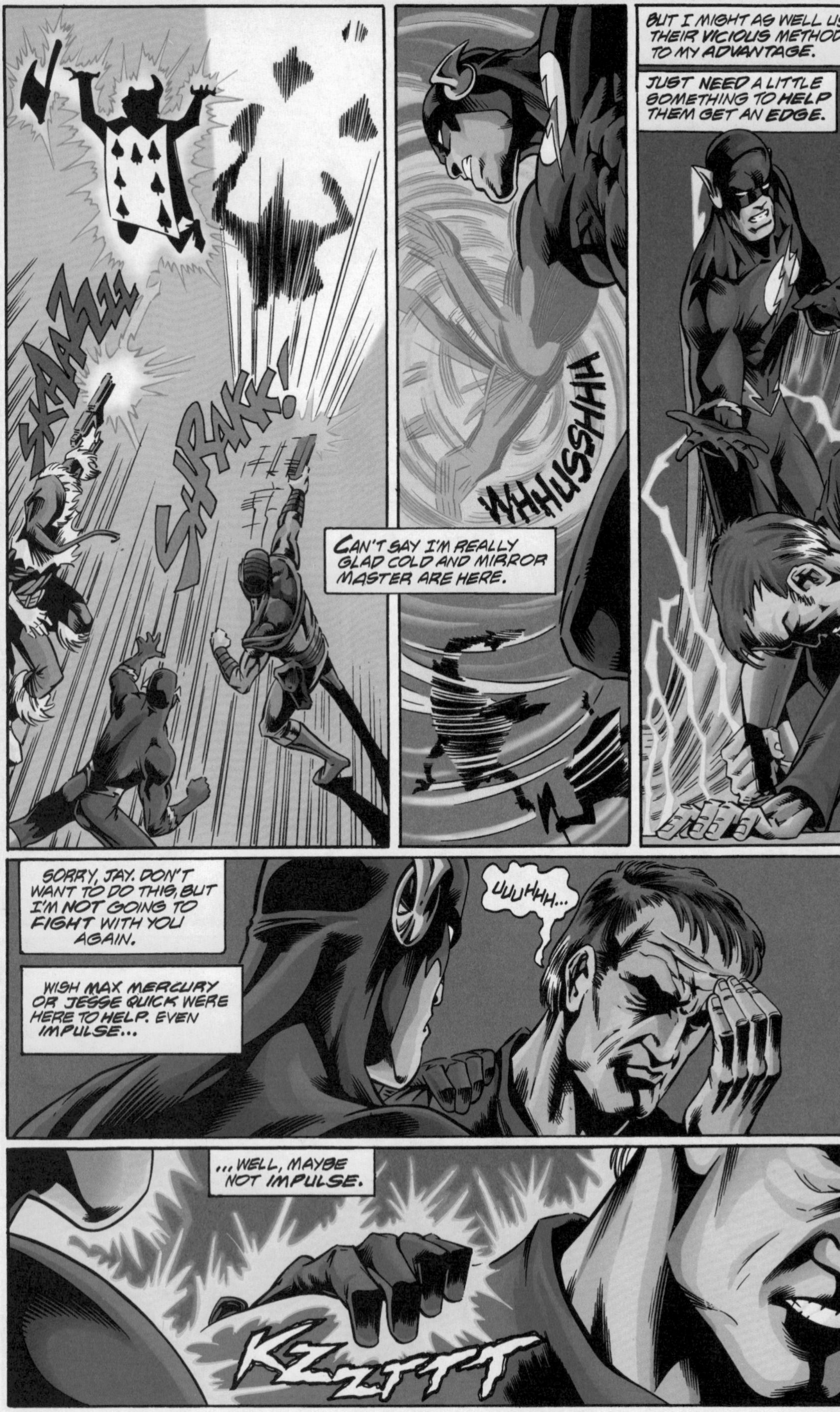
SKAAZZZ
SKRAKK!
CAN'T SAY I'M REALLY GLAD COLD AND MIRROR MASTER ARE HERE.
WHHUSSHHH
BUT I MIGHT AS WELL USE THEIR VICIOUS METHODS TO MY ADVANTAGE.
JUST NEED A LITTLE SOMETHING TO HELP THEM GET AN EDGE.
SORRY, JAY. DON'T WANT TO DO THIS, BUT I'M NOT GOING TO FIGHT WITH YOU AGAIN.
UUUHHH...
WISH MAX MERCURY OR JESSE QUICK WERE HERE TO HELP. EVEN IMPULSE...
...WELL, MAYBE NOT IMPULSE.
KZZTTT

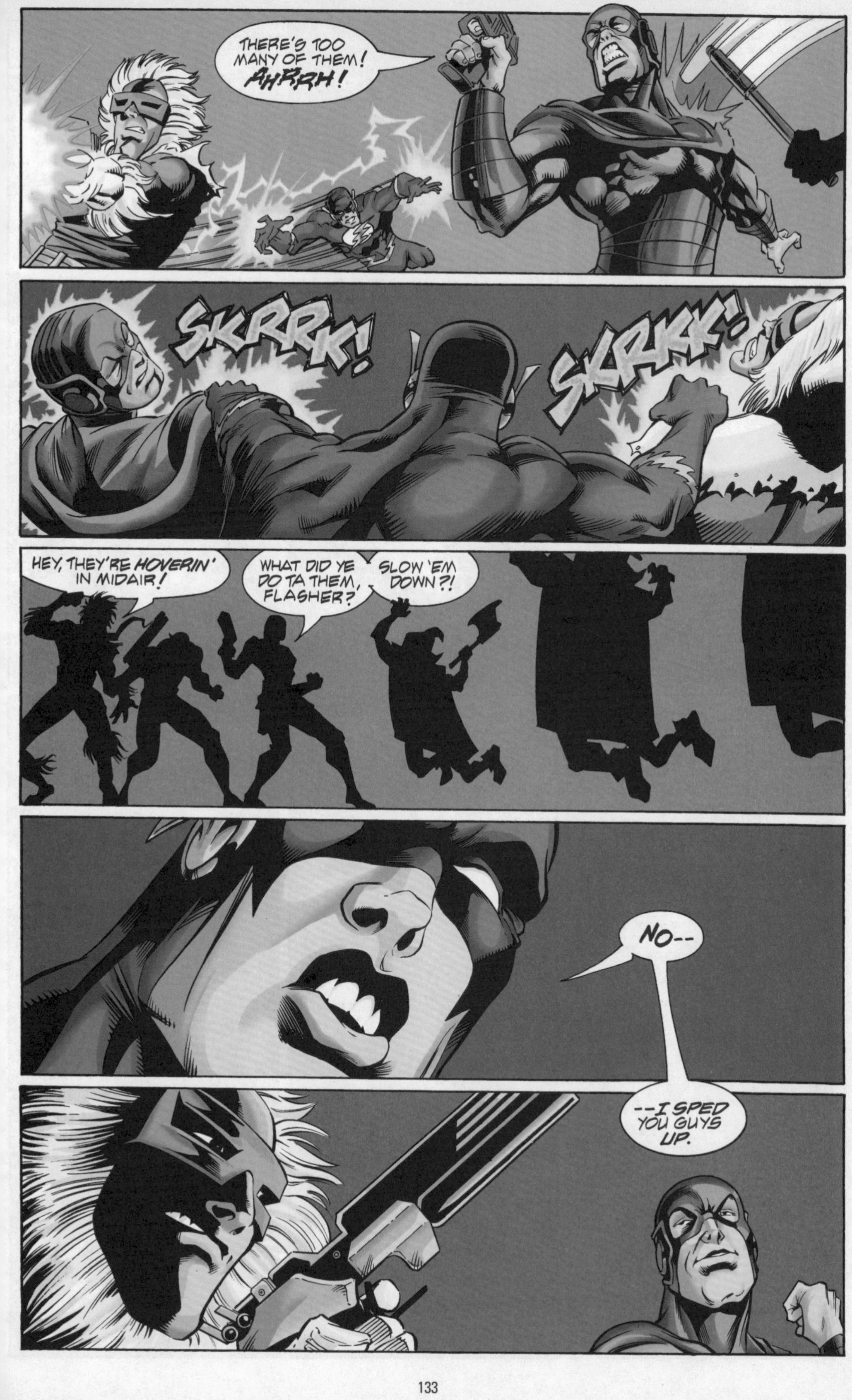
THERE'S TOO MANY OF THEM! AHRRH!
SKRRK!
SKRKK!
HEY, THEY'RE HOVERIN' IN MIDAIR!
WHAT DID YE DO TA THEM, FLASHER?
SLOW 'EM DOWN?!
NO--
--I SPED YOU GUYS UP.

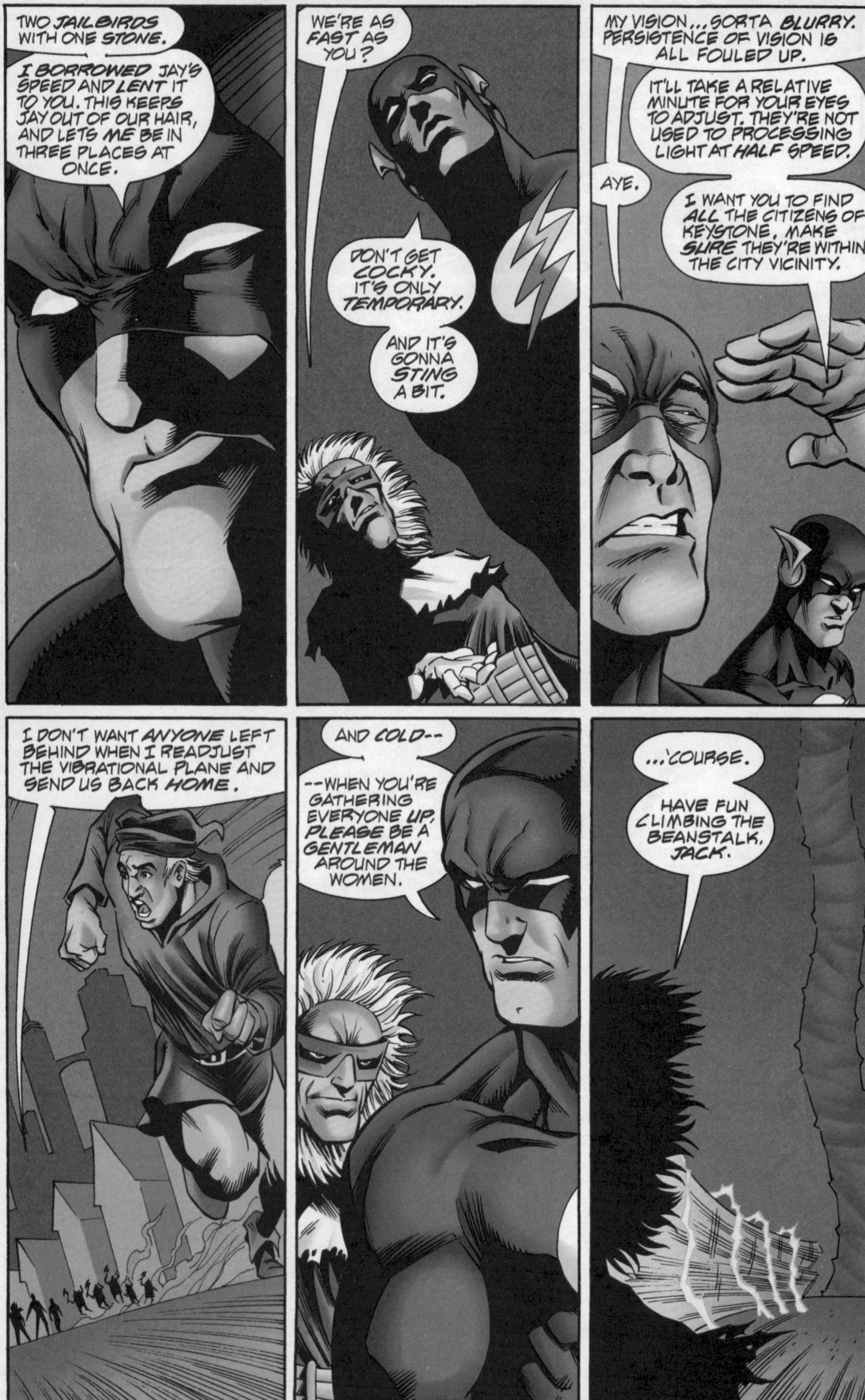
TWO JAILBIRDS WITH ONE STONE.
I BORROWED JAY'S SPEED AND LENT IT TO YOU. THIS KEEPS JAY OUT OF OUR HAIR, AND LETS ME BE IN THREE PLACES AT ONCE.
WE'RE AS FAST AS YOU?
DON'T GET COCKY. IT'S ONLY TEMPORARY.
AND IT'S GONNA STING A BIT.
MY VISION... SORTA BLURRY. PERSISTENCE OF VISION IS ALL FOULED UP.
IT'LL TAKE A RELATIVE MINUTE FOR YOUR EYES TO ADJUST. THEY'RE NOT USED TO PROCESSING LIGHT AT HALF SPEED.
AYE.
I WANT YOU TO FIND ALL THE CITIZENS OF KEYSTONE, MAKE SURE THEY'RE WITHIN THE CITY VICINITY.
I DON'T WANT ANYONE LEFT BEHIND WHEN I READJUST THE VIBRATIONAL PLANE AND SEND US BACK HOME.
AND COLD--
--WHEN YOU'RE GATHERING EVERYONE UP, PLEASE BE A GENTLEMAN AROUND THE WOMEN.
...'COURSE.
HAVE FUN CLIMBING THE BEANSTALK, JACK.

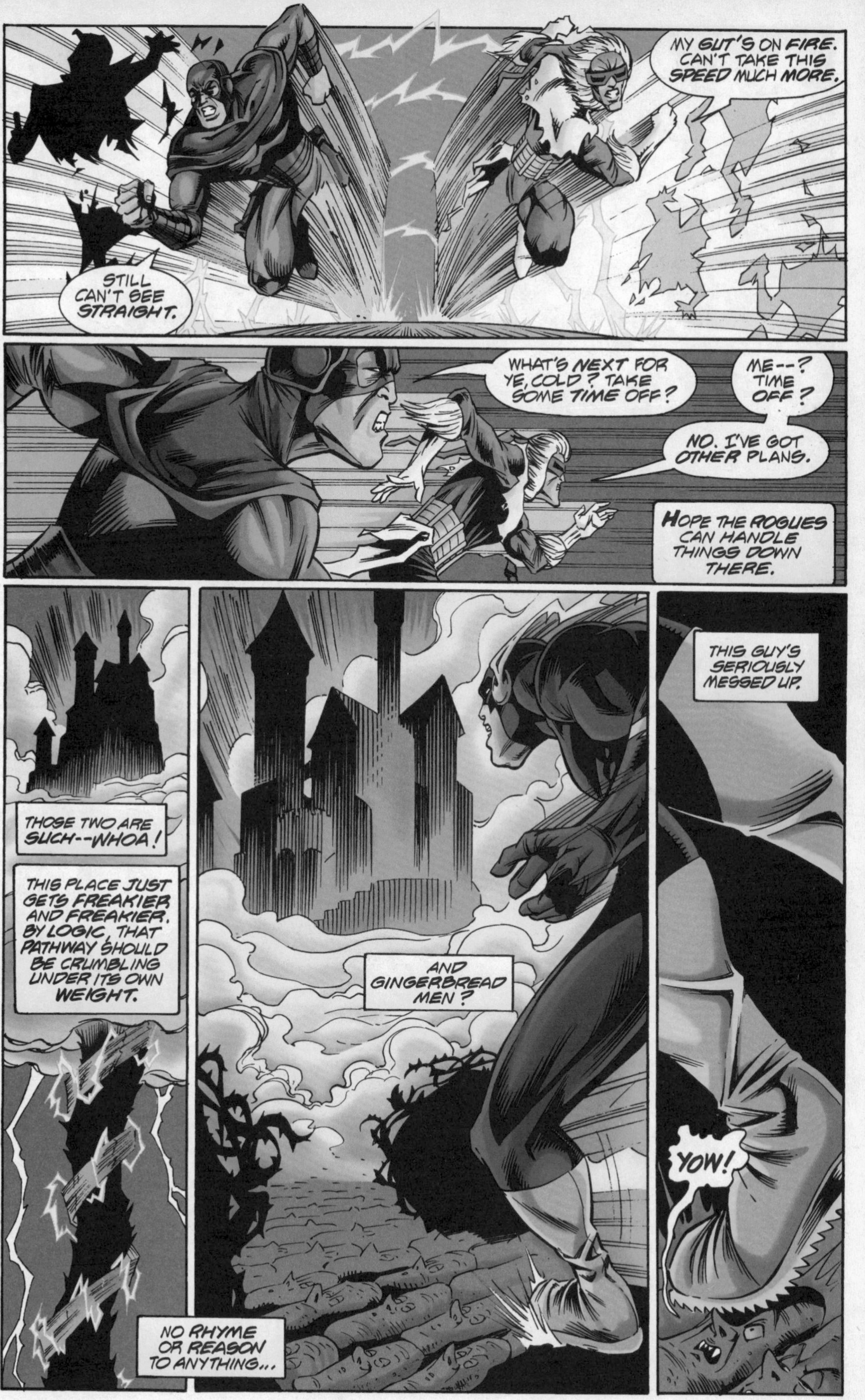
MY GUT'S ON FIRE. CAN'T TAKE THIS SPEED MUCH MORE.
STILL CAN'T SEE STRAIGHT.
WHAT'S NEXT FOR YE, COLD? TAKE SOME TIME OFF?
ME--? TIME OFF?
NO. I'VE GOT OTHER PLANS.
HOPE THE ROGUES CAN HANDLE THINGS DOWN THERE.
THOSE TWO ARE SUCH--WHOA!
THIS PLACE JUST GETS FREAKIER AND FREAKIER. BY LOGIC, THAT PATHWAY SHOULD BE CRUMBLING UNDER ITS OWN WEIGHT.
NO RHYME OR REASON TO ANYTHING...
AND GINGERBREAD MEN?
THIS GUY'S SERIOUSLY MESSED UP.
YOW!

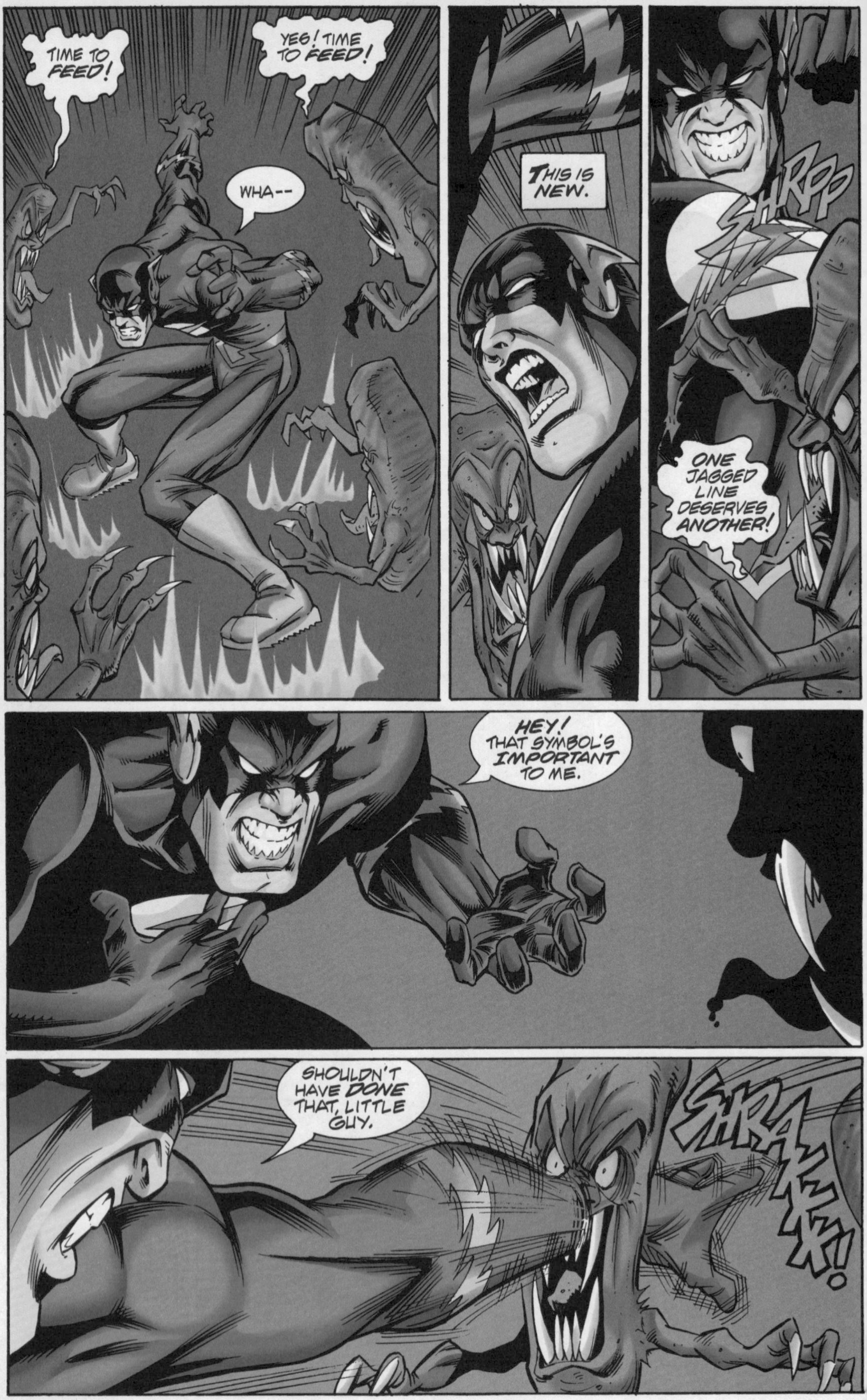
TIME TO FEED!
YES! TIME TO FEED!
WHA--
THIS IS NEW.
SHRPP
ONE JAGGED LINE DESERVES ANOTHER!
HEY! THAT SYMBOL'S IMPORTANT TO ME.
SHOULDN'T HAVE DONE THAT, LITTLE GUY.
SHRAKKK!

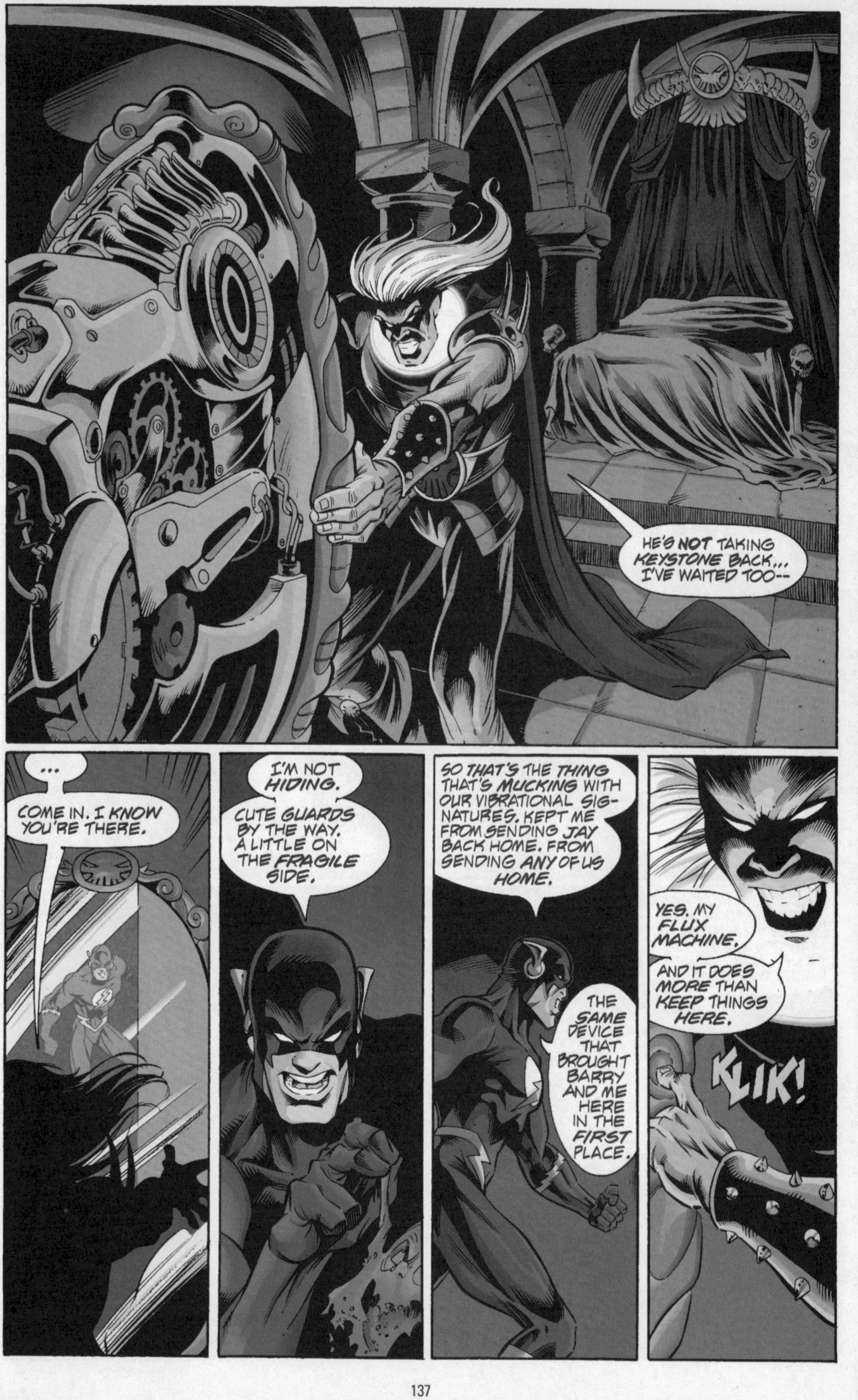
HE'S **NOT** TAKING *KEYSTONE* BACK... I'VE WAITED TOO--
...
COME IN. I KNOW YOU'RE THERE.
I'M NOT *HIDING*.
CUTE *GUARDS* BY THE WAY. A LITTLE ON THE *FRAGILE* SIDE.
SO *THAT'S* THE *THING* THAT'S *MUCKING* WITH OUR VIBRATIONAL SIGNATURES. KEPT ME FROM SENDING *JAY* BACK HOME. FROM SENDING *ANY* OF US *HOME*.
THE *SAME* DEVICE THAT BROUGHT BARRY AND ME HERE IN THE *FIRST* PLACE.
YES. MY *FLUX MACHINE*.
AND IT DOES *MORE* THAN *KEEP* THINGS *HERE*.
KLIK!

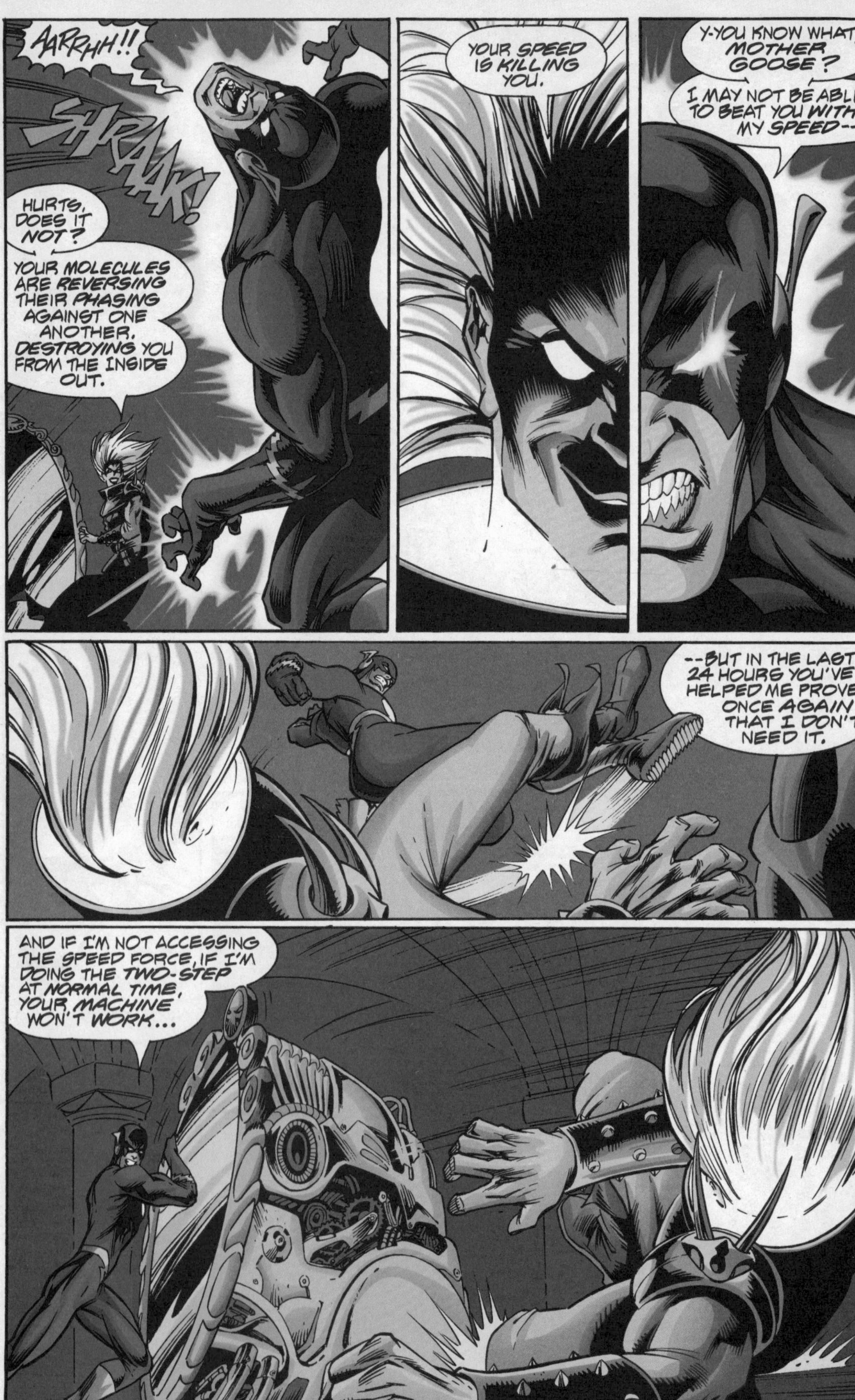
AARRHH!!
SHRAAAK!
HURTS, DOES IT NOT?
YOUR MOLECULES ARE REVERSING THEIR PHASING AGAINST ONE ANOTHER. DESTROYING YOU FROM THE INSIDE OUT.
YOUR SPEED IS KILLING YOU.
Y-YOU KNOW WHAT, MOTHER GOOSE?
I MAY NOT BE ABLE TO BEAT YOU WITH MY SPEED--
--BUT IN THE LAST 24 HOURS YOU'VE HELPED ME PROVE ONCE AGAIN THAT I DON'T NEED IT.
AND IF I'M NOT ACCESSING THE SPEED FORCE, IF I'M DOING THE TWO-STEP AT NORMAL TIME, YOUR MACHINE WON'T WORK...

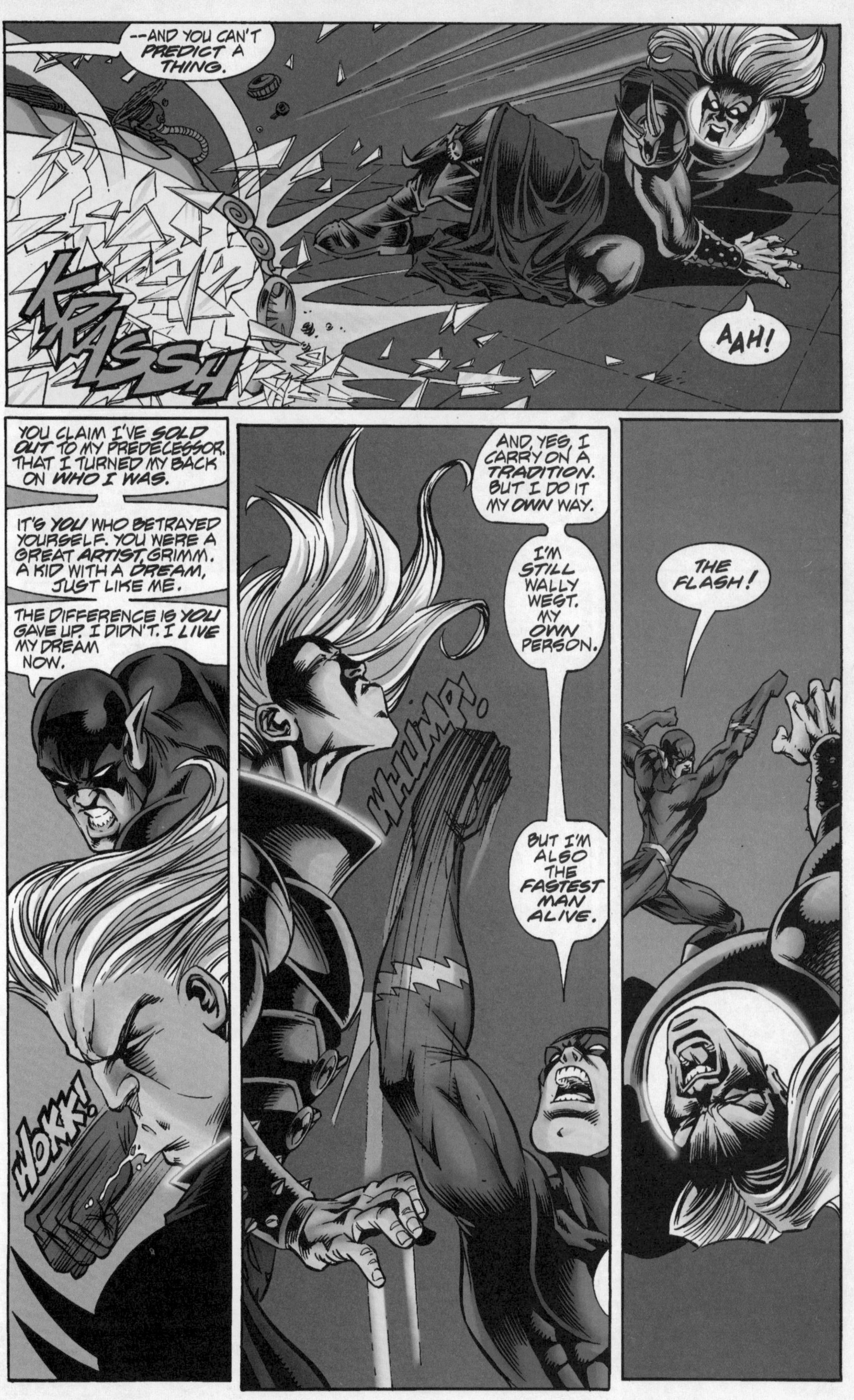
--AND YOU CAN'T PREDICT A THING.
KRASSH
AAH!
YOU CLAIM I'VE SOLD OUT TO MY PREDECESSOR. THAT I TURNED MY BACK ON WHO I WAS.
IT'S YOU WHO BETRAYED YOURSELF. YOU WERE A GREAT ARTIST, GRIMM. A KID WITH A DREAM, JUST LIKE ME.
THE DIFFERENCE IS YOU GAVE UP. I DIDN'T. I LIVE MY DREAM NOW.
WOKK!
AND, YES, I CARRY ON A TRADITION. BUT I DO IT MY OWN WAY.
I'M STILL WALLY WEST. MY OWN PERSON.
WHUMP!
BUT I'M ALSO THE FASTEST MAN ALIVE.
THE FLASH!

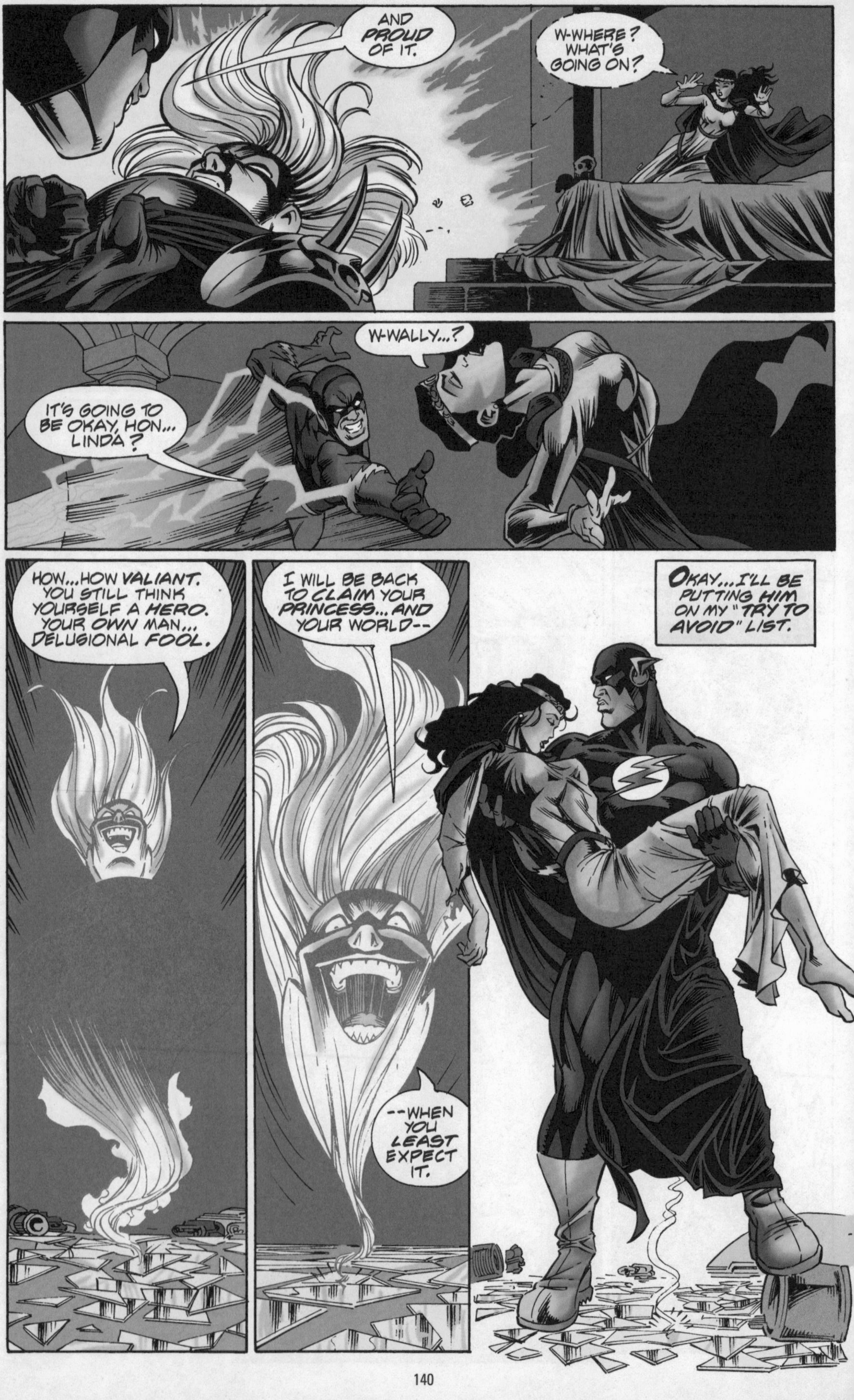
AND PROUD OF IT.
W-WHERE? WHAT'S GOING ON?
W-WALLY...?
IT'S GOING TO BE OKAY, HON... LINDA?
HOW...HOW VALIANT. YOU STILL THINK YOURSELF A HERO. YOUR OWN MAN... DELUSIONAL FOOL.
I WILL BE BACK TO CLAIM YOUR PRINCESS... AND YOUR WORLD--
--WHEN YOU LEAST EXPECT IT.
OKAY... I'LL BE PUTTING HIM ON MY "TRY TO AVOID" LIST.

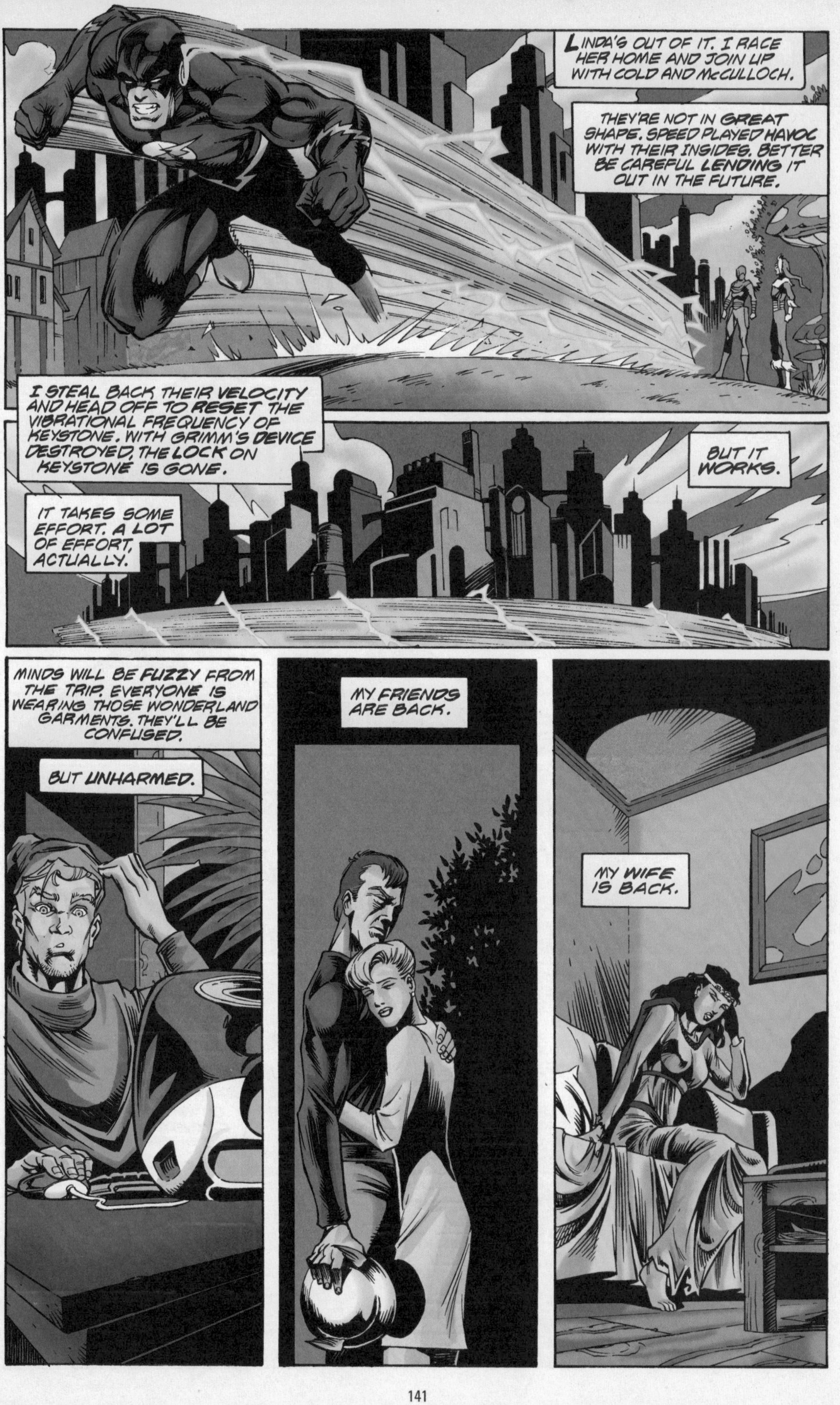
LINDA'S OUT OF IT. I RACE HER HOME AND JOIN UP WITH COLD AND McCULLOCH.
THEY'RE NOT IN GREAT SHAPE. SPEED PLAYED HAVOC WITH THEIR INSIDES. BETTER BE CAREFUL LENDING IT OUT IN THE FUTURE.
I STEAL BACK THEIR VELOCITY AND HEAD OFF TO RESET THE VIBRATIONAL FREQUENCY OF KEYSTONE. WITH GRIMM'S DEVICE DESTROYED, THE LOCK ON KEYSTONE IS GONE.
IT TAKES SOME EFFORT. A LOT OF EFFORT, ACTUALLY.
BUT IT WORKS.
MINDS WILL BE FUZZY FROM THE TRIP. EVERYONE IS WEARING THOSE WONDERLAND GARMENTS. THEY'LL BE CONFUSED.
BUT UNHARMED.
MY FRIENDS ARE BACK.
MY WIFE IS BACK.

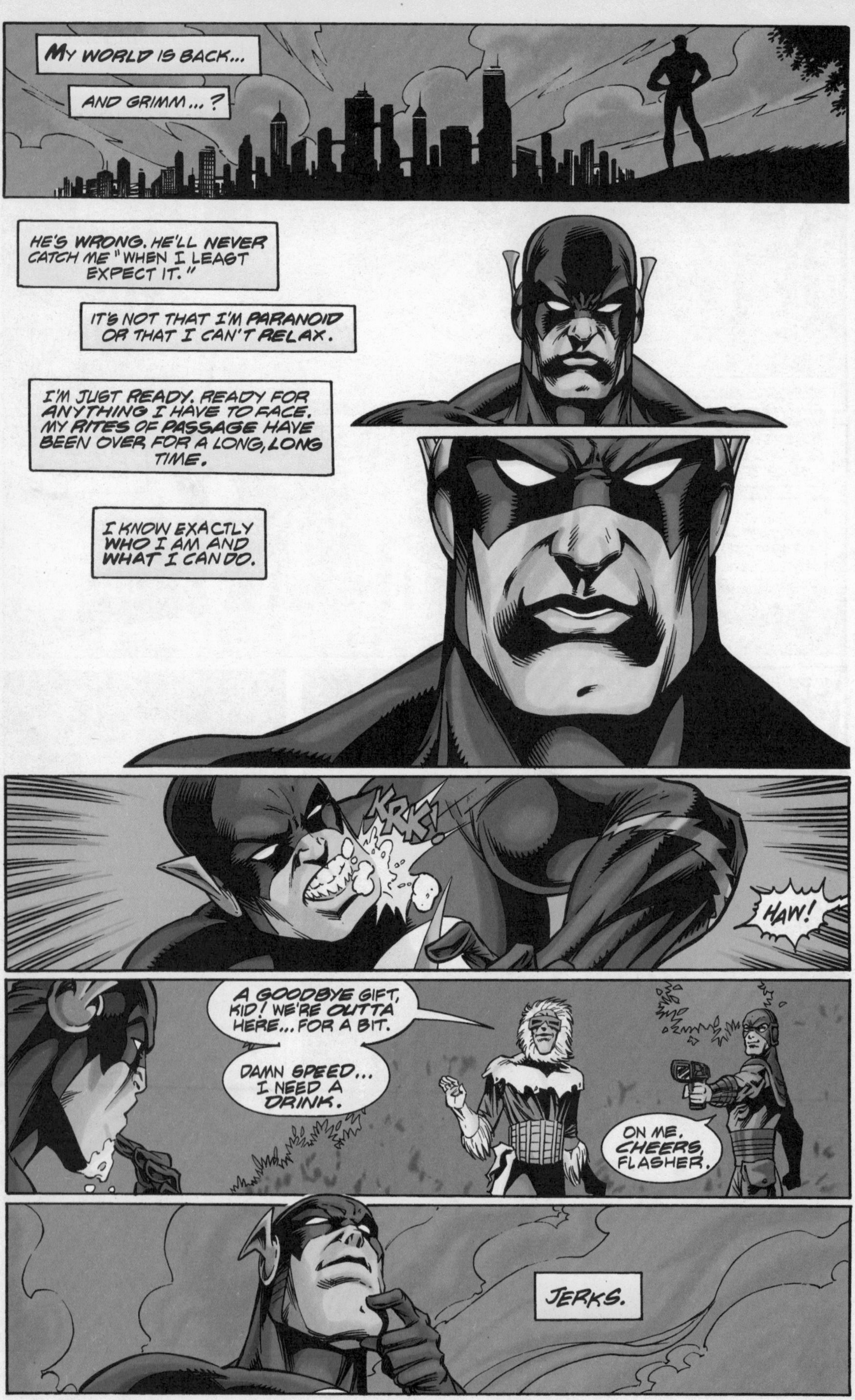

MY WORLD IS BACK...
AND GRIMM...?
HE'S WRONG. HE'LL NEVER CATCH ME "WHEN I LEAST EXPECT IT."
IT'S NOT THAT I'M PARANOID OR THAT I CAN'T RELAX.
I'M JUST READY. READY FOR ANYTHING I HAVE TO FACE. MY RITES OF PASSAGE HAVE BEEN OVER FOR A LONG, LONG TIME.
I KNOW EXACTLY WHO I AM AND WHAT I CAN DO.
KRK!
HAW!
A GOODBYE GIFT, KID! WE'RE OUTTA HERE... FOR A BIT.
DAMN SPEED... I NEED A DRINK.
ON ME. CHEERS, FLASHER.
JERKS.

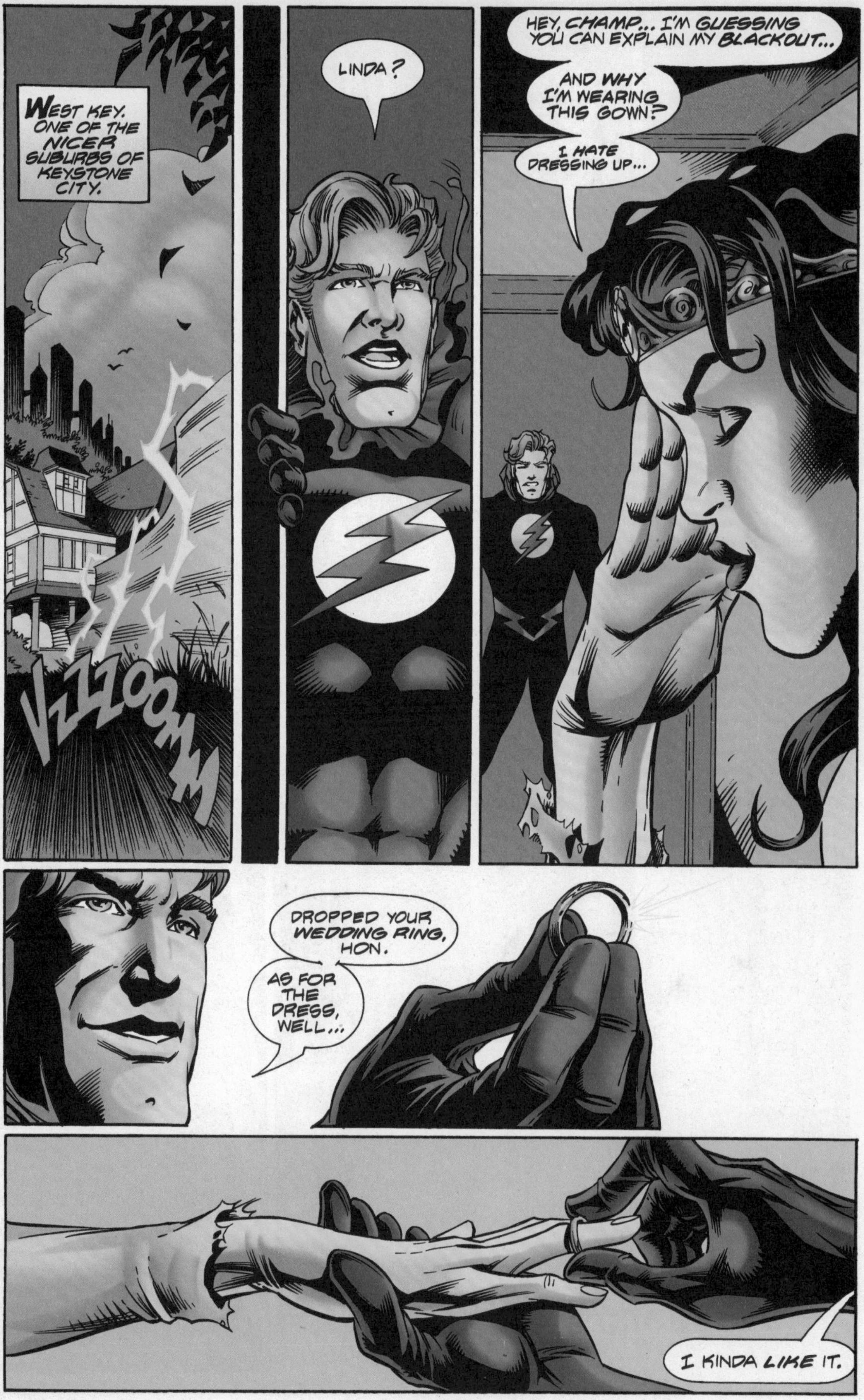
WEST KEY. ONE OF THE NICER SUBURBS OF KEYSTONE CITY.
VZZZOOMMM
LINDA?
HEY, CHAMP... I'M GUESSING YOU CAN EXPLAIN MY BLACKOUT...
AND WHY I'M WEARING THIS GOWN?
I HATE DRESSING UP...
DROPPED YOUR WEDDING RING, HON.
AS FOR THE DRESS, WELL...
I KINDA LIKE IT.

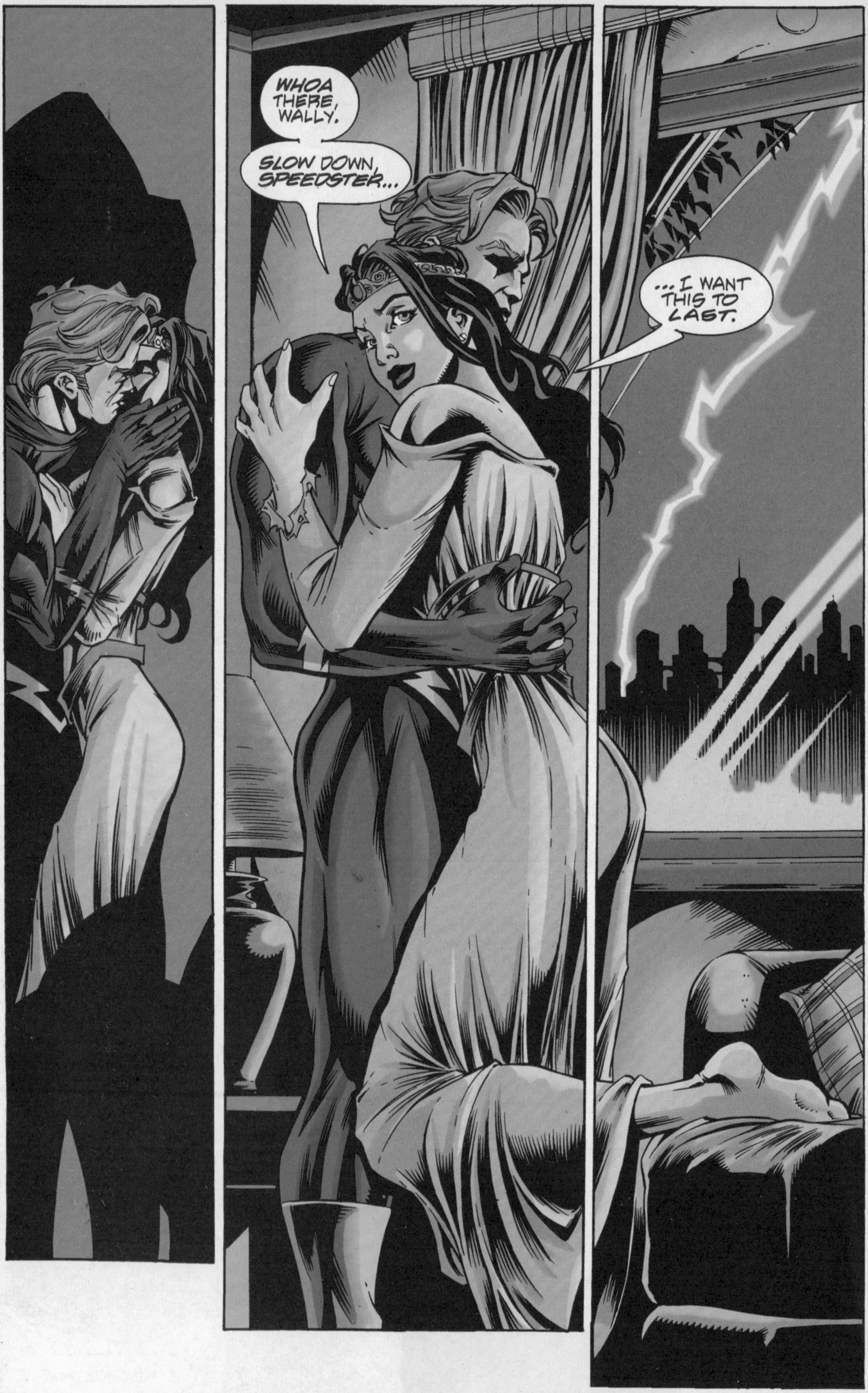
WHOA THERE, WALLY.
SLOW DOWN, SPEEDSTER...
...I WANT THIS TO LAST.